Elementary

Teacher's Book

New Headway English Course

Soars

OXFORD
UNIVERSITY PRESS

OXFORD
UNIVERSITY PRESS

Great Clarendon Street, Oxford OX2 6DP

Oxford University Press is a department of the University of Oxford.
It furthers the University's objective of excellence in research, scholarship,
and education by publishing worldwide in

Oxford New York

Athens Auckland Bangkok Bogotá Buenos Aires Cape Town
Chennai Dar es Salaam Delhi Florence Hong Kong Istanbul Karachi
Kolkata Kuala Lumpur Madrid Melbourne Mexico City Mumbai Nairobi
Paris São Paulo Shanghai Singapore Taipei Tokyo Toronto Warsaw

with associated companies in Berlin Ibadan

Oxford and Oxford English are registered trade marks of
Oxford University Press in the UK and in certain other countries

ISBN 0 19 436665 0

Printed in Spain by Unigraf s.l.

Acknowledgements

The authors and publisher are grateful to those who have given
permission to reproduce the following extracts and adaptations of
copyright material:

p124 *Colours* Words and Music by Donovan Leitch. © Copyright 1965
Donovan (Music) Ltd. Reproduced by permission.
p129 *I Just Called to Say I Love You* Words and Music by Stevie Wonder. ©
1984 Jobete Music Co Inc / Black Bull Music Inc., USA. EMI Music
Publishing Ltd, London WC2H 0EA. Reproduced by permission of IMP Ltd.
p134 *Wonderful Tonight* Words and Music by Eric Clapton © 1977 & 1999
Eric Clapton. Used by permission of Music Sales Ltd. All rights reserved.
International Copyright Secured.
p137 *Summertime* Music and Lyrics by George Gershwin, Du Bose and
Dorothy Heyward and Ira Gershwin. ©1935 (Renewed 1962) George
Gershwin Music, Ira Gershwin Music and Du Bose and Dorothy Heyward
Memorial Fund. All rights administered by WB Music Corp. By permission
of IMP Ltd. All rights reserved.

Illustrations by:
Roger Fereday pp125, 131
Oxford Illustrators pp148, 151

Contents

New Headway Elementary

PHOTOCOPIABLE MATERIALS

Introduction

Why a new version of *Headway Elementary*?

A main reason for producing new versions of *Headway Elementary* and *Headway Pre-Intermediate* was to bring them into line with *New Headway Intermediate* and *New Headway Upper-Intermediate*. Having rewritten the two higher level books, it became increasingly apparent that it was necessary to ring some changes with the two lower levels. We felt that the time had come to give them a much fresher and lighter feel, but at the same time we didn't want to lose those elements that have proved successful with so many teachers. We believe that at lower levels the content and approach of language teaching is inevitably more restricted, and so a lot about the books remains the same.

What remains the same?

- The basic *Headway* methodology is the same. Proven traditional approaches are used alongside those which have been developed and researched more recently.
- The grammatical syllabus is largely unchanged because the requirements of lower level students are usually more predictable than at later levels.
- There is a great variety of practice activities. Some of these have been amended rather than replaced. Nevertheless there are still many new ones.
- Vocabulary is not only integrated throughout but also developed in its own section.
- Skills work is integrated and balanced. It all comes from authentic sources but has been simplified and adapted to suit the level.
- There is an *Everyday English* section.

What are the differences?

- The design is completely new, and this represents a break in what a *Headway* Student's Book traditionally looked like. It is cleaner and fresher, and activities are easier to follow. There is more space on a page, and some of the exercises and activities are shorter.
- The vast majority of the texts are new. We took this opportunity to freshen up the topics. Teachers very easily get fed up with using the same texts year after year. Sometimes we have found a parallel text on the same topic, but more often we have selected a new topic and a new text.
- There are several new features, such as the *Starter* at the beginning of a unit, and the *Grammar Spot*.
- Many of the vocabulary exercises are different, new, or amended, as are the topics of the *Everyday English* section.

STARTER

This is designed to be a warmer to the lesson. It is a short activity and always has direct relevance to the language to be introduced in the unit.

GRAMMAR SPOT

This is a mix of explanation, questions, and self-check tasks to reinforce the grammar being taught. There is a page reference given to the fuller Grammar Reference at the back of the book.

What's in the Teacher's Book?

- **Full teaching notes**, answers, and possible problems.

- *Don't forget!* **section** which refers to relevant exercises in the Workbook, the video, and to the Word list.

- **Tapescripts** in the main body of the teaching notes.

- **Extra ideas and songs section** with notes on how to use them for use after Units 1–4, 5–8, 9–12, and 13–14. You will find the songs on the recording at the end of each section, i.e. at the end of Units 4, 8, 12, and 14.

- **Stop and check tests**
There are four Stop and check revision tests which cover Units 1–4, 5–8, 9–12, and 13–14. These can either be set in class, or given for homework (preferably over a weekend) and then discussed in the next lesson. Students can work in small groups to try to agree on the correct answer, then you can go over it with the whole class, reminding students of the language items covered. It is important that, in the translation sentences which come at the end of each Stop and check test, students translate the ideas and concepts, and not word by word.

- **Progress tests**
There are three Progress tests which cover Units 1–5, 6–10, and 11–14.

What's in the Workbook?

The Workbook is an important component of the course. It revises the grammatical input of the Student's Book and contains the writing syllabus. Many of the exercises are on the Student's Workbook recording, for use in class or at home.

What's in the Teacher's Resource Book?

The Teacher's Resource Book is a new feature for *Headway*. It contains photocopiable games and activities to supplement the main course material.

VIDEO

A *Headway Elementary* Video, Video Guide, and Activity Book are available as an optional accompaniment to the course. The video is linked to the syllabus and consists of mini-documentaries on topics that reflect those in the Student's Book, and situational language such as in a shop and in a pub.

Finally!

There is a lot that is new in the new editions, but there are many aspects that you will be familiar with. We actually try to guide students to an understanding of new language, rather then just have examples of it on the page. We attach great importance to practice activities, both controlled and free, personalized and impersonal. The skills work comes from a wide range of material – newspapers, magazines, biographies, short stories, radio programmes, songs – and features both British and American English. We hope you and your students enjoy using the books, and have success with them whether using *Headway* for the first time or having learned to trust its approach from previous use.

am/is/are • my/your/his/her
Everyday objects • Numbers
Hello and goodbye

Hello everybody!

Introduction to the unit

As you begin *New Headway Elementary*, you are probably starting a new course with a new group of students. The title of Unit 1 is 'Hello everybody!', and one important aim is that students get to know each other and you, and you get to know them. Obviously students will have relatively little English to use at this stage, but nevertheless a convivial classroom atmosphere can be established through quite basic interchanges.

Language aims

Grammar – *am/is/are* The verb *to be* is introduced in all persons, singular and plural. The focus is on the positive and questions with question words (*where*, *what*, and *how*). The negative and *Yes/No* questions are dealt with in Unit 2.

Possessive adjectives *My*, *your*, *his*, and *her* are introduced in the unit. The other possessive adjectives are given in Grammar Reference 1.2 on p124.

Vocabulary Names of countries are introduced as part of the work on introductions. In the *Vocabulary and pronunciation* section, the alphabet is introduced and practised. Students look at the organization of a bilingual dictionary entry, and everyday objects such as *ticket* and *key*. If possible, bring enough bilingual dictionaries for students to share at least one between two. Students are asked to work out the rules for using *a/an* and the formation of regular plurals with *-s*.

Everyday English Numbers 1–20 are revised and practised. The situational focus includes practice on exchanging telephone numbers and work on saying hello and goodbye.

Workbook Nationality adjectives (*German, French*); the numbers 1–20 are practised. The writing syllabus begins in Unit 3.

Notes on the unit

STARTER (SB p6)

1 Say your own name – *I'm (John)* – and point to yourself to make the meaning clear. Then invite students to say their names – *I'm Jean, I'm Keiko*, etc. Encourage students to listen to each other's names and to memorize as many as they can. If appropriate, play a memory game by pointing to individual students and yourself and getting the group to say just the name, e.g. *John! Keiko!* Encourage students in a multilingual group to pronounce each other's names (and your name!) as accurately as possible.

2 Check students understand 'alphabetical order' by putting letters *a–g* on the board in random order and asking students to re-order them alphabetically. (Don't worry too much if students pronounce the letters wrongly as the alphabet is covered later in the unit.) Check by asking students to put the names in *Starter 1* in order.

Ask students to stand up in alphabetical order and say their name. If appropriate, repeat this getting progressively faster each time.

If there are not too many students in the class, put their names on the board so everyone can begin to learn them.

INTRODUCTIONS (SB p6)

am/is/are, my/your

1 **T 1.1** Ask students to read and listen. Play the recording two or three times, repeat as a class first, then practise it in both open (i.e. students ask and answer the question across the room with the rest of the class listening) and closed pairs (i.e. the whole class working in pairs). Make sure students can accurately produce the contracted form *I'm*.

> **GRAMMAR SPOT**
>
> Focus attention on the contractions. Ask students to circle the contracted forms in exercise 1.

2 Ask students to complete the conversation. Remind them to use contracted forms.

T 1.2 Play the recording and let students check their answers. If you feel students need more practice, ask them to say the dialogue in open and closed pairs.

> **Answers and tapescript**
> **A** Hello. My **name's** Richard. What's **your** name?
> **B** Kurt.
> **A** **Where** are you from, Kurt?
> **B** **I'm** from Hamburg. Where **are** you from?
> **A** **I'm from** London.

3 This is a mingle activity. Demonstrate the dialogue first in open pairs, and then get students to move around the class and talk to as many people as possible. Don't let this activity go on too long. If you have a large class, it will be impossible for all the students to talk to everyone.

ADDITIONAL MATERIAL

Workbook Unit 1
Exercises 1–3 These practise *What's your name?*, *Where are you from? I'm from … ,* and *I'm (a) … .*

Countries, *his/her*

If you have access to a world map or a globe, it would be useful for presenting the names of the countries.

4 Focus attention on the table with the names of the countries. Explain stress and the system of stress marks used in *Headway* with an example on the board, e.g. *England.* You could use L1 to explain, and you could perhaps take some examples of words with more than one syllable in L1 (if L1 is stress-timed itself, not syllable-timed) to show how there are stressed and unstressed syllables.

T 1.3 Ask students to read the list of countries as you play the recording. Then they can listen and repeat the second time. Practise the countries as a class, then in closed pairs.

5 Ask students to look at the photographs and read about the people.

> **GRAMMAR SPOT**
>
> Focus attention on the contractions. Ask students to circle the contracted forms in the sentences in exercise 5.

6 Ask students in pairs or groups to write where the people are from. Students are *not* expected to know how to say *Hello!* in all the different languages! This is merely a fun way to introduce countries and the third person singular and plural. Some students will know a few, others will know more.

> **Answers**
> 1 This is Richard.
>   He's from England.
> 2 This is Tomoko.
>   She's from Japan.
> 3 This is Lena and Miguel.
>   They're from Brazil.
> 4 This is Anna.
>   She's from Italy.
> 5 This is Irina.
>   She's from Russia.
> 6 This is László and Ilona.
>   They're from Hungary.
> 7 This is María.
>   She's from Spain.
> 8 This is Kurt.
>   He's from Germany.
> 9 This is Pierre.
>   He's from France.

7 Introduce the questions *What's his/her name?* and *Where's he/she from?* Point to some of the pictures in exercise 6, ask the questions yourself, and let the students reply. Then drill the questions and correct any mistakes in the use of *he/she* and *his/her* carefully. Practise the questions and answers in open pairs.

Ask the students to continue the activity in closed pairs. Monitor and check for correct use of *he/she* and *his/her*, and if necessary, drill the language again using the pictures in the book. At the end of the activity, consolidate the positive form by asking students to say *His/Her name's … , He's/She's from …* or *They're from …* .

Ask students to complete the table with *am*, *is*, and *are*. Check the answers.

Answers		
I	am	
He She It	is	from England.
We You They	are	

Briefly check comprehension of the subject pronouns which are not covered in exercise 6 (*we*, *it*, and *you* plural) by using the photographs and the students themselves. *It* can be checked using international food and drinks, e.g. *champagne – It's from France.*

Read Grammar Reference 1.1 on p124 together in class, and/or ask students to read it at home. Encourage them to ask you questions about it.

PRACTICE (SB p9)

Talking about you

1 Demonstrate the activity by getting students to ask and answer the same questions in open and/or closed pairs about the other people in the class. Obviously this will work better in a multilingual class. In a monolingual class where everyone knows each other, you could make role cards giving students a new country of origin, or the identity of a famous person whose country of origin the class would know. This practises the vocabulary of the exercise, too.

2 Ask the students to introduce their partner to the rest of the class. Check for the correct use of *he/she* and for the correct stress on the names of countries.

Listening and pronunciation

3 **T 1.4** Play the recording. Ask students to tick the sentence they hear. This is an exercise that tests discrimination, but you can make it productive afterwards by asking students in pairs to practise the pairs of sentences. Pay particular attention to the sounds /ɪ/ and /iː/.

Answers and tapescript
1 He's from Spain.
2 What's her name?
3 They're from Brazil.
4 Where's she from?
5 He's a teacher in Italy.

Check it

4 Ask students to work in pairs to put *am*, *is*, *are*, *his*, *her*, or *your* into the gaps. Afterwards, you can ask them to make the contractions in numbers 1, 3, and 7.

Answers
2 Where **are** you from?
3 I **am** from Japan.
4 'What's **your** name?' 'My name's Tomoko.'
5 Max and Lisa **are** from Chicago.
6 This **is** my teacher. **His** name's Richard.
7 Where **is** he from?
8 This is my sister. **Her** name's Emma.

Reading and writing

NOTE
The aim of this section is to allow students to see how much English they already know. In exercise 7, students write about themselves. Encourage them to follow the models in exercises 5 and 6, but also give better students the opportunity to show off!
The verbs *have*, *live*, and *want* appear in their Present Simple form, but you don't need to review this tense at this stage.

5 **T 1.5** Ask students to read and listen to the text about Rafael. Make sure students understand *married* and *children*. You could ask one or two students to read the text aloud, or in closed pairs, and the students can help each other with pronunciation.

6 Ask students to complete the text about Yasmina. Make sure students understand *flat*, *international*, and *language*.

T 1.6 Play the recording to check. Again, you could practise the text around the class and/or in closed pairs.

Tapescript and answers
My name's Yasmina Kamal and I'm a student. I**'m** 19. I'm not married. I have one **sister** and two brothers. I **live** in a flat in Cairo, Egypt. I **want** to learn English because it's an international **language**.

7 Ask students to write about themselves. After quite a lot of oral class work, some silent, individual work provides variety and balance. Ask them to read what they have written to the class. Don't worry if there are a lot of pronunciation mistakes. The aim is for students to show what they can do, and to say a little about themselves and their families. You can't do everything at once!

If you have a large class, not all the students will be able to read out what they have written. Collect it in.

If you have a smaller class, it can be interesting to record the students. Play the recording back and correct mistakes that are common to the whole class.

ADDITIONAL MATERIAL

Workbook Unit 1
Exercises 4 and 5 Third person *is* and *are*, and short and long forms.
Exercises 6 and 7 Possessive adjectives.
Exercises 8 and 9 Countries and nationalities with stress practice.

VOCABULARY AND PRONUNCIATION (SB p10)

SUGGESTION
Some students may be quite familiar with the letters of the alphabet, while others may not remember many of them. Whatever your students' knowledge at this stage of the course, remember that they will all need regular practice in the alphabet and spelling. This can easily be integrated into any lesson when teaching new vocabulary (*How do you think you spell … from the sound?*), or when reviewing vocabulary (*How do you spell … ?*), and by the use of spelling games.

If your group cannot remember much of the alphabet, you may want to write it on the board and drill the letters in groups of five before moving on to the song.

1 **T 1.7** Tell the students that they are going to listen to the alphabet in the form of a song. Ask them to join in where they can. Play the recording and note down the letters students get wrong or don't know, paying particular attention to *a, j, e, g, i, y, u, w, r*, which cause problems for many students. Drill the letters which students found difficult.

Practise the letters as a class and in closed pairs. Listen to the song again and let the students sing it if they want to. It certainly helps them to remember the pronunciation of the alphabet!

> **T 1.7** **The alphabet song**
> A B C D E F G
> H I J K L M N O P
> L M N O P Q R S T
> L M N O P Q R S T
> U V W X Y Z
> That is the English alphabet!

Pre-teach the question *How do you spell … ?* and the use of *double* for spelling (e.g. *apple* = *a*, double *p, l, e*). Get students to practise asking the question and spelling in pairs, using their own names or the names of famous people. Do not focus on the use of *do* to form questions in the Present Simple as in *How do you spell … ?* This will be covered in full in Units 3 and 4.

2 In the previous lesson, check who has a bilingual dictionary. If there are not likely to be enough, bring some yourself. Ask students to find *apple* in the dictionary. You could have a conversation in L1 to compare the dictionary entries, but don't let this go on too long.

3 Students match the words and pictures. Encourage them to work in pairs and match the words that they recognize first. Then they can use a dictionary to complete the activity. Monitor and check for pronunciation.

> **Answers and tapescript**
> a a dictionary   g an apple
> b an orange   h a letter
> c a newspaper   i a magazine
> d a stamp   j a ticket
> e a bag   k a key
> f a camera   l a postcard

T 1.8 Play the recording and get students to repeat the words as a class and individually. If students have problems with incorrect stress, refer them to the table to help them self-correct. If necessary, drill the words, stopping the recording after each example.

4 Demonstrate the activity by saying the letter of some of the photographs and asking a student to tell you what the object is and how you spell it. Students continue in closed pairs.

5 Ask students to look at the words and to work out the rule if they don't already know it.

> **Answers**
> The letters *a, e, i, o,* and *u* are vowels.
> *a* goes before a word with a consonant, *an* goes before a vowel.

Point out the following sound rules:
• when we pronounce *u* /juː/, we use *a*, e.g. *a university*
• when *h* is silent, we use *an*, e.g. *an hour*.

6 Ask students to look at the plurals and work out the rules for the formation of plurals. Refer students to Grammar Reference 1.4 and 1.5 on p124.

> **Answers**
> Most nouns add -*s*. Nouns ending in a consonant + *y*, take away the -*y* and add -*ies*.
> Get students to say the plurals of the other words in exercise 2.

ADDITIONAL MATERIAL

Workbook Unit 1
Exercises 10 and 11 *a/an*
Exercise 12 Check it

Hello and goodbye

1 Get students to say numbers 1–20 around the class. If necessary, drill the numbers and check for correct stress on numbers 13–19, e.g. *thirteen*.

2 **T 1.9** Ask students to read and listen to the telephone numbers. Focus attention on the use of *double* for repeated numbers and the use of 'oh' for 0, rather than *zero*. Make sure students realize that each number is read individually in English, unlike some languages where *94* would be read as *ninety-four*.

3 **T 1.10** Tell students they are going to hear six sentences, each of which contains a number. Ask students to write down the numbers they hear. If necessary, pause the recording after each sentence, or play the recording a second time. Check the answers.

Answers and tapescript
1 Hello. **01913 786 499**.
2 My brother has **four** children.
3 I have **10** stamps in my bag.
4 Hello, extension **4177**.
5 I live at number **19**.
6 Goodbye. See you at **five**.

Get students to practise the numbers in the sentences.

4 Drill the question and answer. Then get students to ask other people what their phone number is and to write a list. If you have a big group, check a few of the numbers across the class. If you have a small group, you could check the numbers by writing up the list on the board.

5 Ask students to write the conversations in the correct order. **T 1.11** Play the recording to check.

Answers and tapescript
1 **A** Hello, extension 3442.
  B Hello, Mary. This is Edward. How are you?
  A I'm fine, thank you. And you?
  B I'm OK, thanks.

2 **A** Goodbye, Marcus.
  B Goodbye, Bianca. Have a nice day.
  A Thanks, Marcus. See you this evening!
  B Yes, at seven in the cinema.

3 **A** Hello, 270899.
  B Hi, Flora! It's me, Leo. How are you?
  A Not bad, thanks. And you?
  B Very well. How are the children?
  A They're fine.

6 Students practise the dialogues in open and then closed pairs. Then ask students to practise again, using their own names and telephone numbers.

Don't forget!

Workbook Unit 1
Exercises 13–14 These are exercises on numbers 1–20.

Word list
Look at the Word list on p135 of the Student's Book as a class. Tell students that the most important words from the unit are here. They could translate the words, or look at them at home, or transfer some of the words to their vocabulary notebook.

Pronunciation Book Unit 1

2

am/is/are – questions and negatives
Possessive *'s* • Family
Opposites • In a café

Introduction to the unit

The title of Unit 2 is 'Meeting people', and various characters are introduced to practise the grammar. The first real fluency activity of *New Headway Elementary* is the reading and listening exercise – Dorita's letter to Miguel. It is important for elementary-level students to be exposed to language in a natural context.

Language aims

Grammar – questions and negatives The verb *to be* is given further practice, with an emphasis on questions, negatives, and short answers. The question words *what, where, who, how old*, and *how much* are revised or introduced.

Note that in the negative, we use the contracted forms of *not*, not the contracted forms of the verb *to be*: i.e. *she isn't, they aren't, you aren't, we aren't*, and not *she's not, they're not, you're not, we're not*. Try to keep to these forms as you speak to the class. The contraction **I amn't* isn't possible, and this is pointed out in the *Grammar Spot* in the *Negative and short answers* section.

Having been introduced to contracted forms, students are tempted to use them in short answers, for example, *Are you married? *Yes, I'm*, but this is not possible. Where other languages will answer an inverted question with simply *yes* or *no*, English prefers to add a short answer. Without the short answer, the speaker can sound rather abrupt.

Possessive *'s* It can come as quite a surprise to students to learn that not only does *s* signify a plural noun, but *'s* is both the contracted form of the verb *to be* and an indicator of possession. This needs to be pointed out very carefully and regular practice given in distinguishing the different forms.

Vocabulary Members of the family (*father, aunt*, etc.), other words for personal relationships (*boyfriend/girlfriend*); plus common adjectives and their opposites.

Everyday English This section practises the language required in a café. *Can I have … ?* is taught idiomatically. Vocabulary to do with food and drink is introduced, and prices are practised. You might feel your students would benefit from doing exercises 13 and 14 in the Workbook before doing the *Everyday English* section.

Workbook The spelling of plural nouns is practised.

Notes on the unit

STARTER (SB p12)

> **POSSIBLE PROBLEMS**
> The *Starter* section revises and practises numbers. Numbers 1–20 and phone numbers were introduced in Unit 1, but you might feel that your students need more classroom work on these areas.
> Learners of English often experience difficulty in recognizing and producing the difference between the 'teen' numbers (13–19) and the corresponding 'ten' numbers (30, 40, 50, etc.). Point out the different word stress.
>
> ●·   ·●
> *thirty*   *thirteen*

1. Get students to count from 1–20 around the class. Repeat so that everyone has a chance to practise or if students make mistakes.

2. Now ask students to count in tens from 10–100 around the class. Check for correct stress, and repeat until students can say the numbers quickly and accurately.

3. Tell students your own age and then briefly revise numbers that reflect the age of your students. Drill the question *How old are you?* Ask students to work in groups of three or four and ask and answer about ages. Ask for a few examples of ages to practise *He's … , She's … , They're … ,* and *We're … .* (Unless your students query the use of *be* as different from how they express age in their own language, do not spend time on this.)

WHO IS SHE? (SB p12)

Questions and negatives

1. Ask students to read about Keesha Anderson. Check comprehension of the key vocabulary: *surname*, *first name*, *address*, and *journalist*.

2. If you think that your students will be familiar with most of the question words in this exercise, you can ask them to do this exercise in pairs. Otherwise, do it as a class.

   T 2.1 Play the recording so students can check their answers. Point out that *isn't* is the negative, and that *n't* is the short form of *not*.

   Tapescript and answers
   1 What's **her** surname? Anderson.
   2 **What's** her first name? Keesha.
   3 **Where's** she from? London, England.
   4 What's **her** job? She's a journalist.
   5 What's **her address**? 42, Muswell Hill Road, London N10 3JD.
   6 **What's her** phone number? 020 8863 5741.
   7 How old **is she**? Twenty-eight.
   8 Is she **married**? No, she isn't.

   Before you ask students to practise the questions and answers in pairs, let them practise in open pairs, focusing on accurate intonation. English has a very wide voice range, and this is apparent in questions. Questions with a question word start high and fall.

   What's her surname?

   Listen to the models on the recording and ask students to imitate them. Point out that the question in number 8 is different as you can answer *Yes/No* and it has a different intonation pattern. Inverted questions usually rise at the end. (Students will practise this more fully in the *Negatives and short answers* section that follows.)

Is she married?

Practise the questions as much as possible without boring the class! Have a mixture of open and closed pairs.

3. Students write questions about Keesha's brother, basing their questions on exercise 2.

   Answers
   Where's he from?   What's his phone number?
   What's his job?   How old is he?
   What's his address?   Is he married?

   Encourage students to ask you questions about Keesha's brother. Insist on accurate intonation. You can give any information you want, but here is a sample profile.

   Keesha's brother
   Surname   Anderson
   First name   Rudi
   Country   England
   Job   Policeman
   Address   70, London Road, Oxford OX3 5AL
   Phone number   01865 753 4991
   Age   21
   Married?   No

Negatives and short answers

4. Tell students they are going to continue asking questions, first about Keesha and then about her brother.

   Asking about Keesha

   T 2.2 Ask students to read and listen to the *Yes/No* questions and short answers. Play the recording. Play the recording again and ask students to repeat, emphasizing the rising intonation on the question and the pronunciation of the contracted form *isn't*.

   Allow students to practise the questions and answers which appear in full in the Student's Book in open and closed pairs. Insist on accurate intonation. Then ask students to ask questions 1 and 2, following the same pattern.

   Answers
   1 Is she a doctor?   No, she isn't.
      Is she a teacher?   No, she isn't.
      Is she a journalist?   Yes, she is.
   2 Is she eighteen?   No, she isn't.
      Is she twenty-one?   No, she isn't.
      Is she twenty-eight?   Yes, she is.

5. **Asking about Keesha's brother**
   Students continue asking about Keesha's brother, following the same pattern and working in closed pairs.

Answers

1	Is his first name Peter?	No, it isn't.
	Is his first name Daniel?	No, it isn't.
	Is his first name Rudi?	Yes, it is.
2	Is he a journalist?	No, he isn't.
	Is he a student?	No, he isn't.
	Is he a policeman?	Yes, he is.
3	Is he sixteen?	No, he isn't.
	Is he thirty?	No, he isn't.
	Is he twenty-one?	Yes, he is.

GRAMMAR SPOT

SUGGESTION

This is the first time that students have seen all the short answers and negative forms of the verb *to be*, so deal with the information in the *Grammar Spot* very carefully. You might want to practise the short answers in open pairs and drill the negative sentences.

1 Students complete the short answers, using the contracted form where possible (*No, it isn't*). Check the answers.

Answers

Is Keesha English?	Yes, she **is**.
Is her surname Smith?	No, it **isn't**.
Are you a journalist?	No, I'm **not**.

Make sure students understand that positive short answers can't be contracted to *Yes, she's.

2 Focus attention on the negative forms and point out especially that we cannot say *I amn't.

Read Grammar Reference 2.1 on p125 together in class, and/or ask students to read it at home. Encourage them to ask you questions about it.

PRACTICE (SB p13)

Who is he?

1 Photocopy the identity cards on p122.

POSSIBLE PROBLEMS

This is the first information gap activity in *New Headway Elementary*, and it might even be the first time your students have ever done such an activity. Students may find it strange that Student A has different information from Student B, so explain this activity very carefully, in L1 if you can. Stress that they mustn't show each other the information! Read the instructions as a class. Allocate the pairs, and give the photocopied card to Student B. You could do the first two questions yourself as an example. Give students enough time to complete the information exchange.

Answers

SURNAME	**Binchey**
FIRST NAME	Patrick
COUNTRY	**Ireland**
JOB	Accountant
ADDRESS	**82, Hill Road, Dublin**
PHONE NUMBER	1232 4837
AGE	**47**
MARRIED?	Yes

2 Students ask and answer questions about Patrick.

POSSIBLE PROBLEMS

Students first saw the short answers *Yes, he/she is, No, he/she isn't*, and *No, I'm not* in *Negatives and short answers*. This speaking exercise and the exercises in *Talking about you* extend and consolidate this focus. It is inadvisable to embark on an explanation of what short answers are and how they operate, as you run the risk of overloading students with too much information. It is better to let students see them in context and use them in controlled exercises. Demonstrate the activity by asking this first question about Patrick's surname and getting students to answer. Students continue to ask and answer in closed pairs. Monitor and check for correct formation of questions and short answers.

Answers

1	Is his surname Smith?	No, it isn't.
	Is his surname Jones?	No, it isn't.
	Is his surname Binchey?	Yes, it is.
2	Is he from Italy?	No, he isn't.
	Is he from England?	No, he isn't.
	Is he from Ireland?	Yes, he is.
3	Is he a policeman?	No, he isn't.
	Is he a teacher?	No, he isn't.
	Is he an accountant?	Yes, he is.

Talking about you

3 Demonstrate the activity by asking students the example questions in the Student's Book. If necessary, remind students of the short answers *Yes, I am* and *No, I'm not*. Get students to ask you the questions for each category on the identity card. Correct mistakes carefully.

4 Photocopy the forms on p122. This is a mingle activity. Read the instructions as a class and get two or three pairs of students to model the examples. Students stand up and ask and answer questions. The students should complete the information exchange with at least two other students, but stop the activity before they get tired.

Ask four or five students to tell the rest of the class about one of the others. They could well have problems with the shift from first and second persons to third person, i.e. *your* to *her*, *are* to *is*, etc., but allow students to feed back without correcting every mistake.

ADDITIONAL MATERIAL

Workbook Unit 2
Exercises 1–7 Verb *to be*, questions, negatives, short answers, short forms, and long forms.

Patrick's family

Possessive 's

1 Focus attention on the vocabulary table and on the example. Make sure students understand that the words are in male–female pairs. Students complete the table working with a partner and using a dictionary if necessary. Monitor and check for correct pronunciation, especially of *daughter* /ˈdɔːtə/ and of *grandmother/grandfather* /ˈgrænmʌðə/, /ˈgrænfɑːðə/. Check the answers. Drill some of the words to practise the pronunciation.

Answers		
husband	**father**	son
wife	mother	**daughter**
brother	uncle	grandfather
sister	**aunt**	**grandmother**

> **SUGGESTION**
> You could begin this presentation with a personalized example. Talk about your own family, e.g. *I have two children, a boy and a girl. The boy's name is Tony and the girl's name is Lucy.*
> Put the last sentence on the board, and draw students' attention to the possessive 's. Say that this isn't the verb *to be*, but that it shows possession. Use L1 if you can.

2 **T 2.3** Focus attention on the photograph. Ask students to read and listen and put the names next to the right person. Check the answers by pointing to each person and asking students for the correct name.

GRAMMAR SPOT

1 Focus attention on the use of 's as the contraction of *is* and as an indicator of possession.

2 Refer students back to the text about Patrick Binchey. Get them to work in pairs and underline the use of possessive 's and circle the use of 's as the contraction of *is*.

Answers	
Possession	*is*
wife's name	She's a teacher.
daughter's name	She's twenty-one
son's name	she's a nurse
Lara's boyfriend	He's nineteen and he's a student.

Refer students to Grammar Reference 2.2 on p125.

3 Students ask and answer questions about Patrick's family.

Answers	
Who's Brenda?	She's Lara and Benny's mother.
Who's Lara?	She's Patrick's/Brenda's daughter.
	She's Benny's sister.
	She's Mick's girlfriend.
Who's Benny?	He's Patrick's/Brenda's son.
	He's Lara's brother.
Who's Mick?	He's Lara's boyfriend.

> **SUGGESTION**
> You could revise the possessive 's and family relationships by referring to famous people and their relations, e.g. *Nicole Kidman – She's Tom Cruise's wife.*

PRACTICE (SB p15)

You and your family

1 Students ask you questions about the names of people in your family, i.e. *What's your mother's name?* not *Who's …*

2 Students write down the names of some of their relatives on a piece of paper. Then they exchange pieces of paper with a partner and ask and answer questions about each other's families.

> **SUGGESTION**
> You could revise the possessive 's at the beginning of the next lesson by asking ten or so students for a personal belonging of theirs. Put them all in the middle of the room. Students then have to point at an object and say *That's Maria's book*, etc.

3 This exercise consolidates the verb *to be* in a range of persons, and allows students to make some sentences about themselves. Check comprehension of *at home*, *at work*, and *coffee bar*.

Check it

4 Students work in pairs or small groups to identify the correct sentence.

Answers
1 I'm a doctor.	5 She's married.
2 I am twenty-nine years old.	6 I'm an uncle.
3 I'm not married.	7 I have two brothers.
4 My sister's name is Lara.	8 Peter's my sister's son.

ADDITIONAL MATERIAL

Workbook Unit 2
Exercises 8 and 9 Possessive *'s*

VOCABULARY (SB p16)

Opposites

1 Students use their dictionaries to match the opposite adjectives.

Answers
big	small	hot	cold
new	old	expensive	cheap
lovely	horrible	fast	slow
easy	difficult		

Drill the words to practise pronunciation. Ask students to mark the stress on words with two syllables or more.

Answers
●∙∙   ∙●∙   ●∙∙
difficult   expensive   lovely
horrible   easy

2 This exercise practises the vocabulary and revises the verb *to be*. Students write sentences for each picture.

T 2.4 Play the recording so students can check their answers. Students practise saying the sentences in pairs.

Answers and tapescript
1 He's old. She's young.
2 It's easy. It's difficult.
3 It's new. It's old.
4 It's fast. It's slow.
5 It's lovely. It's horrible.
6 It's hot. It's cold.
7 They're cheap. They're expensive.
8 It's small. It's big.

READING AND LISTENING (SB p16)

A letter from America

POSSIBLE PROBLEMS
This is the first piece of extensive skills work in *New Headway Elementary*. Students read and listen to the letter at the same time even though this might be deemed an unnatural activity. Learners of English find reading easier than listening because they can recognize cognates without the interference of different pronunciation. However, if they read the letter silently at their own speed, they could become distracted by unknown and not terribly important vocabulary.
The aim of this activity is to show students a lot of the language that they have already been exposed to in a relatively natural context. If you feel your students would not be able to cope with the activity as it stands, you could pre-teach the following items of vocabulary, or set them as a homework task prior to the lesson.

nice	*friendly*	*snow* (*n.*)
apartment	*subway*	*happy*
girl	*use* (*v.*)	*soon*
dancer	*park* (*n.*)	

However, if you feel your students don't need so much support, simply encourage them not to worry about other unknown words.

1 Read the introduction as a class.

T 2.5 Students read and listen to the letter.

2 Ask students to match a picture with a part of the letter. There are more pictures than paragraphs, so students will use words to refer to the relevant part of the letter.

Answers
Picture 1	Central Park is lovely in the snow.
Picture 2	In class with students from other countries
Picture 3	Annie and Marnie
Picture 4	The subway isn't difficult to use.
Picture 5	It's very cold now.

When the students understand the gist, play the recording and ask them to read again.

3 If you feel your students would be happy to correct the false sentences in pairs or small groups, ask them to do this. Otherwise, answer the questions as a class.

Answers
3 ✓
4 ✗ No, she isn't. She's at a language school.
5 ✗ No, it isn't. It's a small class – nine students.
6 ✗ No, they aren't. They're all from different countries.
7 ✗ No, they aren't. Annie is a dancer.
8 ✓

4 Students often have problems with the formation of questions, so it is worth taking the opportunity to provide some practice.

If you feel students would be happy to work in pairs or small groups to answer these questions, let them do so.

Answers
2 Where are the (other) students from?
3 What's her/the teacher's name?
4 Who are Annie and Marnie?
5 How old are Annie and Marnie?
6 Is New York big/exciting/expensive?

You could drill the questions for pronunciation practice. Careful with intonation!

5 **T 2.6** Students listen to three conversations. After each conversation ask and answer the two questions with the students. Then ask them to look at the tapescript on p114 of the Student's Book and play the recording again.

Tapescript
D = Dorita   O = Orlando
1 **D** Hello. My name's Dorita.
  O Hello, Dorita. I'm Orlando.
  D Where are you from, Orlando?
  O I'm from Italy, from Rome. And you? Where are you from?
  D I'm from Argentina.
  O From Buenos Aires?
  D Yes, that's right.

I = Isabel   C = class   D = Dorita
2 **I** Good morning everybody.
  C Good morning, Isabel.
  I How are you all?
  C Fine.
    Good.
    OK.
  I How are you Dorita?
  D I'm fine thank you. And you?
  I Very well. Now listen everybody . . .

M = Marnie   D = Dorita   A = Annie
3 **M** Bye, Dorita. Have a nice day.
  D Pardon?
  A Have a good day at the school of English.
  D Oh, yes. Thank you. Same to you.
  M What's your teacher called?
  D My teacher called?
  A Your teacher's name – what is it?
  D Ah, yes. Her name's Isabel.
  M And is she good?
  D My teacher good?
  A Yeah. Isabel, your teacher, is she a good teacher?
  D Oh yes, yes. Very good, very nice.

Answers
1 She's with the students in her school.
2 She's in school with the teacher.
3 She's at home with Annie and Marnie.

6 This is a free writing activity. Set it for homework, and mark it sympathetically.

EVERYDAY ENGLISH (SB p18)

In a café

> **SUGGESTION**
> The activities in the *Starter* section allow students to focus just on prices before being exposed to them in a fuller context. If you feel your students need to do more work on prices prior to the lesson, see the Workbook Unit 2, Exercises 13 and 14.

1 1 **T 2.7** Students read and listen to the prices to familiarize themselves with the system and pronunciation.

   Play the recording again and get students to repeat the prices. Make sure students realize we only use 'p' for prices under a pound.

   2 **T 2.8** Tell students they are going to hear six prices, each in a context. Get them to write down the prices they hear. (In number 6, they have to write the *correct* price.) Check the answers.

Answers and tapescript
1 That's **five pounds fifty**, please.
2 Look, it's only **twelve pounds**.
3 Here you are. **Twenty p** change.
4 Pizza is **three pounds seventy-five**.
5 **One hundred pounds** for that is very expensive.
6 **Nine pounds fifteen**, not nine pounds fifty.

2 Students read the menu and match the food with the pictures. Drill the pronunciation of the food and drink. Pay particular attention to *hamburger and chips* /ˈhæmbɜːgərən ˈtʃɪps/, *chocolate cake* /ˈtʃɒklət ˌkeɪk/, and *orange juice* /ˈɒrɪndʒ ˌdʒuːs/.

Students practise the menu items in pairs by pointing to the pictures and saying the names.

3 **T 2.9** Students listen and repeat. Do this chorally, stopping the recording, and individually. Check comprehension of the question *How much … ?* Make sure students practise the intonation of the *How much … ?* questions, and draw attention to word-joining, e.g. *an orange juice*.

Students ask and answer questions about the prices. Do this first in open pairs, then in closed pairs. Correct pronunciation carefully.

4 **T 2.10** Students listen to the conversations and fill in the gaps.

> **Answers and tapescript**
> A Good morning.
> B Good **morning**. Can I have **an orange juice**, please?
> A Here you are. Anything else?
> B No, thanks.
> A **Ninety** p, please.
> B Thanks.
> A Thank you.
>
> A Hi. Can I help?
> B Yes. Can I have a **tuna and egg** salad, please?
> A Anything to drink?
> B Yeah. A **mineral water**, please.
> A OK. Here you are.
> B **How much** is that?
> A **Four** pounds **ninety-five**, please.
> B Thanks.

5 Students practise the conversations in pairs. Then make the activity a little freer by roleplaying. Take the role of the person working in the café yourself first and choose one of the students to be the customer. You can increase the vocabulary according to the level of your students, asking for example *Do you want mayonnaise in your sandwich? Diet Coke?* etc.

Then ask students to take both roles and practise the conversations in the Student's Book and their own conversations. You could record some conversations for later examination and correction.

Don't forget!

Workbook Unit 2
Exercise 10 Practice of family vocabulary and possessive *'s*.
Exercise 11 This exercise looks at adjectives and nouns that go together.
Exercise 12 Spelling of plural nouns.

Word list
Remind your students of the Word list for this unit on p135. They could write in the translations, learn them at home, and/or write some of the words in their vocabulary notebook.

Pronunciation Book Unit 2

Video
A video accompanies *New Headway Elementary*. There is a section for every one or two units throughout the course. The first one is called *A Day in London* and features David, who is English, showing his Italian friend, Paola, round London.

3

Present Simple 1 – *he/she/it*
Questions and negatives
Jobs • What time is it?

Introduction to the unit

Work and jobs are the themes of this unit as they lend themselves to the practice of the grammatical aim, which is the introduction of the third person singular of the Present Simple. The skills work includes a reading text about a man who lives on a remote Scottish island and has thirteen jobs! This was chosen to complement both the themes and grammar of the unit. The text also acts as a preview of other forms of the Present Simple in context.

Language aims

Grammar – Present Simple 1 The Present Simple is the most used tense in the English language. It is therefore important to introduce it early in an elementary course. In *New Headway Elementary* the introduction is staged over two units. In this unit only the third person singular with its questions and negatives is presented and practised. All the other persons are introduced in Unit 4.

POSSIBLE PROBLEMS

- The English language does not have many inflections. Unfortunately this seems to mean that the few that exist cause a disproportionate amount of difficulty for foreign learners. The *s* on the third person singular of the Present Simple is a classic example of this. Therefore we introduce it first in the hope that it will be more memorable and students will be less likely to omit it.
- The *s* can be pronounced in three ways:
  comes   /kʌmz/
  works   /wɜːks/
  teaches   /'tiːtʃɪz/
  So you need to spend some time highlighting the /s/, /z/, /ɪz/ endings and practising them.
- The use of *does/doesn't* in the question and negative often seems strange to students, because of the absence of the auxiliary in the positive.

NOTE

For the first nine units of *New Headway Elementary*, the verb *have* is introduced and practised as a full verb with its *do/does* forms. *Have got* is introduced in Unit 10. This is for several reasons:

- By introducing the *do/does* forms, the verb *have* operates like any other verb in the Present Simple (with the exception of *has* in the third person singular).
- When students have just learned the Present Simple and have been introduced to the auxiliary verbs *do/does*, it is very difficult and confusing for them when they come across the verb form *have got*, which operates differently.
- Although *have got* is common, especially in the spoken language, the full verb *have* with its *do/does* forms covers all the uses in a way that *have got* doesn't. *Have got* expresses possession, but it cannot express a habitual action. So students can learn *How many children have you got?*, but then it is very confusing when they are introduced to *What time do you have lunch?* We cannot say **What time have you got lunch?*
- Finally, *have* with its *do/does* forms is becoming more common in spoken British English. It is the standard form in American English.

Vocabulary and pronunciation A variety of jobs with related activities are introduced. Dictionary work is encouraged and there is a certain amount of work on the phonetic spelling of some of the words.

Everyday English Students focus on how to tell the time in English. This is practised in short dialogues.

Workbook The spelling of the third person singular is practised (*watches, goes*).

Question words such as *Where?* and *How much?* are practised.

Verbs of daily routine (*get up, get dressed*) are introduced, and some verbs and nouns that go together (*have a shower, wear a uniform*).

The writing syllabus of *New Headway Elementary* begins in this unit.

Object pronouns (*me, him, them*) are introduced and practised.

Notes on the unit

STARTER (SB p20)

The *Starter* activity recycles the family vocabulary from Unit 2 and allows students to use some of the jobs vocabulary they already know. Give some examples of jobs of the people in your own family and then get students to continue the activity in pairs. If students ask for the names of individual jobs, give some examples that are common to the whole class, but do not let the *Starter* activity go on too long or reduce the usefulness of the *Vocabulary and pronunciation* section.

THREE JOBS (SB p20)

Present Simple *he/she/it*

> **SUGGESTION**
> We suggest that *before* you start this unit you set the following vocabulary homework in preparation for the presentation texts on Ali and Bob. This will save a lot of classroom time where you would have to check vocabulary either by mime, dictionary work, or translation (in a monolingual class), and it will give you more time to focus on the grammar.
>
> **Homework prior to lesson**
> Ask students to write the translation of the following words and *learn* them for the lesson. They can use a bilingual dictionary to look up words they don't know.
>
> **Verbs**   *come fly go help like love speak work*
> **Nouns**   *day hour summer town walk week winter*
> **Adjectives**   *free (time) ordinary*
>
> Pre-teach *scientist* and *flying doctor*.

1 Ask students to look at the photographs. Ask them *What's her job?* (scientist), *What's his job?* (flying doctor).

Then ask them to look quickly at the texts and ask *Where's she from?* (Cambridge, England), *Where's he from?* (England).

T 3.1 Now play the recording and ask your students to read and listen to the texts at the same time. If you think your class will experience some difficulty, you could deal with the texts one at a time, doing the *Grammar Spot* exercises with them for the first text and then asking them to repeat the process on their own for the second.

GRAMMAR SPOT

1 Ask students to work on their own to underline the verbs and then check their answers with a partner before you conduct a full class feedback. You could ask them to call out the verbs for you to write on the board in columns according to their pronunciation.

> **Answers and pronunciation guide**
> /z/   comes flies lives loves is has
> /s/   works likes speaks

2 Ask the whole class what the last letter is and point out that this is the ending for the third person singular – *he, she, it* – of the Present Simple tense.

3 Before you ask your students to practise the verbs in pairs, ask them to chorus them with you from the board and draw their attention to the different pronunciations of the endings.

You may also want to point out that *is* and *has* are irregular.

Now ask them to practise in pairs and read one of the texts to each other. Go round and monitor. You could round off the activity by asking one or two students to read a text aloud to the whole class.

---

2 Ask your students to write in the answers on their own and then check with a partner. Make it clear that each gap represents a word and that number 8 requires a positive verb in the second sentence because of the negative expressed by *never*.

T 3.2 Students listen and check their answers.

> **Answers and tapescript**
> 1 She's a scientist. He's a doctor.
> 2 Alison comes from England. Bob **comes from** England, too.
> 3 She lives in a big city, but he **lives** in a **small** town.
> 4 She **works** three days **a** week. He **works** 16 hours a day **non-stop**.

5 He **speaks** to sick people on his radio. She **speaks** three languages.
6 She loves her job and he **loves his job**, too.
7 She **has a** daughter. He **isn't** married.
8 She **likes** skiing and going **for** walks in her free time.* He never **has** free time.
* Note that *like* + *-ing* is dealt with in Unit 4.

PRACTICE (SB p21)

Talking about people

1 The aim of this activity is to give students the chance not just to produce single sentences, but to speak at some length to describe Philippe. It is both useful and satisfying for low-level students to use language for 'display' purposes in this way and not always engage in the more 'natural' question and answer activities.

Ask the whole class to look at the picture of Philippe and the information about him. Start to build a profile of him orally with contributions from different students.

2 Then ask one or two individuals to speak at length about Philippe.

Sample answer
Philippe is a barman. He comes from France and he lives in Paris. He works in the centre of Paris. He speaks French and a little English. He isn't married, but he has a dog. In his free time he likes walking his dog and playing football.

3 Now ask your students to write some notes about a friend or relative. Students work in pairs and talk about their friend/relative to their partner. Go round the class to check and help them. Bring the whole class together again, and ask one or two students to tell the others about their friend/relative.

ADDITIONAL MATERIAL

Workbook Unit 3
Exercises 1 and 2 These provide further practice of the third person positive of the Present Simple. Exercise 2 focuses on the spelling.
Exercise 3 This is a vocabulary activity in preparation for Exercise 4. It should be done with a dictionary. (It is *not* an opportunity to practise other persons of the Present Simple, only to see the verbs in their infinitive forms!) It would be a good idea to set this exercise for homework and then follow it in class with Exercise 4 – the pictures of Rupert's daily routine are particularly suitable for a classroom activity, where the story is built orally *before* students are asked to write it.

Questions and negatives

NOTE
Be prepared for some students to make mistakes in the use of *does/doesn't* to form the question and negative. In the Present and Past Simple tenses, where there is no auxiliary in the positive, the use of the auxiliary verbs can seem very strange. Many students feel that it would be much more logical to say:
*Lives he in Paris?
*Where lives she?
*She lives not in London.
The short answers *Yes, he does./No, he doesn't.* also cause problems and need highlighting for students.

1 You need to signal that you are going to introduce the question form. You can do this by drawing a large question mark on the board and/or repeating the sentences yourself with exaggerated intonation.

T 3.3 Play the recording and ask your students to read and listen to the questions and complete the answers.

Answers and tapescript

Where does Alison come from?	Cambridge, **in** England.
What does she do?	She's **a** scientist.
Does she speak French?	**Yes**, she does.
Does she speak Spanish?	**No**, she doesn't.

Play the recording again and get students to repeat both chorally and individually. Then get them to ask and answer the questions in open pairs across the class.

NOTE
Encourage good pronunciation at all times. Highlight the pronunciation of *does* and *doesn't*, getting students to repeat the weak and strong forms in isolation and as part of the question and short answers:
the weak /dəz/ in all the questions *What does she do? Does she speak French?*
and the strong form /dʌz/ and /dʌznt/ in the short answers *Yes, she does./ No, she doesn't.*
Also take care with the intonation, falling at the end in the *wh-* questions and rising in the inverted questions.

Where does she come from? /weə dəz ʃɪ kʌm frɒm/

Does she speak French? /dəz ʃɪ spiːk frentʃ/

2 **T 3.4** Ask your students to complete the sentences on their own and then check their answers with a partner. Play the recording and get them to listen and check. Finally, ask individuals to read aloud their answers to the class and check the pronunciation.

> **Answers and tapescript**
> 1 Where **does** Bob **come** from? England.
> 2 What **does** he **do**? He's a doctor.
> 3 **Does** he fly to help people? Yes, he **does**.
> 4 **Does** he **speak** French and German? No, he **doesn't**.

3 Students write similar questions about Philippe and then ask and answer in pairs.

> **Sample questions and answers**
> 1 Where does Philippe come from? France.
> 2 What does he do? He's a barman.
> 3 Does he work in the centre of Paris? Yes, he does.
> 4 Does he speak German? No, he doesn't.

PRACTICE (SB p22)

Asking about people

1 Get students to read about Keiko or Mark. Check comprehension and drill the pronunciation of *interpreter* /ɪnˈtɜːprɪtə/, *journalist* /ˈdʒɜːnəlɪst/, *United Nations* /juːˈnaɪtɪd ˈneɪʃnz/, and *Moscow* /ˈmɒskəʊ/.

2 Get students to say a sentence about each person as an example. Students choose Keiko or Mark and describe her/him to a partner. Go round the class to check and help them. Round off the activity by bringing the whole class together again, and asking one or two students to tell the others about Keiko and Mark.

3 Ask each student in a pair to choose either Keiko or Mark. Students work on their own and write the questions about their character.

> **Answers**
> 1 Where does Keiko/Mark come from?
> 2 Where does Keiko/Mark live?
> 3 What does Keiko/Mark do?
> 4 Where does Keiko/Mark work?
> 5 Does Keiko/Mark speak French/Spanish?
> 6 What does Keiko/Mark do in her/his free time?
> 7 Does Keiko/Mark listen to music?
> 8 How many children does Keiko/Mark have?
> 9 Does Keiko/Mark have a dog?

Check their questions quickly round the class, getting students to read them aloud.

4 Ask your students to close their books. Write the names Keiko and Mark on the board, then ask students to work in pairs and take it in turns to ask and answer questions about them. Don't make the activity too laborious by insisting they ask *every* question about *both* characters, as this would probably take too long. Let your students choose their questions and character they use.

Round off the activity by asking for a few questions and answers in open pairs across the class.

5 This is a personalized activity. Tell students they can answer questions about any relative, e.g. aunt, uncle, or a friend. Feed in any necessary vocabulary, e.g. *cousin*, *(sister)-in-law* if students request this. Go round and check as they do the activity, focusing on the formation of questions. Ask one or two students to tell the whole class about their or their partner's relative.

> **SUGGESTION**
> Students can play a guessing game in which one student describes another (without saying his/her name!) and the rest of the class guess who it is. This can also be used to practise *Yes/No* questions, where the student who has thought of the person replies *Yes* or *No* to the rest of the class and does not give any additional information. This can be set up as a whole-class activity and then continued in groups/pairs.

Listening and pronunciation

6 Do this exercise as briskly as possible with the whole class. Demonstrate the activity by going through the sample sentences with them and practising the responses *Yes, that's right, No, he/she doesn't, No, he isn't.*

T 3.5 Play the recording or read the sentences yourself and nominate individuals in the class to respond.

Encourage other members of the class to correct if a wrong answer is given. It should be quick and fun to do, so *don't* insist on the full correct answer if it slows down the activity. *No, he/she doesn't* is enough.

Answers and tapescript
1 Philippe comes from Paris.
   Yes, that's right.
2 Philippe lives in London.
   No, he doesn't. (He lives in Paris.)
3 He works in the centre of Paris.
   Yes, that's right.
4 He speaks English very well.
   No, he doesn't. (He speaks a little English.)
5 He's married.
   No, he isn't.
6 Keiko lives and works in New York.
   Yes, that's right.
7 She speaks French and German.
   No, she doesn't. (She speaks Japanese, English, and French.)
8 She plays tennis in her free time.
   No, she doesn't. (She goes skiing.)
9 She isn't married.
   Yes, she is. (She's married to an American.)
10 Mark works in an office in Moscow.
   Yes, that's right.
11 He has three sons.
   No, he doesn't. (He has three daughters.)
12 He likes playing football in his free time.
   No, he doesn't. (He likes listening to music.)

7 **T 3.6** This should follow on immediately from the previous exercise. Play the recording. Ask students to tick the sentence they hear. This exercise tests receptive comprehension, but you can make it productive afterwards by asking students to say the pairs of sentences in pairs.

Answers and tapescript
1 She likes her job.
2 She loves walking.
3 He isn't married.
4 Does he have three children?
5 What does he do?

Check it

8 Ask students to work in pairs or small groups and tick the correct sentence. Ask them to work quite quickly, then conduct a full class feedback. Try to get students to correct each other and explain any mistakes they hear.

Answers
1 She comes from Japan.
2 What does he do in his free time?
3 Where does she live?
4 He isn't married.
5 Does she have two sons?
6 He doesn't play football.
7 She doesn't love Peter.
8 What's his address?

ADDITIONAL MATERIAL

Workbook Unit 3
Exercises 4–8 Questions and negatives in Present Simple third person singular.
Exercise 12 Using pronouns.
Exercise 13 Rewriting a short text about Keiko.

READING AND LISTENING (SB p24)

Seumas McSporran – the man with thirteen jobs!

NOTE
This is an important activity because it brings together in a text much of the grammar your students have been studying so far. It should give them great satisfaction to feel that they can already master a piece of continuous prose of this length.
It also acts as a preview of the work on daily routine in Unit 4.
Seumas McSporran is a real person (and a real name), and the text is based on a newspaper article. However, it has been carefully simplified and graded for students of this level.

You could begin the lesson by asking students:
How many jobs do you/most people have?
What time do you/most people start and finish work?

1 Ask students to look quickly at the photographs on the page and tell you a little about what and who they can see. Do not insist on accuracy at this stage – use this as an opportunity for students to get into the topic and predict what they might read in the text.
   Briefly revise the times that go with each photograph.

2 Ask students to work in pairs and match the sentences with the photographs. Tell them not to worry about new vocabulary but to use the words that they recognize and the information in the photographs to help them with the matching.
   Check the answers.

Answers
1 h 2 a 3 e 4 g 5 c 6 b 7 d 8 i 9 f

Check the key vocabulary by giving short definitions accompanied by mime and getting students to tell you the word, e.g. *You eat this in the morning – breakfast; the people who stay in a hotel – guests; you need this in your car to drive it – petrol*, etc.

3   Pre-teach/check some of the key vocabulary before the students start to read, so that they do not stop at every word they do not recognize to ask for an explanation. You can teach/check the following through mime or short definitions: jobs – *policeman, fireman, taxi-driver, school-bus driver, boatman* (a man you pay to take you out in a boat or for the use of a boat), *ambulance man, petrol attendant, undertaker*; verbs – *get up, make breakfast, watch TV, make supper, go to bed.*

Ask students to work in pairs or small groups to find the answers. Tell them not to worry about words they do not recognize and just to focus on the key information. They can consult the text whenever necessary.

Check the answers. Decide according to the speed and ability of your students whether you want quick, short answers or fuller answers (see brackets).

Answers
1   On the Island of Gigha (pronounced /giːə/). (He lives on the Island of Gigha in the north of Scotland.)
2   60. (He's 60 years old.)
3   Thirteen. (He has thirteen jobs.)
4   Margaret. (His wife's name is Margaret.)
5   She works in the shop.
6   120. (120 people live on Gigha.)
7   150. (150 tourists visit Gigha in summer.)
8   He makes breakfast, drives the children to school, collects the post from the boat, and delivers the post to the houses.
9   Margaret makes supper, and Seumas does the accounts. They have a glass of wine and then go to bed.

If appropriate, ask students for their reaction to the text. Ask if they know anyone who has a lot of jobs and what they do.

4   Ask students to look back at the photographs on p24. Demonstrate the activity by getting two students to ask and answer using the example in the Student's Book. Students continue to ask and answer questions about the times in Seumas's day. Go round the class to check. Feed back on any common errors.

5   **T 3.7** Ask students to mask the conversations in exercise 6. Focus attention on the three questions and demonstrate the activity by playing conversation 1 and checking the answers (see below).

Play the remaining three conversations, stopping after each one to allow students to complete their answers. Check the answers with the whole class.

Answers
Conversation 1
1   Afternoon
2   Seumas and a customer in Seumas's shop
3   Shopkeeper
Conversation 2
1   Morning
2   Seumas and a woman who lives on the island
3   Postman
Conversation 3
1   Evening
2   Seumas and Margaret
3   No job – Seumas isn't working
Conversation 4
1   Morning
2   Seumas and schoolchildren
3   School-bus driver

6   Students complete the conversations as far as they can, using what they can remember from the first listening and from the reading text, and the information from exercise 4. Students can then exchange information with a partner.

Play the conversations again to allow students to complete their answers. Then check the answers with the whole class.

Answers and tapescript
1   A   Good **afternoon**. Can I **have** two ice-creams, please?
    B   Chocolate or vanilla?
    A   One chocolate, one vanilla please.
    B   That's **£1.80**. Anything **else**?
    A   No, thank you.
2   A   Only **two** letters for you this **morning**, Mrs Craig.
    B   Thank you very much, Mr McSporran. And **how**'s Mrs McSporran this **morning**?
    A   Oh, she's very well, thank you. She's **busy** in the shop.
3   A   A glass of **wine** before bed, my dear?
    B   Oh, yes please.
    A   **Here** you are.
    B   Thank you, my dear. I'm very **tired** this **evening**.
4   A   Hello, Mr McSporran!
    B   Good **morning**, boys and girls. Hurry up, we're late.
    A   Can I sit here, Mr McSporran?
    C   No, no, I **want** to sit there.
    B   Be quiet **all** of you, and SIT DOWN!

Put students into pairs to practise the conversations. An additional idea is to ask them to choose *one* of the conversations and learn it by heart to act out to the rest of the class. You could also encourage more confident students to improvise some further dialogues. (Asking students to act really seems to help their pronunciation, particularly stress and intonation.)

Jobs

1 Ask students to look at the pictures and tell you any of the jobs they know already. Then get them to work in pairs and match a picture with a job in column A, checking any words that are still unknown in their dictionaries. You could ask them to mark the stress.

Conduct a full class feedback on the correct answers and drill the words both chorally and individually as you go, taking care with the stress (see below). Keep revising as you go by asking *Tell me again! What's 'a'? What's 'd'?* etc.

Answers

1 d	A barman	6 i	A shopkeeper
2 c	A nurse	7 e	An accountant
3 a	A pilot	8 h	An architect
4 b	An interpreter	9 g	A postman
5 f	A journalist		

2 Ask students to work in pairs or small groups and match a job in column A with a line in column B. They will probably need to continue to use their dictionaries *or* if you have a monolingual class and you think dictionary work will take too much time, you could give quick translations of any words they ask about. Afterwards you could either conduct a full class feedback (try not to make this too laborious with too much correction), or ask different students to come to the board and write the answers for the others to comment on and read aloud.

Answers

a A pilot flies planes.
b An interpreter translates things.
c A nurse looks after people in hospital.
d A barman serves drinks.
e An accountant looks after money.
f A journalist writes for a newspaper.
g A postman delivers letters.
h An architect designs buildings.
i A shopkeeper sells things.

3 **NOTE**

The idea of this activity is to give a very short introduction to and practice of the phonetic script. It is also an opportunity to start getting your students familiar with the phonetic symbols chart on p143 of their book.

You need to make clear what exactly phonetic script is, i.e. that it is only the sounds of the words that are transcribed and that it is important to know this in English because the spellings and the sounds often do not relate exactly.

Ask the whole class to look at all the phonetic transcriptions and say if they can recognize any of the words. Ask them to turn to p143, *not* to study it, but so that they get the idea of what phonetic script is.

Now ask them to write the spellings of the words and then check them with a partner and practise saying them together. Let them use the phonetic chart to help them.

Answers

1	nurse	4	shopkeeper
2	postman	5	architect
3	accountant	6	barman

If you have time, you could put a few additional words in phonetic script on the board for students to do after you have asked for feedback on the words in the exercise. For example:

/ˈhɒspɪtəl/	(hospital)
/ˈpiːpl/	(people)
/wɜːks/	(works)
/lʊks/	(looks)
/selz/	(sells)
/pleɪnz/	(planes)
/ˈhaʊzɪz/	(houses)

4 Make this exercise fun, like a game, and do it as quickly as possible. Ask students to learn the sentences by heart, then to close their books. Call out the name of a job and tell your students to call out to complete the sentence.

Teacher	**Student(s)**
A journalist …	*writes for a newspaper!*
A pilot …	*flies planes!* etc.

Finally, ask students to work in pairs for a few minutes with their books still shut, and ask and answer questions about the jobs. Demonstrate the first example yourself to remind them of the question, e.g.

What does an interpreter do? He/She translates things.

Workbook Unit 3
Further vocabulary exercises:
Exercise 9 This practises more verbs and nouns that go together, e.g. *have a shower*.
Exercise 10 This revises a selection of vocabulary from all the units so far. It requires students to sort words into related groups.

EVERYDAY ENGLISH (SB p27)

What time is it?

Introduce the subject of telling the time by asking *What time is it now?* and *What time does the lesson end?* Accept answers in the hour + minutes form, e.g. *five thirty*, but explain that the system used in *New Headway Elementary* uses *past* and *to*.

> **NOTE**
> The first eight clocks on this page are positioned in such a way that those with gaps underneath are next to clocks with *similar* times which students can use to help them write in the correct answers.
> The next eight practise the time in five-minute intervals around the clock. You probably will *not* need to point this out to students. It should be obvious what to do from the pictures.

1 Ask students to work in pairs, look carefully at the clocks, and write in the times.

  T 3.8 Now play the recording for students to check their answers.

> **Answers and tapescript**
> | | |
> |---|---|
> | It's five o'clock. | **It's eight o'clock.** |
> | It's half past five. | **It's half past eleven.** |
> | It's quarter past five. | **It's quarter past two.** |
> | It's quarter to six. | **It's quarter to nine.** |
> | It's five past five. | **It's ten past five.** |
> | **It's twenty past five.** | It's twenty-five past five. |
> | **It's twenty-five to six.** | It's twenty to six. |
> | It's ten to six. | **It's five to six.** |

Get students to practise saying the times either from the recording or repeating them after you. If possible, bring a toy clock with moveable hands to the lesson as an easy way of getting further practice. First, *you* can change the times on the clock and then your students can also have turns, coming to the front of the class, moving the hands, and asking *What time is it?*

2 This exercise introduces *about* as a useful expression for times just before or after an exact division of the clock.

Read through the examples with the class and practise with the toy clock (if you have one!) or by drawing further examples on the board.

3 **T 3.9** Play the recording and ask your students to repeat the sentences giving very special attention to the stress and intonation. Tell them that they must try to sound *very* polite. Really encourage good imitation from the recording, or by giving the sentences yourself. Practise the dialogue across the class with your own examples first, then ask everyone to draw about three clocks on a piece of paper and practise the conversation again in pairs. Round off the lesson by asking one or two pairs to act out the conversations in front of the class. Tell them to imagine that they are stopping someone in the street to ask the time and that they must be very, very polite.

The *more* you insist on good stress and intonation in such activities, the more fun it will be!

Workbook Unit 3
Exercise 11 This gives more practice of telling the time.

Don't forget!

Workbook Unit 3
Exercises 12 and 13 You might want to do the writing activities now, if you haven't done them earlier.

Word list
Remind your students of the Word list for this unit on p136. They could write in the translations, learn them at home, and/or write some of the words in their vocabulary notebook.

Pronunciation Book Unit 3

4

Present Simple 2 – *I/you/we/they*
Leisure activities
Social expressions

Take it easy!

Introduction to the unit

The theme of this unit is free time and leisure activities. This lends itself to much practice, personalized and otherwise, of the main grammatical aim, which is the introduction of all other persons (those without the *s*!) of the Present Simple tense. The skills work includes reading and listening tasks where people from three different countries talk about their favourite season and what they do. This provides the opportunity to bring together and revise all persons of the Present Simple.

Language aims

Grammar – Present Simple 2 This unit follows on from the introduction of the third person in Unit 3 and introduces all other persons of the Present Simple, *I*, *you*, *we*, *they*, and the question and negative. The verb forms with these are all the same, without the inflection *s*, and tend to cause less difficulty as a result. The third person is constantly revised alongside the other persons so that students can perceive the differences in form.

Vocabulary A variety of leisure activities (sports and hobbies) are introduced and these are practised in a personalized activity with the verb *to like*.

Everyday English Some common and useful social expressions are introduced and practised in short dialogues.

Workbook Adverbs of frequency, e.g. *always*, *sometimes*, *never* are practised.

In the vocabulary section, 'opposite' verbs, e.g. *love/hate*, *open/close*, *leave/arrive* are revised.

The writing syllabus continues with an introduction to informal letter writing via a letter to a penfriend.

Notes on the unit

> **SUGGESTION**
> Setting some vocabulary for homework before you start this unit will give you more time to focus on the grammar. It is also worthwhile to get your students used to the idea of taking some responsibility for the learning of vocabulary. Encourage them to enter the new words in their vocabulary notebooks.

Homework prior to the lesson

1   Ask students to learn the days of the week in English. You could give them a handout with phonetic script such as this:

Monday /'mʌndi/	Thursday /'θɜːzdi/	Sunday /'sʌndi/
Tuesday /'tʃuːzdi/	Friday /'fraɪdi/	
Wednesday /'wenzdi/	Saturday /'sætədi/	

2   Give students these new verbs to look up in a bilingual dictionary. Ask them to learn them and write down the translations.

interview _____	go out _____
chat _____	relax _____
cook _____	stay _____
get up _____	visit _____

STARTER (SB p28)

1 Use a calendar that shows the year, months, and days as a visual aid. (Alternatively, write the day, month, and year on the board in abbreviated form, e.g. Tu., Sept., 2000). Focus attention on the year and elicit how we say this in English. Do the same for the month. (Do not spend too long on this, as students will focus on months more fully before the *Reading and listening* section.)

> **POSSIBLE PROBLEMS**
>
> Students often try to say years in English in the same way as in their own language, e.g. 1999 is read as *one thousand nine hundred and ninety-nine* instead of *nineteen ninety-nine*. If necessary, highlight on the board how we divide dates beginning 18-, 19-, into two pairs of numbers and give practise of similar dates.
>
> You may also need to remind students of the use of *and* in dates like 2001 = *two thousand and one*.

2 Use the calendar and get students to go through the days of the week. Say the days yourself and ask them to repeat each one both chorally and individually. This will take less time if you have set the above for homework.

> **POSSIBLE PROBLEMS**
> **Days**
>
> Take particular care with the pronunciation of *Tuesday* /ˈtʃuːzdi/ and *Thursday* /ˈθɜːzdi/ which students can easily confuse because they sound quite similar. Also the pronunciation of *Wednesday* /ˈwenzdi/ can be a problem because of the spelling, and the consonant cluster /nzd/ that results from it being pronounced as *two* syllables not three.

• Ask *What day is it today?* Chorus through the days of the week with the whole class and then make the individual practice fun by getting one student after another to give consecutive days *very* quickly round the class until they are firmly fixed. (If time, you could then ask one or two students to go through the whole week and perhaps also ask them to spell some of the days, to revise the alphabet.)

• Ask *Which days are the weekend?* This will check that students understand the word *weekend* which is needed in the exercises.

• Ask students to ask and answer the *Starter* questions in pairs. Go round and check students' pronunciation and feed back on any common errors.

> **EXTRA SUGGESTIONS**
>
> If you feel your students needs more practice on days, months, and years, try the following activities:
>
> • rearranging the jumbled spelling of days and months
> • matching phonetic script to days and months
> • conducting a favourite day or birthday survey
> • a word association activity for different days/months
> • doing an 'important year' quiz with simple headline-style sentences (to avoid the use of the past simple), e.g. *the first man on the moon*, and students supply the correct year, e.g. *1969*.
> • linking days and months to horoscope signs. This can be done as an information gap activity where students have some of the names of the signs and some of the dates missing.

WEEKDAYS AND WEEKENDS (SB p28)

Present Simple *I/you/we/they*

1 This text reminds students of the third person of the Present Simple before they are introduced to the other persons. Focus attention on the photograph and on the headline. Elicit basic information about Bobbi (*What's her name? Where is she in the photo?*).

> **Answers**
>
> Bobbi Brown **lives** in New Jersey. She **is** thirty-four and **works** for SKY TV in New York City. But she **doesn't work** on weekdays, she only works at weekends. She **interviews** famous people for an early morning news programme called *The World This Weekend*. On Saturdays and Sundays she **gets up** at 3.00 in the morning because she **starts** work at 6.30! She **loves** her job because it is exciting.

Ask a few questions to revise the third person.
Examples

Teacher	Student(s)
Where does Bobbi live?	*In New Jersey.*
How old is she?	*Thirty-four.*
What does she do?	*She works for SKY TV.*
What time does she get up?	*Three o'clock in the morning.*
What time does the programme start?	*Half past six.*
Does she like her job?	*Yes, she does.*
Why does she like it?	*Because it's exciting.*

2 **T 4.1** Tell students that Bobbi Brown is now talking about her weekdays. Ask students to first read and listen to the text and not to write anything. Explain that they will complete the text at the next stage. Check or pre-teach the following vocabulary from the text: *domestic, gym, block, kids*. Play the recording.

3 Ask students to work in pairs and check the verbs in the box. This can be done quite quickly if they have done the preparatory homework. If they haven't, encourage students to look up new words in their dictionary and work together to complete the text with the verbs from the box. You will need to make clear that some of the verbs will need an *s* because they are third person singular. The others can be copied exactly from the box.

T 4.1 Play the recording again so that students can check their answers.

Answers and tapescript
My weekends are fast and exciting. My weekdays are fast and domestic! I **have** two sons, Dylan, 7, and Dakota, 5. Every morning I **get up** one hour before them, at 6.00, and I **go** to the gym. I **come** home and I **make** breakfast, then I **take** them to school. On Mondays I always **go shopping**. I **buy** all the food for the week. I often **cook** dinner in the evenings, but not every day because I don't **like** cooking. Fortunately, my husband, Don, **loves** cooking. On Tuesdays and Thursdays I **visit** my father. He **lives** on the next block. Every afternoon I **pick up** the kids from school. In the evenings Don and I usually **relax**, but sometimes we **visit** friends. We never **go out** on Friday evenings because I **start** work so early on Saturdays.

Ask one or two students to read parts of the text aloud to the rest of the class and, if time, to each other in pairs.

Questions and negatives

4 **T 4.2** Ask students to complete Bobbi's answers and play the recording for them to check their answers.

Answers
In New York.   No, I **don't**.
Yes, I **do**.   **Because** I work.

Play the recording again or model the questions and answers yourself. Practise the questions and answers in open pairs across the class so that you can correct any mistakes. Take particular care with the pronunciation:

Sounds
The weak vowel sound /dʊ/ in the question, and the strong vowel sound /duː/ in the short answer.
Do you like your work?   *Yes, I do.*
/dʒʊ laɪk jə wɜːk/   /jes aɪ duː/

Stress and intonation
The intonation rises at the end of inverted questions and falls at the end of short answers and *wh-* questions.

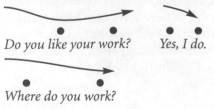

Do you like your work?   Yes, I do.

Where do you work?

5 Tell students to read the texts on p28–9 again first, but then to cover them and try to remember the information about Bobbi's life. Ask students to work in pairs and take it in turns to be Bobbi Brown. Demonstrate the activity by getting two students to ask and answer the first two questions across the class. Ask students to continue the activity in pairs. Go round and check for the correct use of the auxiliary *do/does* and for the correct use of strong and weak forms in the pronunciation of *do*.

GRAMMAR SPOT

1 Ask students to complete the table with the positive and negative forms. Check the answers.

Answers

	Positive	Negative
I	work	don't work
You	work	don't work
He/She	works	doesn't work
It	works	doesn't work
We	work	don't work
They	work	don't work

Ask students to focus on the positive forms in the table. Ask them which have a different form (*he/she/it*) and how they are different (they end in -*s*).

Ask students to focus on the negative forms in the table. Ask them how the *I/you/we/they* forms are different from the positive forms (they use the auxiliary *don't*). Ask students to focus on the *he/she/it* forms and ask them how they are different from the other negative forms (they use the auxiliary *doesn't*).

2 Ask students to complete the questions and answers. Check the answers.

Answers
Where **do** you work?
Where **does** she work?
Do you work in New York? Yes, I **do**.
Does he work in New York? No, he **doesn't**.

Ask students which auxiliary verb is used in questions with *I/you/we/they* (*do*) and which with *he/she/it* (*does*). Remind students that questions can begin with a question word, or have no question word and the answer *Yes/No*. Ask students to give you examples of each type of question from the table.

Read Grammar Reference 4.1 and 4.2 on p127 together in class, and/or ask students to read it at home. Encourage them to ask you questions about it.

3 Students find the adverbs of frequency in the text about Bobbi Brown.

PRACTICE (SB p30)

Talking about you

1 Ask students to work on their own to do this activity. Students who finish early can then check their answers with a partner.

Answers and tapescript
1d What time do you go to bed? At 11 o'clock.
2b Where do you go on holiday? To Spain or Portugal.
3e What do you do on Sundays? I always relax.
4c When do you do your homework? After dinner.
5a Who do you live with? My mother and sisters.
6f Why do you like your job? Because it's interesting.
7g How do you travel to school? By bus.
8h Do you go out on Friday evenings? Yes, I do sometimes.

T 4.3 Play the recording and let students check their answers. As preparation for the next activity, ask students to listen and repeat the questions and answers chorally and individually. Take particular care with intonation.

2 This activity gives practice of the first and second persons only. Ask students to work in pairs to ask and answer the questions in *Practice* 1. Demonstrate the activity by getting a pair of students to ask and answer the first question across the class. Remind students to have the whole question ready before they speak. Go round and check as students do the activity, listening for correct intonation. Students who finish early can be

encouraged to ask similar questions but with different days or question words, e.g. *Do you go out on Saturday evenings? Where do you do your homework?*

3 This activity practises the third person singular alongside the other persons. It also pulls the class together after the pairwork. Ask a few individuals to tell the rest of the class about themselves and their partner. If necessary, remind students they need to use the third person -s when talking about their partner. (Unless you have a small class, it would take too long to give everyone a turn.)

Listening and pronunciation

4 **T 4.4** Play the recording. Ask students to listen carefully and tick the sentence they hear. Play the recording again. Stop after each one and ask students to discuss the answer with a partner before you establish the correct one. You can make this exercise productive by asking students to read aloud the pairs of sentences.

Answers and tapescript
1 What does she do on Sundays?
2 Do you stay home on Thursday evenings?
3 He lives here.
4 What do you do on Saturday evenings?
5 I read a lot.
6 Why don't you like your job?

A questionnaire

5 Focus attention on the verbs in the questionnaire. Check comprehension of *smoke*, *drink wine*, and *have a computer*. Students answer the questions and complete the *Me* column about themselves.

6 Get students to practise the questions and answers from the questionnaire, encouraging good pronunciation with rising intonation for inverted questions. Ask individual students to ask you the questions so that you have the opportunity to help and correct them before they continue working with partners.

Ask all the class to stand up and 'mingle' to do the next part of the activity (if there is enough space to do so!). Tell them to take it in turns with two other students to ask and answer the questions.

7 This part of the activity is designed to revise the third person singular again alongside the other persons. (It could be set for homework or done orally.)

Ask students to use the information they have collected and write and compare themselves with either you or another student. Then ask one or two students to read their answers aloud for the others to comment on.

Positives and negatives

8 This exercise revises the verb *to be* alongside other verbs in the Present Simple. The exercise could be set for homework, but it can be quite fun if done orally and at a brisk pace with the whole class. Students could then write their answers afterwards.

Answers
3 She speaks Spanish.
4 They don't want to learn English.
5 We aren't tired and we don't want to go to bed.
6 Roberto doesn't like watching football on TV, but he likes playing it.
7 I don't work at home because I don't have a computer.
8 Amelia is happy because she has a new car.
9 I don't smoke, I don't drink, and I go to bed early.
10 He smokes, he drinks, and he doesn't go to bed early.

SUGGESTIONS

• You can 'test' how much students can remember about each other's lives by using the ideas in the 'How do you live?' questionnaire and getting the others to guess who is being referred to.

• Students imagine they have a very extravagant and luxurious lifestyle and interview each other, practising *Wh-* and *Yes/No* questions.

Where do you work?	*I don't work.*
What time do you get up?	*About 11 o'clock.*
Where do you live?	*In a very big house in Paris.*
Do you have children?	*Yes, but they don't live with me.*
Do you like cooking?	*No, I never cook. I have a chef at home.*
Do you have a busy life?	*Of course! I go shopping every day and I go to parties every night!*

ADDITIONAL MATERIAL

Workbook Unit 4
Exercise 1 This practises all persons of the Present Simple. Part 3 focuses on question formation.
Exercise 2 This practises *do* and *does*, and the verb *to be*.
Exercises 3–5 Questions and negatives in the Present Simple.
Exercises 6 and 7 More adverbs of frequency.

My favourite season

SUGGESTION
It would save time in the lesson if you could ask your students to learn the names of seasons and months in English for homework before the lesson. You could give them this list to learn by heart and test them in class.

Seasons

spring /sprɪŋ/	*autumn* /'ɔːtəm/
summer /'sʌmə/	*winter* /'wɪntə/

Months

January /'dʒænjəri/	*July* /dʒuː'laɪ/
February /'februəri/	*August* /'ɔːgəst/
March /mɑːtʃ/	*September* /sep'tembə/
April /'eɪprɪl/	*October* /ɒk'təʊbə/
May /meɪ/	*November* /nəʊ'vembə/
June /dʒuːn/	*December* /dɪ'sembə/

1 Ask students to work in pairs and answer the questions in exercise 1. They will obviously find this easier if you set it for homework. Monitor, noting any problems with pronunciation and confusion with the months of the year.

POSSIBLE PROBLEMS
Months and seasons
Students often confuse the months *March* and *May*, and *June* and *July*. They may also need particular help with the pronunciation of *February* /'februəri/ and *autumn* /'ɔːtəm/.

If your students had difficulties with the questions in exercise 1, now is a good time to present the key language again. Use a calendar as a visual aid, and go through the seasons and months. Say them first yourself and ask students to repeat each one in order both chorally and individually. Repeat the months and seasons a few times, making it fast and fun if you can. If necessary, check further by asking:
What's before/after September? etc.
When's your birthday? (Make sure that students give only the month in their answers *not* the actual date.)

Then ask students the questions in exercise 1 again, checking for accurate pronunciation.

If your students had few difficulties with the questions in exercise 1, briefly go through the answers as class feedback, highlighting any specific problems you noted earlier. If necessary, do further spot checks by asking similar questions to those above.

2 Ask students to look at the photographs and see if they can identify the seasons. Ask students which colours they can see.

3 **T 4.5** Ask students to read the text and listen to the recording at the same time. Ask them which seasons are mentioned and the speaker's favourite season (to check whether they were right about the photographs).

It may be wise to pause after *each* text to ask for feedback. You can also ask for the *nationality* of the speaker. (Careful with stress in the nationalities.)

4 Ask students to do this in groups of three if possible. Ask each one in the group to read about a different person. Then they can share the information to answer the questions, which will generate more speaking. Ask someone in each group to write down their answers. Give them 5–10 minutes and then bring the whole class together to conduct the feedback. Encourage them to give short answers where applicable but then to expand on these if possible (see suggestions in brackets in the answer key).

Answers
1 No, they don't. (Toshi doesn't. Al plays baseball and ice hockey and goes ice-skating and sailing. Manuela goes swimming.)
2 Al goes ice-skating and plays ice hockey. Manuela meets friends in restaurants and bars and they chat.
3 Yes, they do. (Manuela likes going to Brazilian bars. Toshi likes relaxing in a bar near his office.)
4 Near a lake.
5 In spring.
6 They drive to the beach, sunbathe, and go swimming.
7 No, we don't. We only know Toshi's job. (He works for Pentax cameras.)
8 Because he likes the colours of the trees.
9 Toshi watches his friend Shigeru. Shigeru likes singing Karaoke in the bars.
Toshi doesn't sing because he is too shy.
10 Red, gold, orange, yellow, brown, grey.
(Ask students to point to things of these colours in the room to check their understanding.)

5 Ask students to remain in their groups to find the six mistakes in the summary and get one or two students to read aloud the corrected version to the rest of the class.

Answers
Al comes from Canada. In winter he plays ice hockey and goes (1) **ice-skating**. He has a holiday home near (2) **a lake**. Manuela comes from (3) **Portugal**. She likes sunbathing and (4) **swimming** in summer.
Toshi comes from Japan. He (5) **doesn't have** a lot of free time. He likes taking photographs, but he (6) **doesn't like** singing pop songs in bars.

6 **T 4.6** Ask students to listen and decide which one is Al, Manuel, and Toshi. Play the recording and stop it after each conversation. Ask *Who is it? Where are they? How do you know?* and let students discuss their answers in pairs before checking with the whole class.

Answers and tapescript
Conversation 1: Manuela. (She is with some Portuguese friends and an English friend called Jane.) They are in a Brazilian bar. We know this because they talk about the music and have drinks.
Conversation 2: Toshi. (He is with a British colleague, Ann Jones from London.) They are in Tokyo in an office (the headquarters of Pentax). We know this because Toshi says *Welcome to Tokyo*.
Conversation 3: Al. (He is with a Scottish friend called Mick.) They are at Al's holiday home, near the lake. We know this because they talk about going sailing and fishing.

T 4.6 **Who's who?**
1 **M = Manuela   J = Jane   F = Manuela's friends**
M Hello, everybody! This is my friend Jane from England.
F Hi!
Hello!
Hello, Jane!
J Hello. Pleased to meet you.
M Sit down here, Jane.
J Thanks.
F Do you like the music, Jane?
J Yes, I do. Is it American?
F No, it's Brazilian jazz!
M Come and have a drink, Jane.

2 **T = Toshi   J = Ann Jones**
T Mrs Jones! How do you do?
J How do you do?
T Please come in. You're from our office in London, aren't you?
J Yes, that's right.
T Welcome to Tokyo! Do you like our headquarters here?
J Yes. It's very big. How many people work here?
T About six thousand people. Do you want to see our offices?

3 **A = Al   M = Mick**
A What do you want to do today, Mick?
M Ooh, I don't know. What do you . . .
A Ah! Do you like sailing?

> **M** Yes, very much. I sometimes go sailing in Scotland but not very often.
> **A** OK – so today it's sailing and fishing on the lake.
> **M** Fantastic. I love fishing too – we go fishing a lot in Scotland.

You could round off the activity by playing the recording again and suggesting that students read the tapescripts on p116 at the same time.

What do you think?

This is an attempt to generate some personalized discussion and give further freer practice of the Present Simple. Don't worry if at this level it turns out to be quite a short activity. Just a little free speaking is still worthwhile.

It can be helpful to ask students to discuss the topic together in small groups first before you conduct feedback with the whole class.

It would also be a nice idea to encourage them to ask *you* questions about *your* favourite season.

SUGGESTIONS

- You could do a favourite month/season survey where students interview each other in groups and then transfer the information into chart form. (This would work well in a class of students from different countries.) Students write notes to accompany the chart and highlight the key information. You will need to feed in expressions like: *Most of the class prefer … because …* , *Nobody prefers …* .

- Students interview each other to find out when the best month/season is for a certain activity in their country: *When's the best month for (skiing, walking, sunbathing, shopping, visiting your city, etc.)?*

- Students write a description of how their home area changes from season to season. Get them to include information on the weather, the colours they can see, the activities people do, and the number of visitors/tourists.

VOCABULARY AND SPEAKING (SB p34)

Leisure activities

1   In pairs or small groups, students look at the pictures and match as many as they can with the names of the activities. Ask them to check the others in their bilingual dictionary. Encourage them to enter any new words in their vocabulary notebooks. Then ask students to tick the activities they like doing.

Answers

1 playing football	3 sailing
5 dancing	10 listening to music
8 skiing	11 swimming
16 watching TV	4 reading
13 going to the gym	15 eating in restaurants
9 taking photographs	14 going to the cinema
6 cooking	7 jogging
12 playing computer games	2 sunbathing

---

2   Highlight the form *like + -ing*. Choose a student and give examples of what you think he/she likes doing. Then ask students what *they* think *you* like doing. Ask them to continue in groups, choosing five activities from the Student's Book.

Encourage students to ask you questions to find out if they were correct about what you like, following the examples in the Student's Book. (Students are often interested to find out about their teacher, but keep this fairly short to allow time for the personalized stage.)

3   First build a dialogue with two students, using the example in the book and highlighting the possible follow-up questions. Then tell the students some true things about yourself, encouraging them to respond to your likes and dislikes as in the example.

Now ask students to continue in pairs and go round the class to check and help them. Make sure they use the *-ing* form.

4   Ask students to think about other activities which are not in the Student's Book. They can look them up in their bilingual dictionary, or ask you or their partner for help. Encourage students to mime or describe the activities rather than ask in L1. Finally, ask a few students in the class to report back on themselves and their partners (thereby practising different persons of the Present Simple).

EVERYDAY ENGLISH (SB p35)

Social expressions

These dialogues introduce and practise little expressions that 'lubricate' day-to-day conversational exchanges.

1   **T 4.7** Ask students to work in pairs and complete the dialogues with the expressions given. Then play the recording for them to listen and check their answers.

Answers and tapescript
1 A **I'm sorry I'm late.** The traffic is bad today.
  B **Don't worry.** Come and sit down. We're on page 25.
2 A **Excuse me.**
  B Yes?
  A Do you have a dictionary?
  B **I'm sorry,** I don't. It's at home.
  A **That's OK.**
3 A It's very hot in here. **Can I open the window?**
  B **Really?** I'm quite cold.
  A OK. **It doesn't matter.**
4 A **Excuse me!**
  B Can I help you?
  A Can I have a film for my camera?
  B How many exposures?
  A **Pardon?**
  B How many *exposures*?
  A **What does 'exposures' mean?**
  B How many pictures? 24? 36? 40?
  A Ah! **Now I understand!** 40, please.

2 Ask students where each conversation takes place and who the speakers are. Play the recording again so that they can copy the stress and intonation. Ask each pair to learn one of the dialogues by heart and then act it out for the rest of the class. Acting out can improve their pronunciation considerably.

Don't forget!

Workbook Unit 4
Exercise 8 Prepositions of time.
Exercise 9 This vocabulary exercise practises verbs with opposite meaning, e.g. *love/hate.*
Exercise 10 Writing an informal letter to a friend.

Word list
Remind your students of the Word list for this unit on p136. They could write in the translations, learn them at home, and/or write some of the words in their vocabulary notebook.

Pronunciation Book Unit 4

Video
There are two video sections that can supplement Units 3 and 4 of the Student's Book.
Report (Section 2) *The Train Drive* A short documentary about a teacher who drives a steam train in his free time.
Situation (Section 3) *The Party* David takes Paola to a party to meet some friends.

EXTRA IDEAS UNITS 1–4
On p123–4 of the Teacher's Book there are two additional activities – a reading text and a song. If you have time and feel that your students would benefit from them, you can photocopy them and use them in class. The reading exercise revises Units 1–4 and could also be done for homework.

An activity to exploit the reading is provided and the answers are on p155.

You will find the song after the tapescript for Unit 4 on the Class Cassette/CD. There are missing words for students to listen and complete, then they can listen again and check their answers.

There is/are • Prepositions
some/any • *this/that*
Furniture • Directions 1

Where do you live?

Introduction to the unit

The theme of this unit is places. Students describe a living room, a kitchen, their classroom, and where they live themselves. There is a reading text about a woman who has an unusual home – a plane! This text consolidates the language of the unit and hopefully students will be interested in the woman and her opinions of her less-than-average living space. There are also four very short listenings about homes around the world, as far apart as Toronto and Samoa.

Language aims

Grammar – *There is/are*

POSSIBLE PROBLEMS

Students often confuse *It's a …* with *There's a …* . The difference is that *It's a …* defines something and gives it a name. *There's a …* expresses what exists. This is quite a subtle area, and we don't suggest that you explore it with students, unless absolutely necessary, and preferably in L1, using translation as a support.

Learners confuse *there* and *their*. For such a short structural item, there are a lot of pronunciation problems. Many nationalities have difficulty with the sound /ð/. In *There's*, the *r* is often silent. In *There are* and the question when the following word begins with a vowel, the *r* is pronounced as a linking sound. Again, students need to be encouraged to start questions 'high' and fall, ending with a rise in inverted questions. It is worth working on these pronunciation areas, but not to the point of exhaustion!

Prepositions Simple prepositions of place, such as *on*, *under*, and *next to*, are introduced and practised.

some/any In this unit, *some* and *any* are presented only with countable nouns. In Unit 9, they are presented with both countable and uncountable nouns.

POSSIBLE PROBLEMS

Some also presents problems of pronunciation with its weak form /səm/.

Some as a concept has a tangible meaning, i.e. a certain, unspecified number of (something). The same cannot be said of *any*. It is a determiner used often (though by no means exclusively) in questions and negatives. We suggest you do not go into the deeper areas of *any* expressing fundamentally negative ideas, or *any* expressing *It doesn't matter what*, as in *Take any book you want*. This is unnecessary, and difficult for elementary-level students.

Vocabulary There is quite a high vocabulary load in this unit, including furniture and electrical appliances, classroom and business items, and local amenities. The vocabulary is taught and recycled alongside the main target structures and, for this reason, there is no self-contained *Vocabulary* section.

It is worth checking from time to time how students are progressing with their vocabulary notebooks. Are they still adding to them? Have they started a new one? Do they try to revise regularly? Have they thought of new ways of organizing their notebooks? Probably not!

Everyday English This is the first activity on directions. This topic is picked up again in Unit 10, where prepositions of movement are introduced.

Workbook There is further practice on *there is/are, some/any,* prepositions, and *this/that/these/those.* There are also exercises to help students distinguish *There's a .../ It's a ...* and *this/that/these/those.*

In the vocabulary section, rooms and objects/appliances are revised through a labelling activity. There is also an exercise on verb and noun collocations.

In the writing section, there is the first exercise on linking words, *and, so, but,* and *because.* Students are invited to write a description of their house or flat.

Notes on the unit

> **SUGGESTION**
> We suggest that you set some vocabulary for homework before you start this unit to maximize classroom time.

Homework prior to the lesson

Ask students to look up the following words in their dictionary, and put them in their vocabulary notebook.

sofa	shelf	fire	bedroom
armchair	cupboard	rug	bathroom
video	curtains	flowers	living room
stereo	lamp	mirror	kitchen

STARTER (SB p36)

1   Focus attention on the vocabulary and ask students to give two or three examples of correct words to go in *The living room* column. Students continue categorizing the vocabulary in pairs. Check the answers with the whole class. (Note that these are the most usual answers and that students may highlight different places for some items, e.g. a television in the kitchen.)

Answers		
The living room	**The kitchen**	**both**
an armchair	a fridge	a shelf
a television	a cooker	a plant
a coffee table	a washing machine	a cupboard
a lamp	a cup	
a telephone		
a stereo		
a sofa		

Drill the pronunciation of the words chorally and individually. Take care with the stress on the compound words •*coffee table* and •*washing machine.* Students may need help with pronunciation of *cupboard* /ˈkʌbəd/ and with distinguishing *cook* and *cooker,* thinking quite logically that *cooker* should be a person and not a thing.

2   Demonstrate the activity by saying what's in your own living room. You can do this in a natural way starting the

sentence *In my living room there's a/an ...* but do not give too much extra detail like size, colour, etc. as the main focus here is the core lexis of furniture and appliances. Students continue the activity in pairs. More able students may be able to include *There is/are ... ,* but do not insist on this and keep the activity brief.

WHAT'S IN THE LIVING ROOM? (SB p36)

There is/are, prepositions

1   You could briefly revise/check the names of the main rooms in a house or flat, *living room, kitchen, bedroom, bathroom,* and *toilet.* Avoid overloading students with relatively low-frequency words like *study, balcony,* etc.

Students look at the photograph of Helen's living room. Call out the following words and get students to point to the objects in the photograph: *armchair, sofa, coffee table, plants, bookshelves, cupboard, television, stereo, telephone, lamps, rug, fire, mirror, magazines, pictures.* (If students have looked up the words for homework, this shouldn't take too long.)

Model the words yourself, and drill them around the class. Correct pronunciation carefully.

Read the example sentences as a class. In a monolingual class, you might want to ask for a translation of *There's* and *There are.* You could ask 'Why *is* and why *are?*' to establish singular and plural.

Again, model the sentences yourself and do some individual drilling. Insist on accurate linking between *There's a/an ...* and *There are ... .* Point out that with plural nouns students need to state the exact number. You do not want them to try to produce *some* at this stage.

Students then work in pairs to produce more sentences. Allow them enough time to give four or five examples each, but do not let the activity go on too long. Monitor and check for correct use of *there is/are.*

Round off the activity by bringing the whole class together again to check the answers. Correct mistakes carefully.

Answers	
There's a sofa.	There's a telephone.
There's a coffee table.	There's a mirror.
There's a cupboard.	There's a fire.
There's a television.	There's an armchair.
There's a stereo.	There are three plants.
There's a table.	There are two lamps.
There's a shelf.	There are two pictures.
There's a rug.	There are three bookshelves.

2 **T 5.1** Students read and listen to the questions and complete the answers.

> **Answers and tapescript**
> A Is there a television?   B Yes, there **is**.
> A Is there a radio?   B No, there **isn't**.
> A Are there any books?   B Yes, there **are**.
> A How many books are there?   B There **are** a lot.
> A Are there any photographs?   B No, there **aren't**.

Play the recording again and get students to repeat. Students then practise the questions and answers in open pairs and then closed pairs. Monitor and check for accurate pronunciation (sounds, intonation, stress).

GRAMMAR SPOT

Focus attention on the tables. Check students are clear about which words are singular and which words are plural. Get students to complete the tables, using contracted forms where they can.

Check the answers with the whole class.

> **Answers**
> **Positive**
> There's a television. There **are** some books.
> **Negative**
> There **isn't** a radio. There **aren't** any photos.
> **Question**
> **Is** there a television? **Are** there any books?

Briefly highlight the use of *some* in the positive plural sentence and *any* in the negative plural and question, but do not go into a long grammatical explanation at this stage. (*Some/any* is covered in the next presentation *What's in the kitchen?*)

Read Grammar Reference 5.1 on p127 together in class, and/or ask students to read it at home. Encourage them to ask you questions about it.

3 Focus attention on the sets of words and make sure students realize that the first set are singular, and the second set are plural and that they are going to ask and answer questions about Helen's living room.

Students work in pairs to ask and answer questions. Go round the class monitoring, helping as necessary. If most students are having problems, drill the question and answers and get students to try again.

Check the answers with the whole class, getting students to repeat their questions and answers in open pairs.

> **Answers**
> Is there a dog?   No, there isn't.
> Is there a fire?   Yes, there is.
> Is there a rug?   Yes, there is.
> Is there a cat?   Yes, there is.
> Is there a mirror?   Yes, there is.
> Is there a computer?   No, there isn't.
> Is there a clock?   No, there isn't.
> Are there any plants?   Yes, there are.
> Are there any lamps?   Yes, there are.
> Are there any flowers?   No, there aren't.
> Are there any pictures?   Yes, there are.
> Are there any newspapers?   No, there aren't.
> Are there any bookshelves?   Yes, there are.
> Are there any photos?   No, there aren't.

4 This exercise practises/revises prepositions. If you think they will be new to your class, you will need to present them first. Do this very simply, perhaps using classroom objects, such as a book or chair (*The book is on the desk*), or the students themselves (*Juan is next to Maria*).

Refer students back to the photo of Helen's living room. Ask students to work in pairs to put a preposition into each gap. Check the answers.

> **Answers**
> 1 The television is **on** the cupboard.
> 2 The coffee table is **in front of** the sofa.
> 3 There are some magazines **under** the table.
> 4 The television is **next to** the stereo.
> 5 There are some pictures **on** the walls.
> 6 The cat is **on** the rug **in front of** the fire.

Point out that *in front of*, like *next to*, is two-dimensional. You can do this by using gestures.

You could practise the prepositions further by using your actual classroom, if you haven't already used this situation to present the items.

PRACTICE (SB p37)

What's in your picture?

1 You will need to photocopy the pictures on p125 of the Teacher's Book, enough copies for half of the class to see picture A and half picture B. Read the instructions as a class. Make sure students understand that each Student B has a complete picture and that each Student A has to draw in objects in the correct place to make a 'mirror' image. These objects are set above Student A's picture so that he/she knows what to ask about. (This is another information gap activity, so use L1 if you want to clarify what students have to do. Naturally, the most important thing is that they don't look at their partner's picture!)

Look at the example questions for Student A, pointing out the use of *Where exactly?* to get precise information about the position of the different objects.

Look at the example answers for Student B, pointing out the use of the prepositions for giving exact positions.

Point out that we say *on the sofa*, but *in the armchair*. Ask students to work in pairs, asking and answering so that Student A can complete their picture. Allow students enough time to complete the information exchange.

When students have finished, get them to compare their pictures and see how well they transferred and interpreted the key information.

Answers
The lamp is on the small table next to the sofa.
The magazines are on the coffee table. Next to the radio.
The photographs are on the bookshelves.
The plants are on the floor. In front of the window.
The clock is on the television.
The rug is on the floor. Under the coffee table.

2 **T 5.2** Ask students to look at the complete picture together. (It's probably wise to ask students to use the printed picture, rather than Student A's completed version just in case there are some objects wrongly located.) Read the instructions as a class. Students listen and shout 'Stop!' when they hear a mistake. You could do some work on contrastive stress as students correct the mistakes.

There aren't three people. There are four people.

Answers and tapescript
These are the mistakes:
1 There aren't three people. There are four people.
2 The girl isn't in the armchair. She's in front of the television.
3 There isn't a cat.
4 There are some photographs on the bookshelves.
5 There aren't any flowers on the table next to the sofa. They're in front of the mirror.

T 5.2
There are three people in the living room. A man and a woman on the sofa and a little girl in the armchair. There's a radio on the coffee table and a rug under it. There's a cat on the rug in front of the fire. There are a lot of pictures on the walls but there aren't any photographs. There are two plants on the floor next to the television and some flowers on the small table next to the sofa.

ADDITIONAL MATERIAL

Workbook Unit 5
Exercises 1–4 *There is/are*, *some/any*, and prepositions.

WHAT'S IN THE KITCHEN? (SB p38)

some/any, this/that/these/those

1 Pre-teach/check the following vocabulary: *plate, glass, fork, spoon, knife.* Check the plural of these words, highlighting the irregular form *knives* and the pronunciation of *glasses.* Ask students to look at the photograph of Helen's kitchen and say what they can see. Take the opportunity for students to recycle *There is/ are … ,* but do not expect or insist on the use of *some.* Correct mistakes in pronunciation.

Answers
(There's) a fridge, a cooker, a table, a shelf
(There are some) cupboards, cups, apples, oranges, knives, forks, flowers

2 **T 5.3** Students listen to the conversation about the kitchen and fill in the gaps. Let them check in pairs, then play the tape again. Ask for feedback. Notice that students are not expected to produce *some* until they have seen and heard it in context.

Answers and tapescript
H = Helen   B = Bob
H And this is the kitchen.
B Mmm, it's very nice.
H Well, it's not very big, but there **are a lot** of cupboards. And **there's** a new fridge, and a cooker. That's new, too.
B But what's **in** all these cupboards?
H Well, not a lot. There are some cups, but there aren't any plates. And I have **some** knives and forks, but I don't have **any** spoons!
B Do you have **any** glasses?
H No. Sorry.
B Never mind. We can drink this champagne from those cups! Cheers!

3 Students now need to practise using *There is/are* and *a/some/any* in context. Focus attention on the photo of Helen's kitchen. Model some sentences yourself in both affirmative and negative and with singular nouns with *a* and noun phrases with *some.* Make sure *some* is weak /səm/. Drill the sentences around the class, correcting mistakes carefully.

Examples
There's a cooker.   *There are some cupboards.*
There aren't any glasses.   *There's a new fridge.*
There are some flowers.   *There aren't any spoons.*

Students continue talking about Helen's kitchen in pairs. You could ask your students to close their books and try to remember what is (and isn't!) in the kitchen. Move on to the personalization fairly quickly, so do not allow this pairwork stage to go on too long.

Briefly describe what is in your own kitchen and how it differs from Helen's. Get students to talk about their own kitchen in pairs. Go round checking and helping where necessary, but don't correct grammar mistakes unless incomprehensible. The emphasis here is on fluency.

Bring the class back together and ask for any interesting examples you heard, e.g. the washing machine being kept in the bathroom, or in a special room on its own, or on a balcony. You could ask follow-up questions like *Where's the fridge? How big is it? Where do you keep food?*, etc.

GRAMMAR SPOT

1   Look at *Grammar Spot* question 1 as a class. Allow students time to think before checking the answer.

2/3 Get students to work in pairs to answer question 2 and complete the sentences in 3.

Check the answers with the whole class.

Answers
1   *Two magazines* gives us the exact number. *Some magazines* doesn't give us the exact number.
2   We say *some* in positive sentences. We say *any* in negative sentences and questions.
3   1   I like **this** champagne.
    2   **These** flowers are lovely.
    3   **That** cooker is new.
    4   Give me **those** cups.

SUGGESTION
If students have difficulty with the use of *this/that/these/those*, use the classroom environment to briefly revise this language focus. Choose objects near to you to demonstrate *this/these*, e.g. *This is my desk. I like these posters* and objects that you have to point to demonstrate *that/those*, e.g. *That cupboard is new. We use those books.* Give students objects to hold or point to objects and get students to say sentences using *this/that/these/those*.

Refer students to Grammar Reference 5.3 and 5.4 on p127–8.

PRACTICE (SB p39)

In our classroom

1   Students work in pairs or small groups to fill the gaps.

Answers
1   In our classroom there are **some** books on the floor.
2   There aren't **any** plants.
3   Are there **any** Spanish students in your class?

4   There aren't **any** Chinese students.
5   We have **some** dictionaries in the cupboard.
6   There aren't **any** pens in my bag.

2   Get students to work in pairs and briefly describe their classroom. If necessary, give word cues to help get a variety of forms, e.g. *television, video, flowers, photos*, etc.

3   Briefly revise the use of *this/that/these/those* and relevant adjectives, e.g. *big, small, new, old*, etc. Get students to continue talking about things in the classroom in pairs.

What's in Pierre's briefcase?

4   **T 5.4**   Focus attention on the photo of Pierre and get students to say who they think he is, where he is, and what his job is. Read the instruction as a class to check.

Students listen to Pierre describing what is in his briefcase, and tick the things they hear.

Answers and tapescript
✔ a newspaper   ✗ a letter
✔ a dictionary   ✔ photos
✗ a sandwich   ✔ a mobile phone
✔ pens   ✗ stamps
✔ a notebook   ✗ an address book
✔ keys
✗ a bus ticket

T 5.4

What's in my briefcase? Well, there's a newspaper – a French newspaper – and there's a dictionary – my French/English dictionary. I have some pens, three I think. Also I have a notebook for vocabulary, I write words in that every day. And of course I have my keys, my car keys and my house keys. Oh yes, very important, there are some photos of my family, my wife and my daughter and there's my mobile phone. I ring my home in Paris every night. That's all I think. I don't have any stamps and my address book is in my hotel.

5   Get students to practise the questions in the Student's Book in open pairs. Students continue working in closed pairs. Ask one or two students to say what is in their or their partner's bag. This can be very interesting! However, try not to be over-curious, as some students may consider it too personal.

Check it

6   Students work in pairs and tick the correct sentence.

Answers
1   There aren't any sandwiches.
2   Do you have a good dictionary?
3   I have some photos of my dog.
4   I have a lot of books.

5 How many students are there in this class?
6 Next to my house there's a park.
7 Look at that house over there!
8 Henry, this is my mother. Mum, this is Henry.

ADDITIONAL MATERIAL

Workbook Unit 5
Exercises 5–8 *this/that/these/those* and *it/they*

READING AND SPEAKING (SB p40)

At home on a plane

You could lead in to the topic of the reading text by asking students:
What type of home do you/most people have?
Do you know anyone who lives in an unusual home? (e.g. on a houseboat, in a windmill, in a lighthouse)

1 Focus attention on the picture of the plane. Demonstrate the activity by asking students for the correct label for number 1 (toilet). Students work in pairs and continue to label the picture. Check the answers with the whole class.

Answers	
1 toilet	5 steps
2 a flight attendant	6 door
3 the first class section	7 windows
4 a cockpit	8 emergency exit

Ask students to give a few examples of things you can find on a plane, e.g. *magazines, newspapers, cups.* Students work in groups and think of as many other examples as they can, including people. Set a time limit for this, e.g. two minutes, so that the activity does not go on too long.

Check answers with the whole class. Accept any realistic answers and correct errors in pronunciation as necessary.

Sample answers		
pilot	cups	presents
passengers	glasses	televisions
knives	drinks	telephones
forks	food	seats
spoons	magazines	
plates	newspapers	

2 Tell students they are going to read a text about a woman with an unusual home. Check comprehension of the questions. Ask students to work in pairs to find the information in the text to answer the questions. Tell them not to worry about words they do not recognize

and just to focus on finding the answers. (You may want to set a time limit for this to discourage students from reading too intensively.)

Check the answers. Decide according to the speed and ability of your students whether to settle for quick short answers or whether you want fuller answers.

Answers
1 54. (She is 54.)
2 On a jet plane. (She lives on a jet plane.)
3 27 years old. (Her home is 27 years old.)
4 Two. (She has two grandsons.)
5 Three. (There are three bedrooms.)
6 Four. (There are four toilets.)

3 Pre-teach/check the following vocabulary: *grandma, passport, luxury, air conditioning, dishwasher, warm, run, party, upstairs/downstairs.*

Get students to answer the true–false questions in pairs. Check the answers with the whole class. Encourage them to correct some of the false answers.

Answers
1 true
2 false
3 false. The bathroom is next to Joanne's bedroom.
4 true
5 true
6 false
7 false
8 false. She wants to buy a Boeing 747.

4 Practise the questions and answers in the Student's Book in open and closed pairs. Drill the pronunciation of the list of things students have to ask about.

Students continue to ask and answer about the things in the list. Monitor and check for accurate use of *Is there a/an … ?* and *Are there any … ?* and feed back on any common errors.

Check the answers with the whole class.

Answers	
Is there a telephone?	Yes, there is.
Is there a dishwasher?	Yes, there is.
Are there any toilets?	Yes, there are.
Are there any flight attendants?	No, there aren't.
Is there an upstairs bedroom?	No, there isn't.

What do you think?

Ask students for a few examples of things they like and don't like and then allow them to continue exchanging opinions in pairs. The aim is to generate some personalized discussion, so do not insist on complete accuracy.

Ask students for any interesting opinions they or their partner gave.

LISTENING AND SPEAKING (SB p42)

Homes around the world

> **POSSIBLE PROBLEMS**
>
> The listening texts contain quite a lot of words that may be new, or that students might not remember. We intend this listening exercise to be for gist understanding only, so students should be encouraged, if possible, not to worry about unknown words.
>
> You *could* ask them to look at the tapescripts while they listen, or you could do this after they have heard the texts once or twice and then study the vocabulary. However, try if possible not to do this – but only you know your class!
>
> Even for gist comprehension, you will need to check the following words first:
>
> *near   river   light (n.)   alone   shops   basement room   swimming pool   sports centre   blinds*
>
> You could ask students to look at the tapescript for homework.

1   Focus attention on the photos of the four places and get students to match the correct names.

> **Answers**
> d   Lisbon
> a   Toronto
> b   Malibu
> c   Samoa

Ask students to give any facts or personal experience of the places. Allow students to continue briefly in pairs. (Again, this is a personalization activity, so do not insist on accuracy.)

2   **T 5.5** Students listen to the five people talking about where they live and fill in the chart, supplying any extra information (see below the chart) that they have understood.

> **Answers and tapescript**
>
> | | Manola from LISBON | Ray and Elsie from TORONTO | Brad from MALIBU | Alise from SAMOA |
> |---|---|---|---|---|
> | **House or flat?** | flat | house | house | house |
> | **Old or modern?** | old | old | we don't know | new house, but in old style |

Where?	in the old town, near the sea	near the city centre	next to the sea	very near the sea
How many bedrooms?	one	three	five	one
Live(s) with?	her cat	each other – children not at home now	alone	her family

Extra information

Manola from Lisbon
- lives in old town called the Alfama
- has beautiful flat – one very big room with one very big window
- bed next to window so can see sea and lights of city when she goes to sleep
- has a cat and lives near shops
- lots of friends visit her
- loves flat

Ray and Elsie from Toronto
- house about 50 years old
- near the city centre
- have living room, quite a big kitchen, but favourite room is their family room
- family room has TV, stereo, large comfortable sofa, some big old armchairs. Love sitting there in winter with snow outside
- children aren't at home now – both have jobs in the USA. Most of the time just Ray and Elsie in house

Brad from Malibu
- house is fantastic
- neighbours very rich – famous film stars. Doesn't see them much but hears parties
- ten rooms in house. Everything white – carpets, curtains, sofa
- also has a swimming pool, cinema, and sports centre
- not married at the moment. Ex-wife is French – lives in Paris with three sons

Alise from Samoa
- house doesn't have any walls because is very hot in Samoa
- have blinds to stop the rain and sun
- new house but in old style
- one room for living and sleeping. Have rugs – sit and sleep on the floor

T 5.5

1   Manola from Lisbon
I live in the old town near the sea. It is called the Alfama. I have a very beautiful flat. There's just *one* room in my flat, one very big room with one very big window. My bed's next to the window so I see the sea and all the lights of the city when I go to sleep. I live alone, but I have a cat and I'm near the shops and lots of friends come to visit me. I love my flat.

2 Ray and Elsie from Toronto

Elsie Our house is quite old, about fifty years old. It's quite near to the city centre. We have a living room, quite a big kitchen and three bedrooms, but the room we all love is our family room.

Ray Yes, there's a TV and a stereo and a large comfortable sofa in there, and some big, old armchairs. We love sitting there in winter with the snow outside.

Elsie Our children aren't at home now, they both have jobs in the USA, so most of the time it's just Ray and me.

3 Brad from Malibu

My house is fantastic. It's right next to the sea. My neighbours are very rich. Some of them are famous film stars. In my house there are ten rooms, five are bedrooms, and everything is white, the floors, the walls, the sofas, everything. I also have a swimming pool, a cinema, and an exercise room. I live here alone. I'm not married at the moment. My ex-wife is French. She lives in Paris now with our three sons.

4 Alise from Samoa

I live with my family in a house near the sea. We have an open house, . . . er . . . that is . . . er . . . our house doesn't have any walls. Houses in Samoa don't have walls because it is very, very hot, but we have blinds to stop the rain and sun. Our house is in the old style. We have only *one* room for living and sleeping, so it is both a bedroom and a living room. We have rugs and we sit and sleep on the floor.

3 Get students to ask you questions about where you live. Then get students to continue in pairs or groups of three. Get students to share any interesting information with the whole class.

4 Students write about where they live for homework. Before you set this, do the writing exercises 10 and 11 in the Workbook, which will prepare them for the task.

EVERYDAY ENGLISH (SB p43)

Directions 1

1 Ask students to look at the street map. Make sure they understand the words on the map. As a class, ask where you can buy the items in the Student's Book.

> **POSSIBLE PROBLEMS**
> There might not be the direct equivalent of a newsagent's in your students' countries. A newsagent sells newspapers, magazines, cigarettes, sweets, and little items such as birthday cards and soft drinks.

Answers
some aspirin at a chemist('s)
a CD (compact disc) at a music shop
a plane ticket at a travel agent('s)
a newspaper at a newsagent('s) or supermarket

a book at a bookshop
some stamps at a post office (sometimes at a supermarket or newsagent)

2 **T 5.6** Students listen to the conversations and complete them. You might want to play them all through first before students begin to write, or pause the tape recorder after each conversation to allow students time to write. Play the tape again to check answers.

Answers and tapescript
1 A Excuse me! Is **there** a chemist **near** here?
   B Yes. It's over **there**.
   A Thanks.
2 A **Excuse** me! Is there a **newsagent** near here?
   B Yes. **It's in** Church Street. Take the first **street on the** right. It's **next to** the music shop.
   A Oh yes. Thanks.
3 A Excuse me! Is there a **restaurant** near here?
   B There's a Chinese one in Park Lane **next to** the bank, and there's an Italian one in Church Street next to the **travel agent**.
   A Is that one **far**?
   B No. Just two minutes, that's all.
4 A Is there a post office near here?
   B Go straight ahead, and it's **on the** left, **next to** the pub.
   A Thanks a lot.

Check that the class understand *Excuse me!*, *over there*, *first/second*, and *near/far*. If necessary, highlight the difference between *next to* and *near* (*next to* is two-dimensional, whereas *near* is three-dimensional.) Students work in pairs to practise the conversations.

3 Students then make more conversations about the places listed. Drill the pronunciation of the places in the list and practise one or two conversations in open pairs across the class. Students continue to work in closed pairs. You could ask some of the pairs to act out their dialogues for the rest of the class.

4 Students talk about their own situation. You could do this as a group activity or as a class.

Don't forget!

Workbook Unit 5
Exercise 9 Vocabulary of rooms and objects found in them, and verbs and nouns that go together.
Exercises 10 and 11 The writing section focuses on basic linking words.

Word list
Remind your students of the Word list for this unit on p137. They could write in the translations, learn them at home, and/or write some of the words in their vocabulary notebook.

Pronunciation Book Unit 5

6

can/can't/could/couldn't • *was/were*
Words that sound the same
On the phone

Can you speak English?

Introduction to the unit

Skills and ability are the themes of this unit. These are particularly suitable topics to introduce and practise *can/can't* (ability). However, the unit has two main aims in that we also introduce some past tenses for the first time: the past of *can* (ability) – *could*, and the Past Simple of the verb *to be* – *was/were*. The skills work includes a jigsaw reading about two ten-year-old geniuses and provides a further context for and practice of the grammar.

Language aims

Grammar – *can/can't* Students have already met the form *can* in the *Everyday English* section of Unit 2, but it is used only as a polite request *Can I have … ?* In Unit 2 it is introduced idiomatically because it is a useful expression, and the grammar is not explored.

Here, in Unit 6, the use is extended to ability, and all aspects of the form (statements, questions, negatives) are fully explored and practised.

> **POSSIBLE PROBLEMS**
>
> 1 Sometimes after all the practising of the Present Simple, students want to use *do/don't* and *does/doesn't* to form the question and negative.
> **Do you can swim?*
> **I don't can swim.*
> 2 A major problem with *can* and *can't* is the pronunciation. Often students find the different realizations of the vowel sounds (/ə/ or /æ/ in *can* and /ɑ:/ in *can't*) confusing and, because the final *t* in *can't* tends to get lost, they can't recognize whether the sentence is positive or negative and they have difficulty producing the correct sounds themselves.
>
> | *I can swim.* | /aɪ kən swɪm/ |
> | *Can you swim?* | /kən ju swɪm/ |
> | *Yes, I can.* | /jes aɪ kæn/ |
> | *I can't come.* | /aɪ kɑ:ŋ kʌm/ |
>
> For these reasons we highlight the pronunciation in the unit and include exercises both for recognition and production.

was/were **and *could/couldn't*** These forms are the first introduction to a past tense. We have chosen to present them in a simple and straightforward manner by having students complete a table about the present and past.

> **POSSIBLE PROBLEMS**
> Again pronunciation is a problem. The vowel sounds in *was* and *were* have both weak and strong realizations: *was* /ə/ and /ɒ/; and *were* /ə/ and /ɜ:/.
> *He was at home.* /hi wəz ət həʊm/
> *Was he at home?* /wəz hi ət həʊm/
> *Yes, he was./No, he wasn't.* /jes hi wɒz/ /nəʊ hi wɒznt/
> *Were they at home?* /wə ðeɪ ət həʊm/
> *Yes, they were./No, they weren't.* /jes ðeɪ wɜ:/ /nəʊ ðeɪ wɜ:nt/

The pronunciation is highlighted and practised in the unit.

Vocabulary and pronunciation We focus on words that sound the same but have a different spelling and meaning, i.e. homophones, for example *see* and *sea*. This provides the opportunity to give more practice of phonetic script.

There are many homophones in English (because of the non-phonetic spelling), and students confuse the two meanings, especially when hearing them (as opposed to seeing them when reading).

Everyday English Language useful for making phone calls is introduced and practised.

Workbook There is further practice on *can/can't, was/were,* and *could/couldn't.* The question *How much ... ?* is practised with *is* and *was.*

In the vocabulary section, more words that commonly go together are practised (*ask a question, get up early*).

There is an exercise to revise and extend coverage of prepositions.

The writing syllabus continues with work on simple formal letters.

Notes on the unit

STARTER (SB p44)

1 Briefly check the pronunciation of the languages. Students work in pairs and say a sentence about where each language is spoken.
Check the answers. If necessary, drill the pronunciation of the countries and languages in pairs, especially where there is a change in stress, e.g. *Japan, Japanese*

Answers
They also speak French in Switzerland, Belgium, and some parts of Africa.
They speak Spanish in Spain, Mexico, parts of South and Central America, Cuba, and the USA.
They speak German in Germany, Austria, and Switzerland.
They speak Italian in Italy and Switzerland.
They speak Portuguese in Portugal, Brazil, Angola, and Mozambique.
They speak Japanese in Japan.
They speak English in Great Britain, the USA, Canada, Australia, New Zealand, Singapore, The West Indies, and India (and in many other countries as the language of tourism, business, and technology).

2 Tell the class which languages you can speak. Students continue to work in pairs or small groups. If you have a small group, allow each student to tell the rest of the class about their language skills. If you have a big group, select just a few students to feed back, but make sure you choose different students at the next feedback stage, so that everyone gets a chance.

WHAT CAN YOU DO? (SB p44)

can/can't

1 This is quite a simple presentation. The aim of the pictures is to illustrate the meaning of *can* and *can't*. The sentences are recorded to provide models of the different realizations of the vowel sounds and to raise students' awareness of these from the start.
First, ask students to look at the pictures and read the sentences. (Most of the vocabulary should be familiar or obvious from the picture, but check that there are no isolated difficulties.) Students then match the sentences to the pictures and write the appropriate sentence number in the boxes provided in the pictures.

T 6.1 Students can discuss their answers with a partner before listening to the recording and checking. Then check the answers with the whole class. Ask students to repeat the sentences after listening to each one.

Answers
1 d 2 a 3 c 4 f 5 e 6 b

GRAMMAR SPOT

1 Focus attention on the *Grammar Spot* questions. Students work in pairs and say all the persons of *can/can't*. Ask them what they notice about the verb form for each person. Check students are clear about the answer.

Answer
Can/can't are the same for all persons, so there is no *-s* added in the *he/she/it* forms.
We do not use the auxiliary *don't/doesn't* to form the negative.

2 **T 6.2** This activity highlights the pronunciation of *can/can't* in the positive, question, and short answers. Play the recording and get your students to read and listen very carefully to the pronunciation of *can* and *can't*. First, ask generally *Can you hear differences?* If necessary, repeat the sentences yourself, exaggerating the vowel sounds in *can* and *can't* and isolating them /ə/, /æ/, /ɑː/, so that your students can fully appreciate the differences. Play the recording again and get students to repeat chorally and individually.

3 Focus attention on the sentence stress in the positive and negative sentences. Drill the sentences and then get students to practise in pairs. Read Grammar Reference 6.1 on p128 together in class, and/or ask students to read it at home. Encourage them to ask you questions about it.

2 **T 6.3** This is a dictation to check that your students
can recognize what they hear. Pre-teach/check *cook*, and
drive. Ask students to listen and write in the answers.
Pause the recording after each sentence. Then ask them
to check their answers with a partner. Play the recording
again as you conduct a full class feedback. (They could
read the tapescript on p117 of their books as you do this.)

Answers and tapescript
1 I **can speak French**, but I **can't speak German**.
2 He **can't dance**, but he **can sing**.
3 '**Can** you **cook**?' 'Yes, I **can**.'
4 They **can ski**, but they **can't swim**.
5 We **can dance** and we **can sing**.
6 '**Can** she **drive**?' 'No, she **can't**.'

Although this is a recognition exercise, you can make it
productive by asking your students to read some of the
sentences aloud to each other.

PRACTICE (SB p45)

Tina can't cook. Can you?

1 This again is a recognition exercise that moves into a
production stage. This time the recording is much more
natural-sounding, not being a series of sentences for
dictation, but a girl talking about her abilities.

T 6.4 Focus attention on the picture of Tina and get
students to say whatever they can about her. Ask your
students to listen to Tina and put a ✔ next to things she
can do or a ✘ next to the things she can't do in the first
column in the chart. Play the recording.

Put students into pairs to compare their answers. Then
conduct a full class feedback to establish the correct
answers. Let students listen again if necessary.

Answers and tapescript

Can ... ?	Tina
drive a car	✘
speak French	✘
speak Italian	✔
cook	✘
play tennis	✔
ski	✔
swim	✔
play the piano	✘
use a computer	✔

T 6.4

Well, there are a lot of things I can't do. I can't drive a car, but
I want to have lessons soon. I can't speak French but I can
speak Italian. My mother's Italian, and we often go to Italy.
My mother's a really good cook, she can cook really well, not
just Italian food, all kinds of food, but I can't cook at all. I just
love eating! What about sports? Er . . . I think I'm good at
quite a lot of sports. I can play tennis, and ski, sometimes we
go skiing in the Italian Alps, and of course I can swim. But
musical instruments – no – I can't play any at all – no I'm not
very musical, but I love dancing! Of course I can use a
computer – all my friends can.

2 The exercise now becomes personalized. Students
complete column 2 of the chart about themselves.

3 This is the productive phase of the activity. Practise the
questions in the Student's Book in open and closed pairs.

SUGGESTION
1 Make sure students use appropriate rising
intonation with the inverted questions, and falling
intonation with the short answers.

Can you ski? Yes, I can.

2 Make sure that they pronounce the *t* on the end of
the negatives. The two consonants *nt* together are
difficult for many nationalities.
Students work in pairs and ask and answer
questions about each of the activities in the chart.
Go round and monitor and help as they do this.
Then round off the activity by asking a few
members of the class to tell the others about their
and their partner's abilities. Highlight the use of
contrastive stress, e.g. *Louis can ski, but I can't.*

What can computers do?

4 **NOTE**
This can be quite a contentious activity because
students tend to disagree about what exactly
computers can do, and/or the degree to which they
can do it. There is a growing belief that the initial
very high expectations of computer ability in terms
of real human-like behaviour have not been met.

Check comprehension of the key vocabulary: *poetry*, *laugh*, *play chess*, *hear*, *feel*, *fall in love*. Put your students into pairs to do this activity. (We are hoping that discussion and disagreement will generate some freer speaking in English, in which case the activity can last some while. However, be grateful at any efforts at expressing their opinions and don't worry if the activity is quite short.)

In the sample answers we have included an extra section (*They can … but …*), which is for your information only. You can choose how/if you deal with the extra information.

Sample answers
They can …
play chess   check spellings
They can … but …
translate (but word for word, not overall meaning)
speak English (only in limited fashion with unnatural intonation)
hear (they can recognize some speech, but limited)
make music (but not like Mozart!)
have conversations (but limited with many misunderstandings of context)
They can't …
write poetry   laugh   feel   think (because they work completely in numbers)   fall in love

Conduct a feedback session with the whole class. This could be quite lively.

5   Ask students what people can do that computers can't do, *or* you could list some things that you think computers can't do and encourage the class to react: *drink*, *eat*, *sleep*, etc.

ADDITIONAL MATERIAL

Workbook Unit 6
Exercises 1 and 2 These practise *can* and *can't*.

WHERE WERE YOU YESTERDAY? (SB p46)

was/were, can/could

This is a very direct presentation of the past of the verbs *to be* and *can*. It revises the present of the verbs and then moves straight to the past tense equivalents.

Pre-teach/check *yesterday*, by doing the first example with the class. Let the students work in pairs to write in the answers. When they have finished, go through the exercise with them, modelling the questions and answers for them to repeat, and highlighting the weak vowel sounds of *was* and *were* (/wəz/ and /wə/) in statements and questions, and the strong vowel sounds (/wɒz/, /wɒznt/, /wɜː/, /wɜːnt/) in short answers and negatives.

POSSIBLE PROBLEM
The negatives
The groups of consonants in the negatives *wasn't* /wɒznt/, *weren't* /wɜːnt/ and *couldn't* /kʊdnt/ may be difficult for some students and may need extra choral and individual repetition.
Also, as you go through, keep backtracking by asking individual students to answer the earlier questions again.
Finally, get your students to ask and answer the questions in open pairs across the class. Use the opportunity to check and correct them carefully. You can move on to practise in closed pairs, unless you think this may prove too laborious.

GRAMMAR SPOT

1   Put your students into pairs to complete the table with the past of *to be*. Quickly check through the answers with the whole class.

Answers		
	Positive	Negative
I	was	wasn't
You	were	weren't
He/She/It	was	wasn't
We	were	weren't
They	were	weren't

2   **T 6.5** This is a repetition exercise with some more questions and answers to help consolidate the pronunciation. There are pauses on the recording for students to repeat. Insist on accurate pronunciation of the strong and weak forms.

3   Students complete the positive and negative forms of *can*.

Answers
Positive could (all persons)
Negative couldn't (all persons)

Read Grammar Reference 6.1 and 6.2 on p128 together in class, and/or ask students to read it at home. Encourage them to ask you questions about it.

PRACTICE (SB p46)

Talking about you

1   Drill the first question and answer in open pairs. Students continue asking and answering the questions in closed pairs. Go round the class to help them. Encourage them to ask about times other than those listed in the

book. Round the activity off by asking one or two students to tell the others about their partner.

2 **T 6.6** Set the scene of the conversation by asking your students to look at the picture and telling them that two friends are talking about parties they've been to. Check that they realize that they can only use *was*, *were*, *wasn't*, *weren't*, and *couldn't* to fill the gaps.

Ask students to work in pairs to do the exercise. Play the recording for them to listen and check their answers. Play it again and ask students to focus on the pronunciation, not only of *was* and *were*, but of the stress and intonation of the questions and answers.

Ask one or two pairs of students to take the parts of Kim and Max and read aloud the conversation across the class. Encourage lively and natural pronunciation.

Answers and tapescript
K = Kim   M = Max
K **Were** you at Charlotte's party last Saturday?
M Yes, I **was**.
K **Was** it good?
M Well, it **was** OK.
K **Were** there many people?
M Yes, there **were**.
K **Was** Henry there?
M No, he **wasn't**. And where **were** you? Why **weren't** you there?
K Oh . . . I **couldn't** go because I **was** at Mark's party! It **was** brilliant!

Now ask the class to practise the conversation again in closed pairs. Go round and help and check them as they do this. (Don't let this go on too long otherwise it will become boring!)

You could move on to some other situations, e.g. *the jazz concert, John's barbecue last Sunday, the disco last Friday evening, the football match last week*. Put some skeletal dialogue prompts on the blackboard and ask pairs of students to come to the front of the class and act out another situation, e.g.

… the jazz concert last Sunday?
… good?
… many people?
… (Tom) there?
… brilliant!

SUGGESTION
Try to personalize the language as much as possible by getting students to use real parties or other events they have been to recently as the basis for similar conversations.

Four geniuses!

This section brings together *could*, *couldn't*, and *was* and it also introduces *to be born* and *until*. It continues the theme of skills and talents, but this time focuses on some famous characters. Students are also given the opportunity to personalize the language.

3 First ask students to look at the pictures and see if they can recognize the people. Do the exercise as a class as a contrast to the pairwork in the previous activity, and so it can be done quite quickly.

Answers
1 Picasso
2 Einstein
3 Nureyev
4 Mozart

POSSIBLE PROBLEM
(I) was born is taught here as an expression, *not* as an example of the passive. Don't be tempted to go into the grammar. Some students translate from their own language and want to say **I am born*.

4 Focus attention on the example. Check comprehension of *was born* and drill the pronunciation. Ask students to give you a complete sentence about Mozart, matching lines in columns A, B, and C, and adding a comparison about themselves.

Check the rest of the answers with the whole class. (It really is true that Einstein couldn't speak until he was eight!)

Answers (Sample personalized sentences in brackets)
1 Mozart was born in Austria in 1756. He could play the piano when he was three. (I couldn't play the piano until I was ten.)
2 Picasso was born in Spain in 1881. He could paint when he was one. (I couldn't paint until I was six.)
3 Nureyev was born in Siberia in 1938. He could dance when he was two. (I couldn't dance until I was seven.)
4 Einstein was born in Germany in 1879. He couldn't speak until he was eight! (I could speak when I was one.)

5 Drill the questions in the Student's Book, highlighting the falling intonation in the *wh-* questions. Students continue working in pairs, asking and answering about the geniuses.

6 This is the personalization stage. Drill the questions in the *you* form, getting students to repeat them in chorus and individually. Make sure the students can hear the difference between *where* and *were*, and again insist on accurate intonation.

Students work in small groups and ask and answer the questions. At the end of the activity, ask a few students to tell you what information they can remember, e.g. *María was born in Barcelona in 1980. She could read when she was five.*

> **SUGGESTION**
> Students could think of some famous talented people that they know and make similar sentences about where/when they were born and what skills they had at different ages.

Check it

This exercise practises the grammar of the unit.

7 Ask students to work in pairs or small groups to choose the correct sentence. Ask them to work quite quickly, then conduct a full class feedback on which are the correct answers. Try to get students to correct each other and explain any mistakes they hear.

> **Answers**
> 1 I can't use a computer.
> 2 Were they at the party?
> 3 I'm sorry. I can't go to the party.
> 4 She wasn't at home.
> 5 He could play chess when he was five.
> 6 I can speak English very well.

ADDITIONAL MATERIAL

Workbook Unit 6
Exercises 3–5 These practise *was* and *were*. Exercise 4 is also very suitable for oral work and could well be used in class either to supplement or replace one of the activities in the Student's Book. Exercise 5 brings together past and present tense forms covered so far.
Exercise 6 This practises *could* and *couldn't* with *was*, *were*, and *can*.

READING AND SPEAKING (SB p48)

Super Kids

This activity is a jigsaw reading. This means that it should result in not only reading practice, but also some freer speaking.

The class divides into two groups and each group reads a different but similar text about a child genius and answers the questions. After this, students from the different groups get together to exchange information about the child in their text. This means that they should get some speaking practice whilst their main attention is on the completion of the reading task.

These texts are based on real newspaper articles but have been simplified and rewritten to include examples of the grammar taught in this and previous units.

You need to be very clear when giving instructions for any jigsaw activity. If necessary and possible, give them in L1.

1 Focus attention on the title of the section *Super Kids*. Ask students what they think the section is about (very talented children). Ask students to look at the photographs of the two children and offer guesses about their age and special talent.

2 Divide the class into two groups. Tell Group A to read about 'Little Miss Picasso' and Group B to read about 'The New Mozart'. Ask each group to read through their text as quickly as possible to get a general understanding of it and to check if their guesses about the children were correct.

3 Get students to read the text again more slowly and find the information in their text to answer the questions about Alexandra or Lukas. Most of the vocabulary in the texts should be known, but allow students to use dictionaries to check if they can't guess from the context.

When they have read the texts, they could either go through the questions on their own and then check with others from the same group, or work with a partner from the same group to answer the questions. Each group has the same questions to answer.

Check the answers with Group A students and Group B students separately. The main idea of these questions is to check understanding, therefore short answers are perfectly acceptable. However, when you have a full class feedback you might want to encourage further language production such as you can see in the brackets in the answers below.

> **Answers**
> **Group A – Alexandra Nechita**
> 1 She's thirteen.
> 2 She paints large, cubist pictures and sells them for a lot of money.
> 3 (She was born) in Romania.
> 4 (She lives) in Los Angeles.
> 5 (She lives) with her family.
> 6 Yes, she does.
> 7 She could paint very well when she was four.
> 8 No, she doesn't, because every day after school she does her homework, plays with her little brother, then paints for two or three hours until bedtime.
> 9 No, she isn't. (She can buy a big house and travel the world.)
> 10 She was in London, Paris, and Rome.

Group B – Lukas Vondracek
1 He's ten.
2 He can play the piano very well. / He's a brilliant pianist.
3 (He was born) in Opava in the Czech Republic.
4 (He lives) in Vienna.
5 (He lives) with his parents.
6 Yes, he does (two days a week).
7 He could play the piano when he was two and he could read music before he could read books.
8 No, he doesn't, because he practises the piano six hours a day and he gives lots of concerts.
9 No, he isn't. (Mozart was poor but Lukas isn't like him at all.)
10 He was in Washington, Chicago, and London.

4 Tell each student to find a partner from the other group and go through the questions and answers together, telling each other about the child in their article. Try not to offer help at this stage – let students exchange the information themselves as far as possible.

5 This stage allows students to summarize the information from both texts and also provides useful consolidation of the *he/she* and *they* forms with various structures. Focus attention on the examples in the Student's Book and then get students to continue discussing similarities and differences in pairs.

Sample answers
They were both born in Eastern Europe. They both travel a lot and have money. Alexandra has a brother but Lukas is an only child. Alexandra goes to school every day, but Lukas goes to school two days a week. Alexandra lives in the USA, but Lukas lives in Vienna. Lukas plays sport but Alexandra doesn't.

Conduct a general feedback session with the whole class. If appropriate, ask students if they know of any other very talented children, or to comment on Alexandra's and Lukas's lifestyle.

POSSIBLE PROBLEM
If students become involved in discussion activities, they often start to talk in L1 in their frustration at not being able to get their point across. Don't worry too much if this happens, at least it shows that they are interested! Gently encourage them to try and express something in English as this is such good practice, and don't correct them too much. If they get their point across, that's enough. The aim of this activity is fluency not accuracy.

Roleplay

SUGGESTION
You might find that time is short for the roleplay or that it might be too difficult for your students as it stands, so an alternative approach is included in the Teacher's Book. Photocopy the interview on p126 of the Teacher's Book and ask your students to complete the gaps either in class or for homework. They can choose which child is being interviewed.

6 Assign roles of the journalist and Alexandra or Lukas, or allow students to choose the role they want. Get students to prepare the interview using the questions in exercise 3 to help them. Allow sufficient time for students to make notes, but discourage them from writing out the interview word for word. Get students to practise the interview in pairs and then act it out in class. (If time is short, use the alternative approach in the *Suggestion* above.)

VOCABULARY AND PRONUNCIATION (SB p50)

Words that sound the same

This activity introduces your students to words that have different spellings and meanings but *sound* the same, i.e. homophones. Of course, it is not important that your students learn the linguistic term *homophone*, but it is important that they are aware of such words, as there are so many in English and they can be particularly confusing when listening. The use of phonetic script in the activity serves not only to continue the process of getting to know it, but also to highlight the fact that there is often no relation between sounds and spellings in English.

1 This is to illustrate what is meant by *words that sound the same*. Ask your students to read aloud the sentences to themselves and then ask for suggestions about the words highlighted in **bold**. They should easily notice that the words sound the same but are spelt differently and have different meanings.
   /aɪ/ = *eye* and *I*
   /nəʊ/ = *no* and *know*

2 Ask students to work in pairs to do this. Most of the words are taken from previous units and should be familiar, but allow them to check new words either with you or in their dictionaries. Whilst they are doing the exercise, write the words in box A on the board in a column.

   Bring the class together to go through the exercise and invite students, in turn, up to the board to write the words that sound the same next to each other.

Answers

A		B
hear	/hɪə/	here
write	/raɪt/	right
there	/ðeə/	their
wear	/weə/	where
see	/siː/	sea
eye	/aɪ/	I
for	/fɔː/	four
hour	/aʊə/	our
by	/baɪ/	buy
too	/tuː/	two
know	/nəʊ/	no
son	/sʌn/	sun

3 This exercise puts some of the words which have the same sound but different spelling in context and should be good fun to do. Again, ask students to work in pairs to do it. Then check through with the whole class, asking individuals to read the sentences aloud and spell the correct word.

Answers

1 I can **hear** you, but I can't **see** you.
2 **There** are three bedrooms in **our** house.
3 I don't **know where** Jill lives.
4 My **son** lives near the **sea**.
5 Don't **wear** that hat, **buy** a new one!
6 **No**, **I** can't come to your party.
7 You were **right**. Sally and Peter can't come **for** dinner.
8 **Their** daughter could **write** when she was three.
9 I **know** my answers are **right**.

4 You could begin this by asking the class to chant through the phonetic transcriptions all together to check their progress in reading them.

Ask students to work on their own to do the exercise and then check their answers with a partner before you go through it.

Answers

1	/nəʊ/	know	no
2	/sʌn/	son	sun
3	/tuː/	too	two
4	/raɪt/	write	right
5	/hɪə/	hear	here
6	/weə/	wear	where

ADDITIONAL MATERIAL

Workbook Unit 6
Exercise 7 This is a vocabulary exercise that practises words that go together, e.g. *paint a picture, get up early*.

EVERYDAY ENGLISH (SB p50)

On the phone

1 Read the introduction as a class.

T 6.7 Focus attention on the first name and address (Nancy Wilson). Students listen and answer the operator's questions and get Nancy's telephone number. Do this as a class activity, getting students to call out the answers.

Answers and tapescript

Operator	International Directory Enquiries. Which country, please?
You	**Australia, please.**
Operator	And which town?
You	**Perth.**
Operator	Can I have the last name, please?
You	**Wilson.**
Operator	And the initial?
You	**N.**
Operator	What's the address?
You	**302 Erindale Road.**
Recorded message	The number you require is **006198 4681133.**

Check students have written Nancy's phone number down correctly.

2 Students work in pairs to roleplay the operator and someone wanting Franziska's and Mauricio's number. Write the numbers on bits of paper to give to the operators:

Franziska Novak's phone/fax number is 004930 369840.

Mauricio Ferreira's phone number is 005511 253 1162, and his fax number is 005511 253 5879.

Briefly check students have exchanged the information correctly.

3 **SUGGESTION**

This activity includes some of the typical expressions used over the phone in English. Make sure students understand that each language uses different expressions over the phone and if they translate from their own language, they may cause confusion or surprise! Point out in particular that in English you cannot say **I'm (Jo)* when saying who is speaking.

Check comprehension of: *get someone* (as in *fetch*), *message*, *Great!*, *Never mind*, *ring back*. Focus on line 1 as an example with the whole class. If students are unsure what would come before this line, tell them they need to make a question with *can* (*Can I speak to Jo, please?*). Ask students to work in pairs and continue the activity. Tell them not to worry about getting exactly the right answers, as you will focus on these at a later stage. Ask them to take the opportunity to exchange their ideas.

Focus attention on the use of *will* to make offers or promises. (Do not focus on other uses of *will*, e.g. simple future at this stage, as this may confuse students.)

Sample answers
1 **Can I speak to Jo, please?**
  This is Jo.
  Hello, it's X here.
2 **I'm afraid X isn't here.**
  Can I take a message?
  Yes, please. Ask him/her to call X.
3 **Sunday is OK for me.**
  Great! See you on Sunday at ten, then. Bye!
  Yes, OK. Bye!
4 **I'm afraid I can't come to your party.**
  Oh, never mind. Perhaps next time. Bye!
  Yes, OK. Bye!
5 **Is that X?**
  No, it isn't. I'll just get her.
  Hello, X speaking.
6 **X isn't here at the moment.**
  I'll ring back later.
  OK. Bye!
7 **Hi, X.**
  There's a party at my house on Saturday. **Can you come?**
  Yes. That's great, thanks.
8 **Hello, (company name).**
  Can I speak to the manager, please?
  Yes, can I ask who's calling, please?

4 Students work in pairs to complete the three telephone conversations, using the lines from exercise 3.

T 6.8 Students listen and check. If necessary, get students to listen and repeat the conversations before continuing to practise in pairs.

Answers and tapescript
1 A Hello.
  B Hello. Can I speak to Jo, please?
  A **This is Jo.**
  B Oh! Hi, Jo. This is Pat. Is Sunday still OK for tennis?
  A Yes. That's fine.
  B **Great! See you on Sunday at ten, then. Bye!**
  A Bye!

2 A Hello.
  B Hello. Is that Liz?
  A **No it isn't. I'll just get her.**
  (pause)
  C Hello, Liz here.
  B Hi, Liz. It's Tom. Listen! **There's a party at my house on Saturday. Can you come?**
  C Oh sorry, Tom. I can't. It's my sister's wedding.
  B **Oh, never mind. Perhaps next time. Bye!**
  C Bye!

3 A Good morning. Barclays Bank, Watford. How can I help you?
  B Good morning. **Can I speak to the manager, please?**
  A I'm afraid Mr Smith isn't in his office at the moment. **Can I take a message?**
  B Don't worry. **I'll ring back later.**
  A All right. Goodbye.
  B Goodbye.

Then ask students to invent more telephone conversations, based on the ones in the Student's Book. They can change the names, times, arrangements, etc. but can keep the basic format of each conversation the same.

Don't forget!

Workbook Unit 6
Exercise 8 Prepositions
Exercise 9 The writing activity is a simple formal letter applying for a job.

Word list
Remind your students of the Word list for this unit on p137. They could write in the translations, learn them at home, and/or write some of the words in their vocabulary notebook.

Pronunciation Book Unit 6

Video
There are two video sections that can supplement Units 5 and 6 of the Student's Book.
Report (Section 4) Heathrow This is a mini-documentary about Heathrow Airport, past and present. It is also suitable for use either before or after the *Everyday English* Unit 14, *At the airport*.
Situation (Section 5) At the bank This is a short situation where Paola exchanges traveller's cheques at a bank.

7

Past Simple 1 – regular verbs
Irregular verbs
Silent letters • Special occasions

Then and now

Introduction to the unit

The past (the early part of the 20th century) and more recent past (the 1990s) are the themes of this unit. Within these contexts both regular and irregular forms of the Past Simple are presented. The formation of the question and negative is introduced, but the latter is only minimally practised because it is one of the main grammatical aims of Unit 8. The skills work includes a jigsaw reading task with texts on two famous leaders – George Washington and Margaret Thatcher – which provides further practice of the Past Simple.

Language aims

Grammar – Past Simple 1 The learning of the Past Simple is facilitated by students' knowledge of the Present Simple, in that both tenses use a form of *do* as an auxiliary in the question and negative. It is not such a big leap to learn that the same auxiliary is used in its past tense form, *did*, to make the Past Simple tense, especially as this form remains constant in all persons.

Many of the exercises in this unit provide opportunities to contrast the Present and Past Simple tenses.

POSSIBLE PROBLEMS

1 Although students should be helped by their knowledge of the Present Simple (see above), the use of *did* still causes problems and students forget to use it, for example:
   * *Where you went last night?*
   * *When she start school?*
   * *She no liked her job.*

2 There are a large number of irregular verbs to learn. From now on students should be encouraged to consult the irregular verb list on p142 and learn the irregular verbs as and when needed. You could start setting some to learn for homework and giving short tests on them at the beginning of some lessons!

3 The different realizations of the pronunciation of -*ed* at the end of regular verbs is a problem. Students always want to pronounce the -*ed* in its entirety – /ed/ – and not the /t/, /d/, /ɪd/ endings, for example:
   cleaned */kliːned/ instead of /kliːnd/
   worked */wɜːked/ instead of /wɜːkt/
   visited */vɪzɪted/ instead of /vɪzɪtɪd/

   There is an exercise to help students perceive the different endings, but we suggest you avoid spending too much time getting students to *produce* the endings at this stage so as not to overload them.

Vocabulary and pronunciation Words with silent letters are focused upon, for example *walk, know, listen*. Again, the point being emphasized is that English spelling is not phonetic. The phonetic script is further practised to highlight words that have silent letters.

Everyday English Common expressions for special occasions, such as *Happy birthday* and *Happy New Year* are introduced and practised. This provides the opportunity for some very interesting discussion on cross-cultural traditions, especially if you have a multilingual class. What occasions different nationalities celebrate, and how they celebrate them, is fascinating!

Workbook More irregular verbs are introduced.
There are exercises to revise the Present Simple alongside Past Simple.

In the vocabulary section, there is an exercise on recognizing parts of speech.

The writing syllabus continues with a piece of narrative writing about *My last holiday*.

Notes on the unit

STARTER (SB p52)

> **SUGGESTION**
>
> You could ask your students to bring to class any old photographs they have of their grandparents when young, and/or you could bring in some of your own family to set the scene and introduce the idea of the past.
>
> It is always interesting looking at old photographs, so take care that the scene-setting doesn't go on too long and take up too much lesson time!

Check comprehension of *great-grandparents*. Demonstrate the activity by telling the class about your own grandparents and great-grandparents, giving as much information as you can about when and where they were born, their names and their jobs. Use photographs you have brought to class if appropriate.

Students work in pairs and talk about what they know about their grandparents and great-grandparents. Get them to talk about photographs they have brought to class if appropriate.

WHEN I WAS YOUNG (SB p52)

Past Simple – regular verbs

1 Focus attention on the photo of Mattie Smith now. Ask students to give you information about her. Pre-teach/check *have a bath, clean the house, verandah, poems*.

T 7.1 Ask students to read and listen about Mattie Smith in text A and complete the text. (This text is about Mattie's life now and revises the Present Simple before moving to the introduction of the Past Simple.) Play the recording and then check the answers.

> **Answers and tapescript**
>
> Mattie Smith is 91 years old. She **lives** alone in Atlanta, Georgia. She **starts** her day at 7.30. First she **has** a bath, next she **cleans** the house, and then she **sits** outside on her verandah and **thinks** about her past life. Then she **writes** poems about it.

Ask a few questions about Mattie now.

How old is she?	*Ninety-one.*
Where does she live?	*In Atlanta, Georgia.*
Does she live alone?	*Yes, she does.*
What time does she start her day?	*At 7.30.*
What does she do every day?	*She has a bath, cleans the house, sits outside and thinks about her past life.*
What does she write poems about?	*Her past life.*

2 **T 7.2** Establish the answer to this last question clearly and tell your students that they are going to listen to and read about Mattie's past. Play the recording and immediately go through the *Grammar Spot* exercises.

> **GRAMMAR SPOT**
>
> Go through the *Grammar Spot* exercises one by one, establishing the answers after each exercise.
>
> 1 Refer students back to text B and get them to find examples of the past of *is* and *can*. Check the answers.
>
> > **Answers**
> >
> > Mattie **was** never at school. . . . She started work when she **was** eight. . . . She **couldn't** read or write but she **could** think, . . .
>
> 2 Students complete the sentence with the correct form of *live*. Check the answers.
>
> > **Answers**
> >
> > Now she **lives** alone, but when she was a child she **lived** with her mother and sisters.
>
> 3 Students work in pairs and find the Past Simple of *start, work,* and *create*. Get them to work out the rule for the formation of Past Simple of regular verbs.
>
> > **Answers**
> >
> > To form the Past Simple of regular verbs, add *-ed* or *-d* to the infinitive.
>
> Read Grammar Reference 7.1 on p129 together in class, and/or ask students to read it at home. Encourage them to ask you questions about it.

3 **T 7.3** Check comprehension of *earn, die,* and *hate*. Students work in pairs to decide on the past form of the verbs in the box and practise the pronunciation.

Play the recording and let students check their answers. Get students to spell the past forms. Pay particular attention to the change of consonant + *y* to *-ied* in *marry–married*.

> **Answers and tapescript**
>
> /t/   looked   worked
>
> /d/   loved   learned   earned   married   died
>
> /ɪd/   hated   wanted

Play the recording again and get students to repeat.

4 **T 7.4** Explain that the next text gives more information about Mattie's past and students have to complete the text using the Past Simple forms of the verbs in the box from exercise 3. You could ask them to try and fill the gaps with the verbs before they listen, then to listen and check their answers with a partner. Or, if you think that it would be too difficult, let them listen to the text and fill in the answers as they go along.

Play the recording without pausing the tape.

Go through the answers as a class, getting students to take turns at reading aloud part of the text. Correct their pronunciation of the past tense verbs in preparation for the exercise on pronunciation in the *Practice* section.

GRAMMAR SPOT

1 Refer students back to the text about Mattie and get them to find a question and negative.

> **Answers**
> And when **did I learn** to read and write? I **didn't learn** until I was 86, . . .

2/3 Go through the notes on the formation of questions and negatives with the whole class.

Read Grammar Reference 7.2 on p129 together in class, and/or ask students to read it at home. Encourage them to ask you questions about it.

5 This exercise focuses on *wh-* questions in the Past Simple. Students work in pairs to complete the questions about Mattie.

T 7.5 Play the recording so that students can check their answers.

Play the questions from the recording one by one (or say them yourself) and get students to repeat them both chorally and individually. Ask other students to provide the answers. These are all *wh-* questions so encourage natural falling intonation on each one.

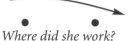

Where did she work?

Students continue practising the questions and answers in pairs.

PRACTICE (SB p54)

Talking about you

1 This activity brings together the past of *be*, *to be born*, and *did* in Past Simple questions, so that students become aware of the difference between the past of the verb *to be* and full verbs. Get students to complete the sentences on their own first and then check in pairs.

Check the answers with the whole class, asking individuals to read out their answers.

Drill the questions, reminding students to use falling intonation.

2 If you have room, ask students to get up and walk round the class asking two or three other students the questions, and answering about themselves in return. Or, if you don't mind a lot of movement, ask students to ask each question to a *different* student. Tell them that you are going to see how much they can remember when they sit down.

3 After a few minutes, students sit down and tell you what information they can remember. Remind them to use the third-person singular forms *was* and *was born*.

You could ask students to write a short paragraph about themselves for homework.

ADDITIONAL MATERIAL

Workbook Unit 7
Exercises 1 and 2 These practise regular verbs, *Yes/No* questions, and short answers in the Past Simple.

Pronunciation

4 **T 7.6** Isolate the sounds /t/, /d/, /ɪd/ for your students and get them to listen and repeat them. Play the recording and ask them to put the verbs in the correct column. Get them to check their answers with a partner and then conduct a full class feedback, asking students to practise saying the verbs.

Answers and tapescript

/t/	/d/	/ɪd/
worked	lived	started
finished	married	hated
looked	loved	visited
liked	died	
	cleaned	

T 7.6

worked	finished
lived	looked
started	died
married	visited
loved	cleaned
hated	liked

THE END OF THE 20TH CENTURY (SB p54)

Irregular verbs

Now the theme moves to the more recent past with a focus on life at the end of the 20th century. This provides the context for the introduction of irregular verbs.

1 Refer students to the irregular verb list on p142. Make sure they understand that it is an important resource that they should refer to regularly.

Ask students to work with a partner. Ask them to use their dictionaries to look up new words and check the list to find out which verb is regular and what the irregular forms of the others are.

Ask students to read out the correct answers.

Answers

have	had
begin	began
come	came
go	went
do	did
leave	left
get	got
study	studied (regular)
become	became
win	won
lose	lost
buy	bought
meet	met

2 **T 7.7** Play the recording (or model the verbs yourself) and ask students to listen and repeat.

3 Write *2000* in large numbers on the board and, if you think your students need to practise dates, ask the whole of your class to chant the years from 1990 to 2000.

Ask your students how old they were in 2000 and what they can remember, not only about their own lives, but also the world, especially sport and politics. You could put them into groups to do this if you have time and if you feel that your students would respond well. Elicit some examples from the class to set the scene for tapescript 7.8 and Simon's reminiscences about the 1990s.

T 7.8 Let students read the texts first and check for any unknown vocabulary – possibly *graphic design*, *advertising agency*, *World Cup*, *the Euro* (the European single currency), *car crash*, and *funeral*. Tell students that the texts are only a summary and that there is more information on tape. Students are required only to select key points to practise certain verbs.

Play the recording. Tell your students to listen to Simon and complete as much of the texts as they can. After listening for the first time, ask students to work in pairs and compare their answers. Now play the recording again so that students can complete or check their answers.

WHAT DID SIMON DO?

He **left** school in 1994. He **went** to university where he **studied** graphic design. Then, in 1997, he **got** a job with Saatchi and Saatchi, an advertising agency in London. He **met** his girlfriend, Zoë, in 1998, and the next year they **bought** a flat together.

WHAT HAPPENED IN THE WORLD?

Sport

France **won** the World Cup in 1998. Brazil **lost**.

Politics

Tony Blair **became** Britain's Prime Minister in 1997. Bill Clinton **had** a lot of problems in his last years in the White House. Eleven countries in Europe (but not Britain) **began** to use the Euro in 1999.

Famous people

Princess Diana **died** in a car crash in Paris in 1997. Millions of people **came** to London for her funeral.

T 7.8

What do I remember of the nineties . . . er . . . well, I left school in 1994 and I went to university. I studied graphic design – it was really good. I had a good time. Then after university, in 1997, I was really lucky. I got a job immediately. A job with Saatchi and Saatchi, they're an advertising agency in London. Soon after that, 1998 it was, I met Zoë, she's my girlfriend. She has a good job, too, and we bought a flat together in 1999.

The only sport I like is football, so I remember when France won the World Cup in 1998. Brazil lost in '98 but they won in '94.

I remember when Tony Blair became Prime Minister in 1997, that was just after I started at Saatchi and Saatchi. Oh, and I remember Bill Clinton and all the problems he had in his last years in the White House. And the Euro – eleven countries in Europe began to use the Euro in 1999, but Britain didn't.

Oh yes – and of course I remember Princess Diana – she died in a car crash in Paris in '97 and millions of people came to London for her funeral. I was there. I can remember it really well.

4 Ask students to give the first question and answer as an example. Ask students to work in pairs to ask and answer the rest of the questions. Insist on full answers so that students get practice with the irregular past forms. Check for accurate question formation and falling intonation. If students have problems, drill the questions and answers in open pairs and then in closed pairs.

Check the answers with the whole class.

Answers

1 When did Simon leave school? He left school in 1994.
2 What did Simon study at university? He studied graphic design.
3 When did Simon get a job with Saatchi and Saatchi? He got a job with Saatchi and Saatchi in 1997.
4 When did Simon meet Zoë? He met Zoë in 1998.
5 What did Zoë and Simon do in 1999? They bought a flat together.

5 Give an example of what you did in the last years of the 20th century and then ask students to write about what they did. If students need a little prompting, you could brainstorm ideas with the whole class, e.g. *have a baby, buy a house/flat, learn to drive, meet boyfriend/girlfriend, marry, start university, get a job*. Students tell the rest of the class about what they did.

PRACTICE (SB p55)

When did it happen?

1 Set up this activity by giving the class a few cues of major events and getting students to form the question and give the corresponding dates, e.g.
the Berlin Wall/fall – When did the Berlin Wall fall? In 1989.
the Second World War/end – When did the Second World War end? In 1945.
the Wright Brothers first fly – When did the Wright Brothers first fly? In 1903.

Students work in groups and list other major events of the 20th century, both nationally and internationally. They then form questions to 'test' the other groups.

Pre-teach expressions like *in the (1950s), in about (1995)* to enable students to give an answer if they can't give an exact year. Get students to ask their questions to another group. Conduct brief feedback with students saying sentences about the most interesting/popular events.

What did you do?

2 Focus attention on the phrases in the box, pointing out we can't use *last* with parts of a day, except *night*. Check pronunciation and then get students to give a few examples of the phrases in context, e.g. *I went to the cinema last night.*

3 Drill the questions in the Student's Book chorally and individually and then get students to ask and answer in pairs. You could suggest that they take notes about each other. Go round the class monitoring and helping.

Bring the class together and briefly check the past form of the verbs as students will need these to report back on their partner. Students tell the class what they learned about their partner.

Check it

4 Ask students to do this exercise on their own and then check with a partner before you go through the exercise as a class.

ADDITIONAL MATERIAL

Workbook Unit 7
Exercises 3–5 These practise irregular verbs in the Past Simple.
Exercise 6 This practises question formation.
Exercise 7 This contrasts Present Simple and Past Simple.

READING AND SPEAKING (SB p56)

Two famous firsts

This is another 'jigsaw' reading activity, so make sure students are clear about which text they should read and how to exchange their information. The mechanics of the activity are made easier by students working on the same true–false statements, irrespective of whether they read about George Washington or Margaret Thatcher.

> **EXTRA INFORMATION**
> The following is some background information on the two leaders:
>
> **George Washington (1732–1799)**
> First President of the USA 1789–97. He was a strong opponent of the British government's policy, and when the War of American Independence started, he was chosen as Commander-in-Chief. After the war, he retired to his Virginia estate, Mount Vernon, but in 1787 he re-entered politics as president of the Constitutional Convention. Although he attempted to draw ministers from a range of political opinion, his aristocratic outlook alienated his secretary of state, Thomas Jefferson, who resigned in 1793, and so created the two-party system.
>
> **Margaret Thatcher**
> British Conservative politician, Prime Minister 1979–90. She was education minister 1970–74 and Conservative Party leader from 1975. She confronted trade union power during the miners' strike 1984–85, sold off many public utilities to the public sector, and reduced the influence of local government. In 1990, divisions in the cabinet forced her to resign.

1 Check students understand the terms *nouns* and *verbs* by translating into L1 or using a simple example sentence and getting students to name the noun and verb, e.g. *The leader died yesterday*. Get students to check the meaning of the words in their dictionary, or use simple explanations and/or L1.

2 Focus attention on the photos. Check students recognize the two people and that they can pronounce their names. Get students to complete the sentences about why each person is an important first. If students are unsure, get them to read the first line of each text. Check the answers.

If students query the terms *president* and *prime minister*, explain that *president* is used for the official leader of a country that does not have a king or queen.

Students work in pairs or groups of three and exchange any information or impressions they have of the two leaders.

3 Divide the class into two groups. Tell Group A to read about George Washington and Group B to read about Margaret Thatcher. Ask each group to read through their text as quickly as possible to get a general understanding of it and to compare the information in the text with what they talked about in exercise 2.

4 Get students to read the text again more slowly and find the information in their text to do the true–false task. Remind them to correct the statements that are false.

When students have read the texts they could either go through the statements on their own and then check with others from the same group, or work with a partner from the same group to do the exercise. Each group has the same statements to work on.

Check the answers with Group A students and Group B students separately.

5 True
6 False. She had twins – a girl and a boy.
7 False. She was in office for eleven years.
8 False. She didn't want to resign and left 10 Downing Street in tears.

5 Tell each student to find a partner from the other group and go through the statements together, telling each other about the leader in their text. Encourage students to exchange their information in a meaningful way, by comparing and contrasting the two leaders, rather than simply saying *true/false* about each statement, e.g.

A *George Washington came from a rich family. What about Margaret Thatcher?*

B *No, her father worked hard for little money.*

Check the answers with the whole class. Again, get students to give complete sentences, comparing and contrasting the two leaders, using *They both …* for comparing, and linking contrasting information with *but*.

Answers
1 George Washington came from a rich family, but Margaret Thatcher didn't.
2 Margaret Thatcher loved being a politician, but George Washington didn't.
3 They both worked hard.
4 George Washington had a lot of other interests, but Margaret Thatcher didn't.
5 Margaret Thatcher had a good education, but George Washington didn't.
6 Margaret Thatcher had twins – a girl and a boy, but George Washington didn't have any children.
7 George Washington was in office for eight years, but Margaret Thatcher was in office for eleven years.
8 George Washington was tired of politics, but Margaret Thatcher didn't want to resign.

6 Get students to complete the questions about the other leader, i.e. Group A complete the questions about Margaret Thatcher and Group B about George Washington. Students can work in pairs or small groups to do this. If students have problems finding the correct words, you could put them on the board in two groups clearly headed *George Washington* and *Margaret Thatcher* (the words are in **bold** below).

Check the answers with Group A students and Group B students separately.

Answers
About George Washington
1 How many jobs did he **have**?
2 When did he **become** President?
3 What did he **like** doing in his free time?

4 Did George and Martha have any **children**?
5 What **did** he build?
6 How long **was** he President?

About Margaret Thatcher
7 What **was** her father's job?
8 When did she **marry** Denis?
9 How many children did they **have**?
10 How much sleep **did** she need?
11 When did the terrorists **bomb** her hotel?
12 How long **was** she Prime Minister?

Students then work with the same partner as in exercise 5 and ask and answer the questions. Check the answers with the whole class, getting students to give full statements where possible in order to practise past forms, e.g. *George Washington had three jobs.*

Answers
About George Washington
1 George Washington had three jobs.
2 He became President in 1789.
3 He liked dancing and going to the theatre in his free time.
4 No, they didn't.
5 He built The White House.
6 He was President for eight years.
About Margaret Thatcher
7 Her father was a grocer.
8 She married Denis in 1951.
9 They had two children/twins.
10 She needed four hours' sleep a night.
11 The terrorists bombed her hotel in 1984.
12 She was Prime Minister for eleven years.

What do you think?

Get one or two students to give an example and then ask students to continue to talking about famous leaders. This will obviously work well in a multilingual group, but can also create quite a lot of discussion in a monolingual group, as students are likely to disagree about which leader was the most important!

VOCABULARY AND PRONUNCIATION (SB p58)

Spelling and silent letters

The aim of this exercise is to show students yet again that English spelling is not phonetic through an exercise on silent letters. It is useful to have a convention when writing words on the board to show students a silent letter. This might be by writing the silent letter in a different coloured pen, or by crossing out the silent letter, e.g. bomb.

You could encourage your students to do the same in their vocabulary notebooks.

The silent *r* in mid-position (e.g. *hard*) and in the end position (e.g. *daughter*) is practised. We do not advise you to explain the rule about silent *r* in end position unless the following word begins with a vowel sound e.g. *daughter and son*. This would probably overload students at this level.

Also, pronunciation work here and on the recording is based on RP. If you are a native-speaker teacher with a different accent, you may like to point this out and explain a little about the many and varying accents of spoken English!

1 Read the instructions as a class. Practise the words from the texts on p57 chorally and individually.
Students work in pairs to cross out the silent letters.

T 7.9 Students listen and check.

Answers and tapescript

1	walk	5	eight	9	island
2	listen	6	farm	10	build
3	know	7	work	11	resign
4	write	8	walk	12	daughter

Students practise saying the words in pairs. Monitor and check.

2 Students look at the phonetics and write in the words from exercise 1.

Answers

1	work	4	build
2	farm	5	write
3	listen	6	daughter

3 Students work in pairs to write other words with silent letters. They are all words students have met in earlier units or should recognize.

T 7.10 Students listen and check.

Answers and tapescript

1	born	5	knives
2	bought	6	wrong
3	world	7	cupboard
4	answer	8	Christmas

Students practise saying the words in pairs. Monitor and check.

EVERYDAY ENGLISH (SB p58)

Special occasions

This exercise can provide a lot of fascinating information if you have students from different countries, or if some of your students know foreign countries.

1 Students look at the list and decide which are special days. They match the special days to a picture and/or object.

Answers

1	New Year's Eve	6	Mother's Day
2	wedding day	7	birthday
3	Thanksgiving	8	Valentine's Day
4	Christmas Day	9	Hallowe'en
5	Easter Day		

Ask your class if they have the same customs for the same days. Here are some notes on what the days mean to British people (though not all British people, of course).

British and American customs
Birthday
There is often a birthday cake, with candles to be blown out and everyone sings *Happy birthday*. People send birthday cards, and there is perhaps a birthday party with friends.

Wedding day
People get married in a church for a religious ceremony or a registry office for a civil ceremony. Rice or confetti is thrown at the bride and groom to wish them luck, and the bride often carries a horseshoe, again to symbolize good luck. (We have no idea why the horseshoe is a symbol of good luck!) There is a party afterwards called a reception, and the bride and groom may go on a holiday called a honeymoon.

Christmas Day
This is the 25 December, the main day for celebrating Christmas in Britain, when presents are exchanged. There is a large dinner, traditionally with turkey and Christmas pudding, which is made from dried fruit. We decorate the house, and have a Christmas tree. Young children believe that Santa Claus (or Father Christmas) visits during the early hours of Christmas morning and leaves presents by the children's beds or under the tree.

New Year's Eve
In Scotland this is a more important celebration than in the rest of Britain. People go to parties and wait for midnight to come, when they wish each other 'Happy New Year'. In London many thousands of people celebrate New Year in Trafalgar Square where they can hear Big Ben (the clock on the Houses of Parliament) strike midnight.

Easter Day
There is no fixed tradition of ways to celebrate Easter. Children receive chocolate Easter eggs and usually eat too many of them!

Mother's Day
This is on a Sunday towards the end of March. Children give cards and a present such as some flowers or chocolates.

Thanksgiving

This is a national holiday in the US (fourth Thursday in November) and Canada (second Monday in October) first celebrated by the Pilgrim settlers in Massachusetts after their first harvest in 1621. Most families enjoy a large meal together.

Valentine's Day

People send Valentine cards to the person they love. They are usually sent with no name on!
People also put messages in newspapers to their loved one. These can often be quite funny!

Hallowe'en

This is the evening of 31 October, when it was believed that the spirits of dead people appeared. Customs associated with Hallowe'en in Britain and the US are fancy dress parties where people dress up as ghosts, witches, etc. Children often celebrate by wearing masks or costumes and going 'trick or treating' – going from house to house collecting sweets, fruit, or money.

2   Students work in pairs to complete the conversations with the days, and match them to the days and occasions in exercise 1.

T 7.11 Students listen and check their answers, then practise the conversations with a partner.

> **Answers and tapescript**
> 1   **Monday**
>   A Ugh! Work again! I hate **Monday** mornings!
>   B Me, too. Did you have a nice weekend?
>   A Yes. It was brilliant.
> 2   **birthday**
>   Happy **birthday** to you.
>   Happy **birthday** to you.
>   Happy **birthday**, dear Tommy,
>   Happy **birthday** to you.
> 3   **Valentine's Day**
>   A Did you get any **Valentine** cards?
>   B Yes, I did. Listen to this.
>   Roses are red. Violets are blue.
>   You are my **Valentine**
>   And I love you.
>   A Oooh-er! Do you know who it's from?
>   B No idea!
> 4   **wedding day**
>   A Congratulations!
>   B Oh . . . thank you very much.
>   A When's the happy day?
>   B Pardon?
>   A Your **wedding** day. When is it?
>   B Oh! We're not sure. Perhaps some time in June.

> 5   **New Year's Eve**
>   A It's midnight! Happy **New Year** everybody!
>   B Happy **New Year**!
>   C Happy **New Year**!
> 6   **Friday**
>   A Thank goodness! It's **Friday**!
>   B Yeah. Have a nice weekend!
>   A Same to you.

3   **T 7.12** Students listen to the lines and give an answer. They can choose what they say.

> **Sample answers and tapescript**
> 1   A Did you have a nice weekend?
>   **B Yes, very nice, thank you. What about you?**
> 2   A Did you get any Valentine cards?
>   **B Only one, from my husband. What about you?**
> 3   A Congratulations!
>   **B Thank you very much!**
> 4   A Happy New Year!
>   **B And Happy New Year to you too!**
> 5   A Have a nice weekend!
>   **B Thank you. Same to you.**

Don't forget!

Workbook Unit 7

Exercise 8 Vocabulary of parts of speech, such as *adjective*, *noun*
Exercise 9 Prepositions: *about, after, for*
Exercise 10 This is the writing activity: describing a holiday. It provides more practice of the Past Simple.

Word list

Remind your students of the Word list for this unit on p138. They could write in the translations, learn them at home, and/or write some of the words in their vocabulary notebook.

Pronunciation Book Unit 7

Video

There are two video sections that can supplement Units 7 (and 8) of the Student's Book.
Report (Section 6) *Shakespeare* This is a short documentary about the life of Shakespeare.
Situation (Section 7) *The pub* David takes Paola to an English pub. (This section can also be used with Unit 9 as its topic is food and drink.)

8

Past Simple 2 – negatives/*ago*
Which word is different?
What's the date?

How long ago?

Introduction to the unit

This is the second unit on the Past Simple tense, and it provides further practice and reinforcement of the input in Unit 7, focusing particularly on the negative. The title of this unit is 'How long ago?' and the topics in the unit lend themselves to practice of the Past Simple. The unifying theme of the unit is how things began, with reading texts on inventions, and listening texts on the start of two different relationships. This main listening exercise is one of the first extensive listening exercises where students do not have the support of the written word.

Language aims

Grammar – Past Simple 2 See the introduction to the Past Simple and problems associated with it on p51 of the Teacher's Book. There is considerable practice of the positive in this unit, but there is also much emphasis on question forms and negatives. These present few problems of concept, but there can inevitably be mistakes of form.

Common mistakes
*When you went home?
*When did you went home?
*Where did go Peter?
*I no went out last night.

ago *Ago* is an adverb which is used when the point of reference is the present. It means 'before now', and is used only with past tenses, not present tenses or present perfect tenses. *Ago* always comes after an expression of time.

Different languages realize this concept in various ways.

two years ago – *il y a deux ans* (French)
          – *vor zwei Jahren* (German)
          – *hace dos años* (Spanish)
          – *due anni fa* (Italian)

Common mistakes
*I went there ago two weeks.
*I went there before two weeks.
*My cat died for two years.

Time expressions There is a focus on preposition and noun collocations, such as *on Saturday* and *in summer*. These prepositions can cause a lot of confusion and so will need a lot of practice and regular reviewing.

Vocabulary There is quite a lot of vocabulary input throughout the unit. The first part of the vocabulary section is an 'odd one out' exercise which revises vocabulary from this and previous units, as well as preparing students for the listening exercise *How did you two meet?* There is also further work on word stress and phonetic script.

Everyday English This section introduces and practises ordinals and dates.

Workbook In the vocabulary section, there is a focus on words which are both nouns and verbs, e.g. *dance*, and revision and extension of machines and inventions. There is also a section on numbers 100–1,000.

In the writing section, there is further work on linking words, and students are invited to write about an old friend.

Notes on the unit

STARTER (SB p60)

Students work in pairs and say the Past Simple of the verbs in the box. If they have problems with the form of any of the irregular verbs, refer them to the irregular verb list on p142.

Check the answers with the whole class, getting students to spell the past forms and making sure they can pronounce them correctly.

Answers

eat	ate
drink	drank
drive	drove
fly	flew
listen to	listened to
make	made
ride	rode
take	took
watch	watched
wear	wore

FAMOUS INVENTIONS (SB p60)

Past Simple – negatives/*ago*

1 Focus attention on the photographs and get students to name each of the items shown. Check pronunciation carefully, especially of the 'international' words which are the same or very similar in other languages, e.g. *hamburger* /ˈhæmbɜːɡə/, *Coca-Cola* /ˈkəʊkə ˈkəʊlə/, *jeans* /dʒiːnz/, *television* /ˈtelɪvɪʒn/, and *photograph* /ˈfəʊtəɡrɑːf/. Check students stress the noun form *record* correctly /ˈrekɔːd/.

Students work in pairs and match the verbs from the *Starter* activity to the nouns.

Check the answers with the whole class.

Answers

1 **drink** Coca-Cola
2 **take** photographs
3 **listen to** records
4 **fly** planes
5 **wear** jeans
6 **eat** hamburgers
7 **drive** cars
8 **make** phone calls
9 **watch** television
10 **ride** bikes

2
SUGGESTION

You might want to pre-teach *ago*. You could ask questions such as the following to feed this in:

When was your last English lesson? (On Tuesday.)
How many days ago was that? (Two days ago.)
When did you last have a holiday? (In June.)
How many months ago was that? (Five months ago.)
When did you last go to the cinema? (Last Friday.)
How many days ago was that? (Five days ago.)

You could then highlight and explain *ago* (see *Language aims* on p60 of the Teacher's Book). Translation might help.

Model the example question yourself, and get lots of repetition practice. Then practise the question and the three sample answers in open pairs. Do the same for five of the photographs and then ask students to ask and answer questions about the remaining five in closed pairs.

3 Students give you their opinions about what people did and didn't do 100 years ago.

4   **SUGGESTION**

This activity requires students to use the Past Simple passive in the question: *When was/were … invented?* Point out that students will need to use *was* to ask about *Coca-Cola* and *television*. You can drill the question forms, but do not do a full presentation of the passive at this stage.

Get students to ask you about each of the items in the photographs and give them the correct date. Get them to write the dates down and work out how long ago the item was invented. You may get some surprised reactions and even disagreement from students, as there is a big difference between, say, the invention of the car and when cars became generally available.

Answers (The number of years ago will depend on the year you are using the course)
1 Coca-Cola was invented in 1886.
2 The camera was invented in 1826.
3 The record player was invented in 1878.
4 The first plane was invented in 1903. The first flight across the Channel was in 1909.
5 Jeans were invented in 1873, made by Levi Strauss.
6 Hamburgers were invented in 1895.
7 Cars were invented in 1893. A Benz went at 18 miles an hour.
8 The phone was invented in 1876.
9 The television was invented in 1926.
10 Bikes were invented in about 1840.

GRAMMAR SPOT

Focus attention on the *Grammar Spot* table. Get students to work through the answers orally first. Then check the answers with the whole class, writing the sentences on the board for students to copy.

Answers

Present Simple	Past Simple
He lives in London.	He lived in London.
Do you live in London?	Did you live in London?
Does she live in London?	Did she live in London?
I don't live in London.	I didn't live in London.
He doesn't live in London.	He didn't live in London.

Highlight that *he/she/it* has a different form in the Present Simple from the other persons, but that all forms in the Past Simple are the same.

Read Grammar Reference 8.1 and 8.2 on p129 together in class, and/or ask students to read it at home. Encourage them to ask you questions about it.

PRACTICE (SB p62)

Three inventors

1 Ask students to look at the three photos and say what they can see. Students read the three texts, checking new words in their dictionaries. The following words will probably be new: *cloth, workmen, fashionable, transmitted, workroom, produced, arthritis, best-selling, painkiller, astronaut, philosopher, century, age* (= era).

Tell students they are going to read the texts again, focusing on the dates. Stress that all three dates in each text are incorrect, and get students to discuss in pairs what the correct dates might be. Remind them that they already have some of the correct dates from *Famous inventions*, exercise 4 and point out that they aren't expected to know the correct dates, just have fun guessing.

T 8.1 Students listen, correct the dates, and see if they guessed any of them correctly. You could either play the recording all the way through, or stop it after each text. Ask students to make a negative and a positive sentence about each date. Drill the example sentence in the Student's Book chorally and individually, highlighting the contrastive stress and the use of the pronoun:

They didn't make the first jeans in nineteen twenty-three.

They made them in eighteen seventy-three.

Briefly revise the pronouns *them* and *it* and then get students to continue working in pairs. Check the answers with the whole class, either by getting students to read out the pairs of sentences with the correct stress or asking different students to read the texts aloud with the correct information. Correct any pronunciation mistakes.

Answers and tapescript
They didn't make the first jeans in 1923. They made them in 1873.
Jeans didn't become fashionable for women in 1965. They became fashionable for women in 1935.
Calvin Klein didn't earn $12.5 million a week from jeans in the 1990s. He earned $12.5 million a week from jeans in the 1970s.

Baird didn't transmit the first television picture on 25 November, 1905. He transmitted it on 25 October, 1925.

Baird didn't send pictures from London to Glasgow in 1929. He sent them in 1927.

Baird didn't send pictures to New York in 1940. He sent them in 1928.

Felix Hofman didn't invent Aspirin in 1879. He invented it in 1899.

Aspirin wasn't the best-selling painkiller by 1940. It was the best-selling painkiller by 1950.

The Apollo astronauts didn't take aspirin to the moon in 1959. They took it to the moon in 1969.

T 8.1

JEANS

Two Americans, Jacob Davis and Levi Strauss, made the first jeans in 1873. Davis bought cloth from Levi's shop. He told Levi that he had a special way to make strong trousers for workmen. The first jeans were blue. In 1935 jeans became fashionable for women after they saw them in *Vogue* magazine. In the 1970s, Calvin Klein earned $12.5 million a week from jeans.

TELEVISION

A Scotsman, John Logie Baird, transmitted the first television picture on 25 October, 1925. The first thing on television was a boy who worked in the office next to Baird's workroom in London. In 1927 Baird sent pictures from London to Glasgow. In 1928 he sent pictures to New York, and also produced the first colour TV pictures.

ASPIRIN

Felix Hofman a 29-year-old chemist who worked for the German company Bayer, invented the drug Aspirin in March 1899. He gave the first aspirin to his father for his arthritis. By 1950 it was the best-selling painkiller in the world, and in 1969 the Apollo astronauts took it to the moon. The Spanish philosopher, José Ortega y Gasset, called the 20th century 'The Age of Aspirin'.

2 Look at the example in the Student's Book and highlight the negative form and the correct answer. Students work on their own and continue the activity.

T 8.2 Play the recording and let students check their answers.

Answers and tapescript

1 Two Germans didn't make the first jeans. Two Americans made them.
2 Davis didn't sell cloth in Levi's shop. He bought cloth from Levi's shop.
3 Women didn't see pictures of jeans in *She* magazine. They saw them in *Vogue*.
4 Baird didn't send pictures from London to Paris. He sent pictures from London to Glasgow.

5 Felix Hofman didn't give the first aspirin to his mother. He gave it to his father.
6 A Spanish philosopher didn't call the 19th century, 'the Age of Aspirin'. He called the 20th century 'the Age of Aspirin'.

Play the recording again and get students to practise the stress and intonation.

Did you know that?

3 **T 8.3** Pre-teach/check the following vocabulary: *spaghetti*, *really*, *incredible*, *true*, *afraid*, and *believe*. Students read and listen to the conversations. Draw their attention to the wide voice range of the second speaker as he/she expresses incredulity. Practise the conversations in open pairs, and really encourage students to sound surprised!

4 You will need to photocopy the lists of incredible information on p127 of the Teacher's Book. They are repeated to help you save paper.

Pre-teach/check the following vocabulary: *painting*, *alive*, *actress*, *millionaire*, *spell* (past tense *spelled*) *snow* (*v*), *marijuana*, *wall*, *voice*, *novelist*.

Take care also with the pronunciation of the following words:
van Gogh (in British English) /ˌvæn ˈɡɒf/
spelled /speld/
Sahara Desert /səˈhɑːrə ˈdezət/
Louis /ˈluːi/
marijuana /ˌmærɪwˈɑːnə/

Also, point out how we say kings and queens in English. (Students might not understand Roman numerals.)
King Louis the fourteenth
King Henry the eighth
King Francis the first

Divide the class into pairs. Give out the lists of incredible information to Student A and B in each pair. Do an example from Student A's information and one from Student B's. Remember that students will have difficulty in selecting the correct short answer (*wasn't*, *didn't*), so you might want to go through them as a class first. On the other hand, you might decide that as a teacher you can't do everything at once! If students produce a good, wide voice range, and enjoy doing the exercise, maybe that's enough! (This is primarily a pronunciation exercise.)

Sample answers

Did you know that Vincent van Gogh sold only two of his paintings while he was alive?

Really (etc.)? He didn't! I don't believe it (etc.)!

Did you know that the actress Shirley Temple was a millionaire before she was ten?

Really? She wasn't!

Did you know that Shakespeare spelled his name in eleven different ways?

He didn't! Really? That's incredible!

Did you know that in 1979 it snowed in the Sahara Desert?

It didn't!

Did you know that King Louis XIV of France had a bath only three times in his life?

He didn't! I don't believe it!

Did you know the American President George Washington grew marijuana in his garden?

He didn't!

Did you know that it took 1,700 years to build the Great Wall of China?

It didn't!

Did you know King Henry VIII of England had six wives?

Really? He didn't!

Did you know that Walt Disney used his own voice for the character of Mickey Mouse?

He didn't!

Did you know that Shakespeare and the Spanish novelist Cervantes both died on the same day, 23 April 1616?

They didn't! Really?

Did you know that King Francis I of France bought the painting *The Mona Lisa* to put in his bathroom?

He didn't! That's incredible!

Did you know when Shakespeare was alive, there were no actresses, only male actors?

There weren't! I don't believe it!

ADDITIONAL MATERIAL

Workbook Unit 8
Exercises 1–4 Past Simple, regular and irregular
Exercise 5 Past time expressions
Exercise 6 *ago*

Time expressions

5   Ask students to identify the correct preposition for the time expressions. Some they will know, some will be new. If mistake follows mistake, you can expect some frustration, and possibly amusement, from students. Give them these rules to help:
on + day/day of the week plus part of the day, e.g. *on Saturday morning*
in + part of the day (except *night*)/month/season/year/ century
at + time

This leaves only *at night* and *at weekends* that do not fit any of the categories. Check the answers.

Answers
at seven o'clock
in the morning
on Saturday
on Sunday evening
at night
in September
at weekends
in summer
in 1994
in the twentieth century

6   Demonstrate the activity by getting students to practise the examples in the Student's Book in open pairs. Students continue in closed pairs asking questions with *when*, and answering the questions in the two different ways. Monitor and check that the questions are well formed, and that the voice starts high. Feed back on any common errors in grammar or pronunciation.

7   Get students to tell the class about their day so far. If you have a small group and sufficient time, you could ask each student to give their example. If you have a lot of students, you could get students to work simultaneously in small groups, making sure the students who worked together in exercise 6 talk to different students.

VOCABULARY AND PRONUNCIATION (SB p63)

Which word is different?

The aim of this activity is to revise and extend vocabulary from this and previous units, and to pre-teach some words that will come up in the listening exercise *How did you two meet?* on p64 of the Student's Book.

1   Read the instructions and the example as a class. Students work in pairs to find the words that are different, using their dictionaries.

Answers
Students might decide that they have alternative answers, which is fine if they can justify them!
2   *Recipe* /ˈresəpi/ is different. You can eat all the others.
3   *Television* is different. The others are machines for housework.
4   *Kissed* is different. All the other verbs are irregular. (Students may need prompting with this one.)
5   *CD player* is different. All the others are ways of communicating.
6   *Delicious* is different. All the others are colours.
7   *Leg* is different. All the others are parts of the face.

8 *Laugh* is different. All the others are ways of communicating with words.
9 *Clock* is different. All the others are periods of time.
10 *Funny* is different. All the others are emotions.
11 *Go to a party* is different. The others are all possible stages in a relationship.

2 Students look at the words in phonetic script. Tell them not to panic as all the words have been taken from exercise 1, so they should recognize most of them! Students work in pairs and practise saying the words. Monitor and check pronunciation, particularly of the more difficult words – *recipe, delicious, sandwich.*

Answers and tapescript
1 recipe
2 chat
3 shy
4 funny
5 face
6 worried
7 delicious
8 sandwich
9 machine
10 century

T 8.4 Students listen and check.

3 Students work in pairs to put one of the words from exercise 1 (not necessarily the odd ones out) into each gap.

T 8.5 Students listen and check.

Answers and tapescript
1 A Why didn't you **laugh** at my joke?
  B Because it wasn't very **funny**. That's why!
2 A Hello. Hello. I can't hear you. Who is it?
  B It's me, Jonathon . . . JONATHON! I'm on my **mobile phone**.
  A Oh, Jonathon! Hi! Sorry, I can't **chat** now. I'm in a hurry.
3 A Good luck in your exams!
  B Oh, thank you. I always get so **nervous** before exams.
4 A Mmmmm! Did you make this chocolate cake?
  B I did. Do you like it?
  A Like it? I *love* it. It's **delicious**. Can I have the **recipe**?
5 A Come on, Tommy. Say hello to Auntie Mavis. Don't be **shy**.
  B Hello, Auntie Mavis.

Students practise the conversations in pairs.

How did you two meet?

POSSIBLE PROBLEMS
This is one of the first extensive listening exercises in *New Headway Elementary* where students are not encouraged to read and listen at the same time. They have to listen to the recording only. Students often find listening to recordings very difficult for the obvious reason that they have no visual support. They cannot see the speakers, or their lips. However, there are several pre-listening tasks, and students are guided to comprehension via the questions.

1 Students work in pairs to put the sentences in order. Ask for some feedback. You will probably get lots of different ideas!

Sample answers
1 Wilma and Carl met at a party.
2 They chatted for a long time. (Make sure students realize that we also use the verb *chat* when people communicate informally over the Internet.)
3 They kissed.
4 They fell in love.
5 He invited her to meet his parents.
6 They got engaged.
7 They got married.
8 They had two children.

2 **SUGGESTION**
With a weaker group, or to help get students started, you might like to give your ideas about one of the people as an example, e.g.
I think this woman is Rosa because she looks Spanish. She has dark hair and dark skin. She is also on a beach. I think she is married to Vincent because they both like the sea. I think they met when he went to Spain on his boat.
Feed in useful language like: *dark hair/eyes/skin, fair hair/skin, blond, tall/short, he/she/it looks . . . , I think . . . and . . . are husband and wife because . . . , I think they met . . . .*

Students look at the photos of the four people and answer the questions in pairs. Point out that they are not expected to give correct answers at this stage and any suggestions they make are valid provided they give a reason.

3 Students read the introductions about how the couples met and see if their ideas in exercise 2 were correct. Get students to give a brief reaction to each introduction – were they surprised or amused, and which story do they think is the more romantic?

Tell students to decide individually what they think happened next in each story. Again, give a brief example if you think this will help, e.g. *I think Per and Debbie chatted on the Internet for a long time. Then they fell in love.* Then get students to compare in pairs or small groups.

4 **T 8.6** Tell students they are going to listen to each couple talking and they should try to understand just what happened next in each relationship and not to panic if they don't understand every word. Pause the recording after Debbie and Per and allow students to check in pairs. Then play the recording of Rosa and Vincent and again let students check briefly in pairs.

Answers and tapescript
Per and Debbie chatted on the Internet for a year.
Rosa asked a friend to translate the letter and then she wrote to Vincent and sent a photo.

T 8.6

Debbie	I'm really quite shy. I find it difficult to talk to people face to face. But I find it easy to chat on the Internet. I met Per there about a year ago. It was on a chatline called 'the Chat Room'. He was so funny.
Per	But I'm only funny on the Internet! Anyway, we chatted on the Internet for a year, we exchanged hundreds of e-mails and some photographs. I wanted to phone Debbie but . . .
Debbie	I said no. I was worried. I didn't want it to end.
Per	She didn't even give me her address. But finally she said OK, I could phone, so I did, and we spoke for an hour. It was very expensive! That was six months ago. Then she sent me her address and . . .
Debbie	. . . that was three months ago and one week later, there was a knock at the door and I knew before I opened it. Somehow I wasn't worried any more. I opened the door and . . .
Per	. . . and I stood there with some flowers . . .
Debbie	. . . lots of flowers. Red roses. Beautiful . . . and . . .
Per	. . . and well, we fell in love and . . .
Both	. . . and we got married last Saturday.
Rosa	I love the sea. I like walking on the beach. One day, it was five years ago now, I was on the beach and I stood on something, it was a bottle, a green bottle. I could see something inside. Some paper, so I broke the bottle, it was a letter but . . .
Vincent	. . . but you couldn't read it . . .
Rosa	No, I couldn't. You see it was in English and I couldn't speak English then.
Vincent	You can speak it well now . . .
Rosa	No, not really, but anyway. I asked a friend to translate the letter for me. We couldn't believe it. A man in America – he wanted a wife, but the letter was ten years old.

Vincent	And I still wasn't married!
Rosa	But I didn't know that. Anyway for a joke I wrote and sent a photo . . .
Vincent	And now, I couldn't believe it. I got this letter and a photo. She looked beautiful. I wrote back immediately and we wrote every week for six months . . . and we spoke on the phone and . . .
Rosa	. . . and finally I flew to America and we met face to face. I was very shy but it was good, very good and now . . .
Vincent	. . . now, we have three children. We have a house by the sea . . .
Rosa	We're very happy. You see, we both love the sea!

SUGGESTION

Try to get students used to listening for gist from this first extensive listening exercise and so only repeat the recording if students have really failed to follow what happened next in the stories. They will probably tell you they didn't understand anything, but get them to pool their ideas in pairs or small groups before feeding back, as this will help build up their confidence.

5 Get students to read through the questions and check comprehension of the expression *face to face*, and *stood* (past of *stand*). Make sure they understand that in question 6 they need to write the initial of the person who says the sentences.

T 8.6 Ask students to listen again for the information they need to answer the questions. Play both recordings straight through and get students to complete their answers. Get them to check in pairs and exchange any information they missed. Only play the recording a third time if most of your students have missed a lot of key information. Check the answers with the whole class.

Answers
1 Per and Debbie met about a year ago. Rosa and Vincent met five years ago.
2 Because she is shy (and she finds it difficult to talk to people face to face).
3 It was in a green bottle on the beach. It said Vincent wanted a wife.
4 She couldn't speak English.
5 No. Rosa and Vincent have three children but Per and Debbie don't have any.
6 a **D** I'm really quite shy.
     R I was very shy.
   b **D** I find it difficult to talk to people face to face.
     R I flew to America and we met face to face.
   c **R** I stood on something.
     P I stood there with some flowers.
   d **P** We chatted on the Internet for a year.
     V We wrote every week for six months.

Speaking

6 Students work in pairs. Tell them they are going to roleplay being one of the characters from the listening. Let students alone or in pairs choose their character. If you can, ask the boys/men to imagine they are Per/Vincent, and similarly the girls/women to imagine they are Debbie/Rosa. Make sure that each student is paired with the husband/wife of the *other* couple, i.e. Per and Rosa and Debbie and Vincent. Students tell their partner about how they met their husband/wife from their character's point of view. The partner can ask them questions for more details and the student roleplaying must answer in character.

7 To encourage students to feel comfortable about talking about their own life, give an example about how your own relationship started and/or how your parents/grandparents met. Students continue working in pairs.

Ask students to give the whole class examples of romantic, unusual, or amusing starts to a relationship.

ADDITIONAL MATERIAL

Workbook Unit 8
Exercise 7 This is a gap-fill and comprehension exercise on the same theme of *How did you two meet?*

EVERYDAY ENGLISH (SB p65)

What's the date?

1 Students work in pairs to put the correct ordinal next to the numbers.

Answers

1st	first	13th	thirteenth
2nd	second	16th	sixteenth
3rd	third	17th	seventeenth
4th	fourth	20th	twentieth
5th	fifth	21st	twenty-first
6th	sixth	30th	thirtieth
10th	tenth	31st	thirty-first
12th	twelfth		

T 8.7 Students listen and practise saying the ordinals. Stop the recording after each one and drill them around the class, correcting carefully.

2 Students ask and answer questions about the months of the year. You don't need to let this go on for very long.

3 Focus attention on the Caution Box and highlight the different ways of writing and saying the dates. Students practise saying the dates both ways. Students often have a lot of difficulties saying dates, for the reasons explained

on p61 of the Teacher's Book, so do the activity as a class and correct mistakes very carefully.

T 8.8 Students listen and check.

Answers and tapescript
1 The first of April
  April the first
2 The second of March
  March the second
3 The seventeenth of September
  September the seventeenth
4 The nineteenth of November
  November the nineteenth
5 The twenty-third of June
  June the twenty-third
6 The twenty-ninth of February, nineteen seventy-six
7 The nineteenth of December, nineteen eighty-three
8 The third of October, nineteen ninety-nine
9 The thirty-first of May, two thousand
10 The fifteenth of July, two thousand and four

4 **T 8.9** Students listen and write down the dates they hear. Tell them there are seven dates in total. Let them check in pairs before you give the answers.

Answers and tapescript
1 4 January
2 7 May, 1997
3 15 August, 2001
4 13 July
5 30 November
6 23 April, 1564
  23 April, 1616

T 8.9
1 The fourth of January.
2 May the seventh, 1997
3 The fifteenth of August, 2001
4 A It was a Friday.
  B No, it wasn't. It was a Thursday.
  A No, I remember. It was Friday the thirteenth. The thirteenth of July.
5 A Oh no! I forgot your birthday.
  B It doesn't matter, really.
  A It was last Sunday, wasn't it? The thirtieth. November the thirtieth.
6 A Hey! Did you know that Shakespeare was born and died on the same day?
  B That's not possible!
  A Yes, it is. He was born on April the twenty-third fifteen sixty-four and he died on April the twenty-third, sixteen sixteen.

5 Students work in pairs to answer the questions about dates. Monitor and feed back on any common errors before checking the answers with the whole class.

Don't forget!

Workbook Unit 8

Exercise 8 A vocabulary exercise on words that are both nouns and verbs

Exercise 9 A puzzle activity on machines and inventions.

Exercises 10–12 Revision of numbers 100–1,000

Exercises 13 and 14 The writing syllabus continues with a further exercise on linking words, *because*, *when*, and *until*. Students are invited to write about an old friend.

Word list

Remind your students of the Word list for this unit on p138. They could write in the translations, learn them at home, and/or write some of the words in their vocabulary notebook.

Pronunciation Book Unit 8

Video

There are two video sections that can supplement Units 7 and 8 of the Student's Book.

Report (Section 6) is about Shakespeare (if you haven't already played it whilst doing Unit 7). It is a short documentary about his life.

Situation (Section 7) The Pub David takes Paola to an English pub. (This section can also be used with Unit 9 as its topic is food and drink.)

EXTRA IDEAS UNITS 5–8

On p128–9 of the Teacher's Book there are two additional activities: a reading text and a song. If you have time and feel that your students would benefit from them, you can photocopy them and use them in class. The reading exercise revises Units 5–8 and could also be done for homework. Activities to exploit the reading are provided, and the answers are on p155.

You will find the song after Unit 8 on the Class Cassette/CD. Students choose the correct words to complete the song, then listen and check their answers.

9

Count and uncount nouns
I like/I'd like • *much/many*
Food • **Polite requests**

Introduction to the unit

The theme of this unit is food and drink, which lends itself to the presentation and practice of the target items – count and uncount nouns with a review of the determiners *some* and *any* (in Unit 5 they were introduced with countable nouns only) and a focus on *much/many*. The verb *like* is contrasted with *would like*, and the *Everyday English* focus *Polite requests* carries through the food and drink theme. The skills material includes a reading text about food around the world, and an invitation to discuss eating habits in different countries. There is also a *Listening and Speaking* section on *My favourite food*.

Language aims

Grammar – count and uncount nouns Students often need help with the concept of count and uncount nouns, and need regular practice with the articles and determiners that can be used with them. Students also need to understand that a lot of nouns can be both countable and uncountable, depending on the context in which they are used, e.g.
Two coffees, please. (countable and meaning two cups of coffee)
Coffee is expensive. (uncountable and meaning coffee in general)
Students also have to get to grips with interference from their own language where some nouns which are uncount in English are countable. This can lead to misuse, e.g.
*They gave me advices.
* I'd like some informations.

like and **would like** *Would like* is introduced for the first time, and this is the first time that students have seen the modal verb *would*. It is easy for students to confuse these two forms. Here are some common mistakes.
*Do you like a coffee?
*I like a cup of tea, please.
Are you hungry? *You like a sandwich?
It is relatively easy for students to perceive the difference between a general expression of liking and a specific request, but you can expect many mistakes for a long time as students confuse the two forms, especially the two auxiliary verbs *do* and *would*.

some/any *Some* and *any* were first introduced in Unit 5, but only with count nouns. This unit introduces them with uncount nouns as well.

The often-repeated rule that *some* is used in positive sentences and *any* in questions and negatives is not entirely true, but it's still useful at this level. However, in this unit the use of *some* in requests and offers is also introduced. It is quite a subtle concept for students to grasp that *some* can be used in questions when there is no doubt about the existence of the thing requested or offered. The use of L1 might help to clarify this.

As in Unit 5, we do not suggest that you explore the use of *any* to mean *it doesn't matter which*, as in *Take any book you want*.

much/many The focus on indefinite quantities is extended with a focus on *much/many*. The question forms *How much … ?* and *How many … ?* are also practised.

Vocabulary There is quite a heavy vocabulary load in this unit, largely to do with food and drink. Words to do with food and drink are introduced as part of the presentation of count/uncount nouns, and there is more lexis to do with food in the language practice and skills work. For this reason, there is no separate *Vocabulary* section.

Everyday English Polite requests with *Can/Could you … ?* and *Can/Could I … ?* are introduced and practised.

Workbook There are exercises on count and uncount nouns, *I like/I'd like*, and *some/any*, *much/many*.

The vocabulary of the unit is recycled and extended through a menu and related activities.

In the writing section, there is the second focus on formal letters, and students are invited to write a letter to a hotel.

Notes on the unit

STARTER (SB p66)

Give examples of your own favourite fruit, vegetable, and drink. Then get students to write their own answers. Students compare their answers in pairs.

Ask students to tell the rest of the class their answers, checking and drilling pronunciation as necessary. Revise the alphabet by getting students to tell you the spelling of each word. Build up lists on the board for each category and get students to copy into their vocabulary notebooks.

FOOD AND DRINK (SB p66)

Count and uncount nouns

1   Students match the food and drink in columns A and B to the pictures.

Answers			
A		**B**	
20 tea	3 spaghetti	8 apples	6 carrots
15 coffee	9 yoghurt	10 oranges	2 tomatoes
11 wine	7 pizza	19 bananas	17 hamburgers
12 beer	1 cheese	14 strawberries	18 chips
4 apple juice	16 chocolate	5 peas	13 biscuits

GRAMMAR SPOT

Focus attention on the *Grammar Spot* and look at the questions as a class. Don't hurry this part. Allow students time to think. If one student knows and wants to give the answer before the others have had time to think, ask him or her to wait a little.

Answers
1   List B has plural nouns.
2/3 We cannot count the things in the sentences in A, but we can count the things in the sentences in B. (You might want to feed in the terms *count* and *uncount* nouns.)

Read Grammar Reference 9.1 on p130 together in class, and/or ask students to read it at home. Encourage them to ask you questions about it.

2   The aim of exercise 2 is to revise *like* with count and uncount nouns, but more especially to reinforce the idea of *like* to express an 'all time' preference, in preparation for the presentation of *would like* in the next section which expresses a preference/request at a specific time.

T 9.1 You can tell students that they are going to listen to two children talking about what they like and don't like to eat and drink. Students listen to Daisy and Tom and tick the things they *both* like in lists A and B on p66. Check the answers.

Answers and tapescript
They both like apple juice, apples, oranges, bananas and strawberries, hamburgers, chips, spaghetti, pizza (though Daisy eats hers without tomatoes or cheese!), ice-cream, and chocolate.

T 9.1

D = Daisy   T = Tom
D I don't like tea.
T Oh, I do. Well, sometimes, with sugar. But coffee's horrible!
D Yeah. Disgusting. I don't like wine or beer either.
T Well – I don't like wine but I like beer. My dad has beer every day after work and sometimes I have a bit.
D Beer! Yuk! But apple juice is nice. I really like apple juice. It's delicious.
T Mmmm! Yeah, it's delicious and it's good for you. Apples are too! I love all fruit – apples, oranges, bananas, strawberries.
D Yeah. OK. I like fruit, but I hate all vegetables, 'specially carrots.
T Yeah, vegetables are disgusting. Eh – but not all of them, – I quite like peas. Hamburgers, chips, and peas. Mmm! That's one of my favourite meals.
D Yeah – hamburgers, I like. Chips, I like. But peas – yuk!
T My very favourite meal is spaghetti. Spaghetti, then ice-cream after. Yummy! . . . Or yoghurt. I love strawberry yoghurt.
D Ice-cream – OK, yes. Yoghurt, no! Spaghetti – yes. I like all pasta and pizza! But I don't like it with tomatoes or cheese. I don't like tomatoes very much and I hate cheese.
T Mmmm! Pizza. The best. But . . . you can't have pizza without tomatoes and cheese.
D You can.
T You can't!
D Can!
T Can't!
D Well, I can. I don't like cheese at all!

T 9.1 Play the recording again and get students to decide who says which sentence. Students write *D* for Daisy or *T* for Tom. Check the answers.

After students have listened, ask if they can remember what the children said to express that they liked something or didn't like it! The answers are the exclamations *Yummy!* and *Yuk!* Ask what children say in other languages. Ask the class if they can remember any of the other things the children said. Ask what they argue about (Tom says you can't have pizza without tomatoes and cheese).

3 Drill the pronunciation of the food and drink in the lists on p66. Also practise the sentences in exercise 2, paying particular attention to stress.

I don't like wine but I like beer.

I really like apple juice. It's delicious.

I quite like peas.

I don't like tomatoes very much.

I don't like cheese at all.

Students look at the lists of food and drink, and decide what they like and don't like. Students work in pairs and talk about their likes and dislikes Encourage them to use the expressions from exercise 2, rather than simply *I like/I don't like* . . . . Monitor and check.

Get students to feed back briefly, encouraging them to talk about their partner and so practise the third person *-s*, e.g. *Ana likes fruit, but I don't.* Correct mistakes in grammar and pronunciation carefully.

I like . . . and *I'd like* . . .

1 **T 9.2** Focus attention on the photo and get students to describe briefly what they can see. Students read and listen to the conversation.

GRAMMAR SPOT

Look at the *Grammar Spot* questions as a class.

1 Question 1 is intended to guide students to the difference between *I like* and *I'd like*. Do not attempt to go into a full presentation of the uses of *would* at this stage, just highlight it as a polite way of making requests and offers.

Point out that when we talk about things in general, we do not use an article/determiner with plural count nouns or with uncountable nouns. You could write these examples on the board:

I like biscuits. (NOT *I like some biscuits.)
I don't like tea very much. (NOT *I don't like any tea very much.)
Do you like Chinese food? (NOT * Do you like any Chinese food?)

2 Question 2 highlights the use of *some* with both count and uncount nouns when saying what you want.

3 Question 3 highlights the special use of *some* in requests and offers, and *any* in other questions and negatives.

Read Grammar Reference 9.2 on p130 together in class, and/or ask students to read it at home. Encourage them to ask you questions about it.

2 Students practise the conversation in exercise 1 and make similar conversations. If students have problems with pronunciation, play the recording again and get students to repeat.

You could record students' conversations and play them back for intensive correction. Pay attention to all aspects of pronunciation – sounds, stress, and intonation.

a or some?

The aim of this section is to consolidate the concept of count and uncount nouns and practise the use of *a/an* and *some*. Use the section to check how well students have grasped the concept and be prepared to explain further, using L1 if possible.

1   Students work in pairs to write *a*, *an*, or *some* before the nouns.

Answers

3	**a** mushroom	8	**some** rice
4	**some** bread	9	**some** money
5	**some** milk	10	**a** dollar
6	**some** meat	11	**a** notebook
7	**an** apple	12	**some** homework

2   Students work in pairs to write *a*, *an*, or *some*. The aim of this exercise is to show that some nouns (*coffee*, *cake*, and *ice-cream*) can be both countable and uncountable.

Answers

1	**an** egg	5	**some** cake
2	**some** eggs	6	**a** cake
3	**a** coffee	7	**an** ice-cream
4	**some** coffee	8	**some** ice-cream

Questions and answers

3   Focus on number 1 as an example with the whole class. Students work in pairs or small groups to choose the correct form.

T 9.3   Students listen and check.

Answers and tapescript

1   **Would you like** a cigarette?
    No, thanks. I don't smoke.
2   **Do you like** your teacher?
    Yes. She's very nice.
3   **Would you like** a drink?
    Yes, please. Some Coke, please.
4   Can I help you?
    Yes. **I'd like** a book of stamps, please.
5   What sports do you do?
    Well, **I like** swimming very much.
6   Excuse me, are you ready to order?
    Yes. **I'd like** a steak, please.

Students practise the conversations in pairs.

4   **T 9.4**   Students listen to the questions and choose the correct answers. Let students listen and discuss their answers in pairs, then play the recording again.

Tapescript

1   Good afternoon. Can I help you?
2   Who's your favourite writer?
3   What would you like for your birthday?
4   Do you like animals?
5   Here's the wine list, sir.
6   Have some ice-cream with your strawberries.

T 9.5   Students listen and check their answers. Then get them to practise the conversations in pairs.

Answers and tapescript

1   **A** Good afternoon. Can I help you?
    B **Yes. I'd like some fruit, please.**
2   **A** Who's your favourite writer?
    B **I like books by John Grisham.**
3   **A** What would you like for your birthday?
    B **I'd like a new bike.**
4   **A** Do you like animals?
    B **I like cats, but I don't like dogs.**
5   **A** Here's the wine list, sir.
    B **We'd like a bottle of French red wine.**
6   **A** Have some ice-cream with your strawberries.
    B **No, thanks. I don't like ice-cream.**

ADDITIONAL MATERIAL

Workbook Unit 9
Exercises 1 and 2 Count and uncount nouns
Exercises 3 and 4 *like*
Exercises 5 and 6 *would like*, and *like* or *would like*

GOING SHOPPING (SB p69)

some/any, much/many

The aim of this section is to practise *some/any*, and introduce *(not) much/many* with both countable and uncountable nouns.

1   Read the instructions and focus attention on the picture. Make sure students understand *sausages* and *chewing gum*, and briefly revise the other items in the picture (see Answers below). Focus attention on the examples. Drill the examples around the class. Students look at the picture and make positive and negative sentences, working as a class. Correct mistakes carefully, and pay attention to the weak *some* /səm/.

Answers

There are some newspapers.
There are some sausages.
There's some yoghurt.
There's some apple juice.
There aren't any tomatoes.
There aren't any carrots.
There isn't any bread.
There isn't any pizza.
There aren't many sandwiches.
There aren't many eggs.
There aren't many mushrooms.
There aren't many magazines.
There isn't much chewing gum.
There isn't much coffee.
There isn't much orange juice.
There isn't much rice.

GRAMMAR SPOT

Look at the *Grammar Spot* section as a class. As well as the notes in the Student's Book, highlight the use of *many* with the plural verb *are* and *much* with the singular verb *is*.

Read Grammar Reference 9.3 on p130 together in class, and/or ask students to read it at home. Encourage them to ask you questions about it.

2 Before students work in pairs to ask and answer questions, highlight the use of *any* in the questions and the contrastive use *some/many* with count nouns in the answers, e.g. *Yes, there are some. but there aren't many,* and *some/much* with uncount nouns, e.g. *Yes, there is some, but there isn't much.* Drill the questions in open and closed pairs. You might want to make this exercise a little more challenging by asking students to close their books, so they have to remember the picture. Either one student at a time can close his/her book, or you can put all the food as prompts on the board so that both students keep their books closed.

3 **T 9.6** Focus attention on the shopping list. Students listen to the conversation in the shop, and tick what Barry buys. The conversation is supposed to be funny, so if students laugh they are probably understanding it!

If necessary, play the recording a second time to allow students to focus on the reasons why he doesn't buy certain items. Check the answers.

Answers and tapescript

Orange juice	✔	Cheese	
Milk		Pizza	
Coffee	✔	Bread	
Apples			

He doesn't buy . . .
. . . milk because Miss Potts sold the last bottle a few minutes ago.
. . . apples because Miss Potts doesn't sell them.
. . . pizza because Miss Potts doesn't have pizza on Thursdays.
. . . bread because there isn't any.
. . . cheese because Miss Potts doesn't sell it.

T 9.6

B = Barry   MP = Miss Potts

MP Good morning. Can I help you?
B Yes. I'd like some orange juice, please.
MP Er . . . sorry. There's apple juice but no orange juice.
B What's that then? Isn't that orange juice?
MP Oh, yes. So it is! My eyes! Here you are.
B Thank you, and some milk, please.
MP Sorry. I sold the last bottle two minutes ago.
B Oh, dear! What about some coffee?
MP Yes. Here you are.
B Thanks. That's orange juice, coffee . . . er . . . and . . . er . . . a kilo of apples, please.
MP I don't sell apples.
B You don't sell apples! That's strange. What about cheese. Can I have some cheese?
MP I don't sell cheese, either.
B You don't sell cheese! That's amazing. Now, I want some pizza, but I'm sure you don't sell pizza, do you?
MP Oh, yes I do. What would you like? Pizza with mushrooms, pizza with cheese and ham, pizza with sausage, or pizza with tomatoes?
B Wow! Can I have . . . er . . . some pizza with cheese and tomatoes, please?
MP Oh, sorry. I forgot. Usually, I have pizza but not on Thursdays. Today's Thursday, isn't it?
B Yes, it is. Mmm . . . OK, . . . er . . . OK, forget the pizza. What about bread? I don't suppose you have any bread?
MP Yes, you're right.
B Pardon?
MP You're right. There isn't any bread.
B Tell me. Do you do a lot of business?
MP Oh, yes sir. This shop is open 24 hours.
B Really! What do people buy?
MP All the things you see.
B Mmmm. OK. That's all for me. How much?
MP That's £5.60, please.
B Thank you. Goodbye.
MP Goodbye sir. See you again soon.
B I don't think so.

The conversation is meant for gist understanding only, but if you want to look more closely at the language you could play the recording again, and ask students to look at the tapescript. With a strong group, you could ask students to talk about similar experiences in a shop!

ADDITIONAL MATERIAL

Workbook Unit 9
Exercise 7 *some* or *any*?
Exercise 8 *How much … ?* or *How many … ?*

PRACTICE (SB p70)

much or *many*?

1 Students work in pairs to complete the questions using *much* or *many*. The word *petrol* might be new.

> **Answers**
> 1 How **many** people are there in the room?
> 2 How **much** money do you have in your pocket?
> 3 How **many** cigarettes do you smoke?
> 4 How **much** petrol is there in the car?
> 5 How **many** apples do you want?
> 6 How **much** wine is there in the fridge?

2 Students choose an answer for each question in exercise 1.

> **Answers**
> 1e Twenty. Nine men and eleven women.
> 2d Just fifty pence.
> 3c Ten a day.
> 4f It's full.
> 5a A kilo.
> 6b There are two bottles.

Check it

3 Students work in pairs to find the mistakes.

> **Answers**
> 2 I don't like ice-cream./I wouldn't like an ice-cream.
> 3 Can I have some bread, please?
> 4 I'm hungry. I'd like a sandwich.
> 5 I don't have much milk left.
> 6 I'd like some fruit, please.
> 7 How much money do you have?
> 8 We have a lot of homework today.

Roleplay

4 Demonstrate the activity by writing a shopping list on the board and getting two confident students to roleplay the conversation. Drill the language in the Student's Book and briefly revise realistic prices for a small amount of shopping. Then students continue in pairs. You could ask some of the pairs to act out the dialogue.

READING AND SPEAKING (SB p70)

Food around the world

> **SUGGESTION**
> You might want to set some vocabulary for homework prior to this lesson – the pictures on the page can then be used to check vocabulary in the lesson.
>
> | | | |
> |---|---|---|
> | *move on* | *environment* | *sardines* |
> | *pick up (food)* | *farm (v.)* | *depend on* |
> | *course (of a meal)* | *transport (v.)* | *land (n.)* |
> | *noodles* | *chopsticks* | *control (v.)* |
> | *herrings* | *fingers* | |

1 In a monolingual group, answer the questions as a whole-class activity. In a multilingual group, students can work in pairs or small groups and exchange information about their country.

2 Focus attention on the photographs. Ask students to name the places or nationalities represented by the food.

> **Answers** (clockwise from the left)
> India – curry
> Japan – *sushi* and *tempura*
> Thailand – bananas in market
> France – café in Lyon
> Venezuela – strawberries
> China – rice harvest
> Saudi Arabia – desert tribe sharing meal
> Sudan – rice
> China – noodles

3 Get students to read the text through quickly and match the correct headings to paragraphs 2, 3, and 4. Encourage students to focus on just matching the headings and tell them not to worry about new vocabulary at this stage. (If they have done the above homework task, they should not have too many difficulties.) You might want to set a time limit to encourage students to read extensively.

> **Answers**
> Paragraph 2: WHAT DO WE EAT?
> Paragraph 3: HOW DO WE EAT?
> Paragraph 4: WHERE DOES OUR FOOD COME FROM?

4 Students read the text again more slowly and answer the questions. Get them to check in pairs before checking answers with the whole class.

Speaking

5 Read through the questions as a class. Quickly revise the meaning and pronunciation of *breakfast*, *lunch*, and *dinner* and check comprehension of *main meal*.

Students work in small groups and discuss the questions. This will obviously be a very productive activity in a multilingual group, but students in a monolingual group can also discuss food habits in their own country and their own family, and compare with other countries they have visited.

Conduct a brief feedback session with the whole class, encouraging students to highlight different eating habits in different countries.

Writing

6 Students write a short paragraph about meals in their country. This can be given as a homework activity if you do not have time to do it in class. When you correct this, don't correct too harshly. The idea is to give students an opportunity for some freer writing, and they will inevitably make a lot of mistakes.

LISTENING AND SPEAKING (SB p72)

My favourite food

1 Focus attention on the photographs. Students work in pairs and decide where each type of food is from and which one(s) they like.

Answers
1 America
2 Italy
3 India
4 England
5 China

2 **T 9.7** Tell students they are going to hear the five people in the photographs talking about their favourite food. Ask them to match each person with the photographs of the different food. Play the recording through once and then check the answers.

Answers and tapescript
Marian: Chinese food; Graham: English cooked breakfast; Lucy: Italian food; Gavin: Indian food; Sally: chocolate

T 9.7
Marian
Well, I love vegetables, all vegetables – I eat meat too – but not much. I think this is why I like Chinese food so much. There are lots of vegetables in Chinese food. Yes, Chinese is my very favourite food, I like the noodles too. Can you eat with chopsticks? I can!

Graham
Now in my job, I travel the world, and I like all kinds of food . . . but my favourite, my favourite is . . . er . . . I always have it as soon as I come home . . . is a full English breakfast. Bacon, eggs, sausage, mushrooms, tomatoes, and of course toast. I love it, not every day but when I'm at home we have it every Sunday. Mmmm! I'd like it right now – delicious.

Lucy
Oh, no question, no problem. I know exactly what my favourite food is. Pasta. All pasta. Especially spaghetti. Pasta with tomato sauce – and I like it best when I'm in Italy. I went on holiday to the Italian lakes last year. The food was wonderful.

Gavin
. . . er . . . I'm not sure. No, I know what it is. My . . . favourite . . . food is Indian food. Friday night I like to go to the pub with friends from work and . . . have a few beers, . . . er . . . no, not too many, . . . and after we always go to an Indian restaurant and I have a chicken curry with rice. It's the best! I like it more than chips!

Sally
Well, shhh! But my very, very favourite food is chocolate. Chocolate anything, I love it. Chocolate ice-cream, chocolate biscuits, chocolate cake, but especially just a big bar of chocolate. Mmmm! Terrible isn't it? Go on! Have some of this! My friend brought it back from Switzerland for me!

3 Focus attention on the questions about the people in exercise 2. Students work in pairs and answer as many questions as they can. If necessary, play the recording again to let students complete their answers. Check the answers with the whole class.

Answers
Graham travels a lot.
Sally likes sweet things.
Lucy had her favourite food on holiday.
Marian prefers vegetables.
Graham likes food from his own country.

4 Students discuss the questions in pairs and then feed back to the rest of the class.

Workbook Unit 9

Exercise 9 Food vocabulary; ordering a meal in a restaurant.

EVERYDAY ENGLISH (SB p73)

Polite requests

> **POSSIBLE PROBLEMS**
>
> This section introduces *Can I … ?/Could I … ?* and *Can you … ?/Could you … ?* for the first time. If you think your students will not be familiar with it, present it yourself, using the classroom to illustrate meaning: *Jean, can you open the window, please? Maria, could you clean the board, please? Emma, could I borrow your pen, please?* etc.
>
> You could tell students that *Can I … ?* and *Could I … ?* mean the same, but *could* is usually more polite. Point out that although *could* looks like the past tense, the concept is in fact present. However, if you think your class is strong enough, you could use the situations in the Student's Book as a vehicle for presentation.

1 Look at the photograph and get students to say what they can see.

2 Pre-teach/check *pass* (the salt), *fizzy/still* (water). Ask students to match the questions and responses, using the singular and plural forms, e.g. *It's/They're delicious* to help them.

> **T 9.8** Students listen and check their answers.

> **Answers and tapescript**
>
> 1 Would you like some more carrots?
>   Yes, please. They're delicious.
> 2 Could you pass the salt, please?
>   Yes, of course. Here you are.
> 3 Could I have a glass of water, please?
>   Do you want fizzy or still?
> 4 Does anybody want more dessert?
>   Yes, please. I'd love some. It's delicious.
> 5 How would you like your coffee?
>   Black, no sugar, please.
> 6 This is delicious! Can you give me the recipe?
>   Yes, of course. I'm glad you like it.
> 7 Do you want help with the washing-up?
>   No, of course not. We have a dishwasher.

Students practise the questions and responses in pairs. Monitor and check pronunciation mistakes.

Read the information in the caution box as a class.

3 Students look at the requests and complete them, using *Can/Could I … ?* or *Can/Could you … ?*

> **Answers**
>
> 1 **Can/Could I** have a cheese sandwich, please?
> 2 **Can/Could you** tell me the time, please?
> 3 **Can/Could you** take me to school?
> 4 **Can/Could I** see the menu, please?
> 5 **Can/Could you** lend me some money, please?
> 6 **Can/Could you** help me with my homework, please?
> 7 **Can/Could I** borrow your dictionary, please?

4 Students work in pairs to practise the requests in exercise 3 and give an answer.

> **T 9.9** Play the recording and get students to compare their answers with those on the tape.

> **Tapescript**
>
> 1 Can I have a cheese sandwich, please?
>   Yes, of course. That's £1.75.
> 2 Could you tell me the time, please?
>   It's just after ten.
> 3 Can you take me to school?
>   Jump in.
> 4 Can I see the menu, please?
>   Here you are. And would you like a drink to start?
> 5 Could you lend me some money, please?
>   Not again! How much would you like this time?
> 6 Can you help me with my homework, please?
>   What is it? French? I can't speak a word of French.
> 7 Can I borrow your dictionary, please?
>   Yes, if I can find it. I think it's in my bag.

Don't forget!

Workbook Unit 9

Exercise 10 Formal letters 2. Students are invited to write a letter to a hotel.

Word list

Remind your students of the Word list for this unit on p139. They could write in the translations, learn them at home, and/or write some of the words in their vocabulary notebook.

Pronunciation Book Unit 9

Video

This unit can be supplemented by the following video section, if you haven't already used it.

Situation (Section 7) *The Pub* David takes Paola to an English pub.

10

Comparatives and superlatives • *have got* •
Town and country • Directions 2

Introduction to the unit

This unit is unusual in that it has three presentation sections, each one revising the grammar of the one before.

The theme is describing places: towns and cities, the countryside, and hotels. These are useful contexts to practise comparatives and superlatives. Now we introduce *have got* (see *Note* in Unit 3, p18 of the Teacher's Book) in a direct comparison with *have* (for possession), which students are already familiar with. The skills section includes a jigsaw reading about three cities which are famous for their links to music, New Orleans, Vienna, and Liverpool, and provides further practice of the grammatical aims.

Language aims

Grammar – comparative and superlative adjectives The following aspects of comparatives and superlatives are introduced:

- the use of *-'er/-est* with short adjectives, such as *cheap, cheaper, cheapest.*
- the use of *-ier/-iest* with adjectives that end in *-y*, such as *noisy, noisier, noisiest.*
- the use of *more/most* with longer adjectives, such as *more expensive, most expensive.*
- irregular adjectives such as *good, better, best.*

The presentation of these is staged. In the first presentation, pairs of opposite adjectives are revised/introduced and this leads to the introduction of comparative forms. These forms are then revised in the second presentation when *have got* is introduced. Finally, superlatives are introduced in the third presentation and at the same time comparatives and *have got* are revised.

Students usually experience little difficulty with the concept of comparatives and superlatives but experience more difficulty in producing and pronouncing the forms because of all the different parts involved. Utterances often sound very laboured and unnatural because equal stress is given to each word and syllable. For this reason we practise natural-sounding connected speech.

Common mistakes
*She's more tall than me.
*He's the most tall student in the class.
*She's taller that me.
*He's tallest student in the class.

have got The verb *have* for possession was introduced in Unit 3. We purposely have delayed the introduction of *have got* for possession until now because of the complications of production it causes if introduced alongside the Present Simple of *have*, particularly in the question and negative. (See the *Note* in the *Language Aims* of Unit 3, p18 of the Teacher's Book.)

In this unit there are many exercises that contrast *have* and *have got*.

Vocabulary and pronunciation Pairs of opposite adjectives are introduced as part of the presentation of comparative adjectives.

In the vocabulary section, town and country words are introduced and practised in contexts which provide an opportunity to review comparatives and superlatives.

There is further practice in recognizing phonetic script.

Everyday English There is further practice of getting and giving directions, and prepositions of movement such as *along* and *down* are introduced.

Workbook There is further practice on comparatives and superlatives, and *have got.*

In the vocabulary section, compound nouns to do with towns are introduced such as town *centre*, *railway station*.

The writing syllabus includes work on relative pronouns. Then students study a model text about London before being guided to write a short piece about *their* capital city.

Notes on the unit

STARTER (SB p74)

> **POSSIBLE PROBLEMS**
> This activity aims to remind students of the concept of comparatives and to help you assess how well students can cope with simple comparative statements. It is also intended to be good fun, so don't worry too much if students slip into mistakes like **more tall* or if the pronunciation is a little stilted. Students will get plenty of practice in the activities that follow.

Demonstrate the activity by standing next to one of your students who is taller or shorter and highlighting the difference in height. Then ask the same student *How old are you?* and get him/her to ask you the same question. Write the ages on the board and then give a full example, e.g. *I'm smaller and older than (Carlos). (He) is taller and younger than me.*

Students work in pairs and compare heights and ages. Encourage students who are of a similar height to stand next to each other or back to back to check.

CITY LIFE (SB p74)

Comparative adjectives

> **SUGGESTION**
> You could set exercise 1 for homework if you need to save class time. If you do, begin the lesson by going through the answers and practising the pronunciation of each word.

1   If students haven't done this exercise as homework (see *Suggestion* above), put your students into pairs and get them to match the adjectives with their opposites. Check the answers and the pronunciation first before students categorize the words into 'city' and 'country'.

Be prepared for students to want to pronounce the *ie* of *friendly* separately */frɪendli/ and make sure they say it correctly, /frendli/.

> **Answers**
> In these pairs of words the opposite of *old* is *modern* (it could also be *new*) not *young*, because in the context of the presentation the adjectives are being used to talk about buildings not people.
>
> | | | | |
> |---|---|---|---|
> | fast | /fɑːst/ | slow | /sləʊ/ |
> | big | /bɪg/ | small | /smɔːl/ |
> | dirty | /ˈdɜːti/ | clean | /kliːn/ |
> | dangerous | /ˈdeɪndʒərəs/ | safe | /seɪf/ |
> | noisy | /ˈnɔɪzi/ | quiet | /ˈkwaɪət/ |
> | modern | /ˈmɒdən/ | old | /əʊld/ |
> | unfriendly | /ʌnˈfrendli/ | friendly | /ˈfrendli/ |
> | exciting | /ɪkˈsaɪtɪŋ/ | boring | /ˈbɔːrɪŋ/ |
> | expensive | /ɪkˈspensɪv/ | cheap | /tʃiːp/ |

Ask students to think about which words describe life in the city and life in the country. You could put the headings *CITY* and *COUNTRY* on the board and write in your students' suggestions as to which adjectives belong where, or you could ask individual students to come up to the board to write in the suggestions themselves. Be prepared for some debate and discussion as there are obviously no prescribed right answers. A lot is to do with personal opinion and experience. Welcome any freer speaking that results.

2   This exercise focuses on the main target language for this section, so make it clear to your class that this is an important moment and that this is the structure in English that compares things. If necessary and possible, use translation to do this.

Ask students to look at the chart and to work in pairs to make sentences comparing life in the city and country. (You may need to point out the use of *more* with longer adjectives, but don't go into the rules in too much detail at this stage. They are dealt with more fully later on.)

At this stage, don't worry too much about pronunciation as long as students understand the meaning of the structure, just let them try to produce sentences that express their opinions. Get some feedback from the whole class.

3   **T 10.1** Now is the moment to concentrate on the pronunciation. Ask your students to look at the example sentence in the Student's Book and say it in chorus either using yourself or the recording as a model. Focus particularly on the /ə/ sound at the end of the comparative and in the pronunciation of *than* /ðən/. Isolate *safer* and *than* and then drill them together as connected speech:

> *cheaper than* /ˈtʃiːpəðən/
> *safer than* /ˈseɪfəðən/

Drill the other sentences from the recording or by saying them yourself. If necessary, break up the sentences to drill them, particularly the comparative forms + *than*.

Try to get a natural 'flow' in the repetition of the sentences as on the recording.

4   Get students to discuss their opinions in pairs. Monitor and check for accurate use of comparatives and acceptable pronunciation.

Students share their opinions with the rest of the class. If most of your students had problems with the comparative forms, write their sentences on the board including the mistakes and get students to correct them as a class. Major problems with pronunciation can be dealt with by drilling the students' sentences with the whole class.

GRAMMAR SPOT

1   This is to reinforce and make clear to your students the rules governing the formation of comparative adjectives. Get students to work individually to complete the comparative sentences and try to formulate any rules they can. They may have got a clear idea from doing exercise 2 or they may need a bit of prompting and guiding, but try not to just give them the rules. You could write the rules up on the board as you go along.

Answers
I'm **older** than you.
Your class is **noisier** than my class.
Your car was **more expensive** than my car.

-*er* is used with short adjectives such as *old, older*.
-*ier* with adjectives that end in -*y* such as *noisy, noisier*.
more ... is used with longer adjectives such as *expensive, more expensive*.

2   Students work in pairs to write the comparative forms of the adjectives in exercise 1, using dictionaries to help them if appropriate. Some of the comparative forms have already been given in exercise 2.

Check the answers with the whole class, getting students to spell the comparative forms. Highlight *bigger* as an example of the doubling of the consonant in short adjectives with a short vowel sound. (You don't need to go into this rule in detail, but do check that they have noticed the doubling of the consonant.)

Answers

fast	**faster**	slow	**slower**
big	**bigger**	small	**smaller**
dirty	**dirtier**	clean	**cleaner**
dangerous	**more dangerous**	safe	**safer**
noisy	**noisier**	quiet	**quieter**
modern	**more modern**	old	**older**
unfriendly	**unfriendlier***	friendly	**friendlier**
exciting	**more exciting**	boring	**more boring**
expensive	**more expensive**	cheap	**cheaper**

*This is the comparative usually given by dictionaries, but *more unfriendly* is also often used.

3   Ask students for the irregular forms of *good* and *bad*, and check the pronunciation of *worse* /wɜːs/ carefully.

Answers
good **better**   bad **worse**

Read Grammar Reference 10.1 on p131 together in class, and/or ask students to read it at home. Encourage them to ask you questions about it.

PRACTICE (SB p75)

Much more than ...

1   This exercise is also good for stress and intonation practice. Put the conversations in a context and tell your students that two people are discussing different cities that they know.

NOTE
In this exercise we bring in the use of *much* to emphasize comparatives. The students are only asked to recognize it at first, and not produce it until later.

Do the example with your students to illustrate the activity. Then ask them to work in pairs to complete the conversations. Point out that the students have to fill in the opposite adjectives in B's comments to those A uses.

T 10.2 Play the recording and get students to check their answers. Tell them to also focus on the pronunciation, particularly the stress and intonation.

Answers and tapescript
1   A Life in the country is **slower than** city life.
    B Yes, the city's much **faster**.
2   A New York is **safer than** London.
    B No, it isn't. New York is much **more dangerous**.
3   A Paris is **bigger than** Madrid.
    B No, it isn't! It's much **smaller**.

4 A Madrid is **more expensive than** Rome.
   B No, it isn't. Madrid is much **cheaper**.
5 A The buildings in Rome are **more modern than** the buildings in New York.
   B No, they aren't. They're much **older**.
6 A The Underground in London is **better than** the Metro in Paris.
   B No! The Underground is much **worse**.

Get individual students to practise the conversations across the class in open pairs. Encourage the Bs to sound really indignant when they disagree with A. Give them exaggerated models yourself or play the recording again to make clear that you want them to produce good stress and intonation and connected speech:

Examples

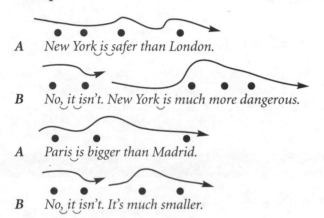

A New York is safer than London.

B No, it isn't. New York is much more dangerous.

A Paris is bigger than Madrid.

B No, it isn't. It's much smaller.

2 This is the personalization stage. Decide on two town/cities that you and all, or most, of the students know and demonstrate the activity. Students continue in pairs and decide which town/city they prefer. Monitor and check for accurate use of comparative forms and pronunciation.

Get a few students to feed back to the rest of the class. Highlight any common mistakes in grammar or pronunciation from the pairwork stage.

ADDITIONAL MATERIAL

Workbook Unit 10
Exercises 1 and 2 consolidate the work on comparatives.

COUNTRY LIFE (SB p75)

have got

In this presentation, comparatives are revised and *have got* is introduced in the context of a telephone conversation where someone has moved from the city to the country.

Read the introduction about Mel and Tara aloud to the class to set the scene. You could ask your students *Why do you think Mel moved to Seacombe?*

1 **T 10.3** Tell students they are going to read and listen to the telephone conversation between Mel and Tara. For the moment, don't focus on the examples of *have got* in the text – just tell students to complete the conversation with the missing adjectives. Make it clear that some of them are comparatives and some are not.

Play the recording through once and then ask students to check their answers in pairs. Play the recording again for students to add in any answers they missed. Check the answers with the whole class.

Answers and tapescript
Tara Why did you leave London? You had a **good** job.
Mel Yes, but I've got a **better** job here.
Tara And you had a **big** flat in London.
Mel Well, I've got a **bigger** flat here.
Tara Really? How many bedrooms has it got?
Mel Three. And it's got a garden. It's **nicer** than my flat in London and it's **cheaper**.
Tara But you haven't got any friends!
Mel I've got a lot of friends here. People are much **friendlier** than in London.
Tara But the country's so **boring**.
Mel No, it isn't. It's much **more exciting** than London. Seacombe has got shops, a cinema, a theatre, and a park. And the air is **cleaner** and the streets are **safer**.
Tara OK. Everything is **wonderful**! So when can I visit you?

GRAMMAR SPOT

This *Grammar Spot* highlights the form and use of *have got* compared with *have*.

1 Read through the notes with the whole class. You will need to highlight the fact that the *have* in *have got* contracts but that it doesn't in *have* for possession. Students may have trouble saying the contracted and negative forms, especially next to the following consonant, so practise saying the examples in the box. You could drill them chorally and individually.

I've got a dog.	/aɪv gɒt ə dog/
He's got a car.	/hiːz gɒt ə kɑː/
Have you got a dog?	/hæv (həv) juː gɒt ə dɒg/
Has she got a car?	/hæz (həz) ʃiː gɒt ə kɑː/
They haven't got a flat.	/ðeɪ hævnt gɒt ə flæt/
It hasn't got a garden.	/ɪt hæznt gɒt ə gɑːdn/

2 Highlight the past of *have* and *have got*. Elicit a few examples from the class of things they had when they were younger, e.g. *I had a dog. I had a bike.*

3 Ask your students to study the conversation and underline all the examples of *have got* and *had*. Make it clear that they are looking for questions and negatives and not just the positive. Ask students to check in pairs, and then check with the whole class.

Read the Grammar Reference 10.2 on p131 together in class, and/or ask students to read it at home. Encourage them to ask you questions about it.

2   Ask students to work in pairs and take the parts in the dialogue to practise *have got*. If necessary, play the recording again and let students listen and repeat, before practising in pairs.

You can then ask students to go through the dialogue again and encourage them not to follow the dialogue exactly, but to replace the adjectives with others that are suitable. If they have the confidence, encourage them to improvise completely without their books.

PRACTICE (SB p76)

have/have got

This is a very straightforward transformation exercise designed to focus students' attention solely on the difference in form between *have* and *have got* for possession. It is worth bearing in mind that focusing on the form of *have got* at this stage should help students when they meet the Present Perfect Simple in Unit 14.

1   We suggest that you refer students back to Grammar Reference 10.2 on p131 as they do the exercise. Ask them to do the exercise on their own, writing the contracted forms where possible. Then get students to check with a partner, before you conduct a full class feedback.

I've got more than you!

> **NOTE**
> You will need to photocopy the information about the multi-millionaires' possessions on p130 of the Teacher's Book.

2   This roleplay should be a fun (and not very realistic!) activity. Ask your students to look at the pictures of the two millionaires. Ask *What have millionaires usually got?* and elicit a few suggestions from the whole class.

Possible answers	
money	horses
(big) houses	boats
(fast) cars	servants
planes	

Say the first line yourself and then in open pairs. Encourage exaggerated stress and intonation as students boast about their possessions!

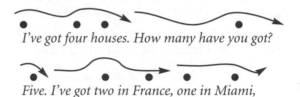

I've got four houses. How many have you got?

Five. I've got two in France, one in Miami,

one in the Caribbean, and a castle in Scotland.

Ask your students to work in pairs. Give out the rolecards on p130 of the Teacher's Book and get students to exchange information about their possessions. Go round the class checking grammar and pronunciation. Only correct where absolutely necessary, in order to encourage fluency. Then get feedback as to who is the richer! (Millionaire B is.)

ADDITIONAL MATERIAL

Workbook Unit 10
Exercises 3–5 These give further practice of *have got*.
Exercise 6 This brings together comparatives and *have got*.

THE WORLD'S BEST HOTELS (SB p76)

Superlative adjectives

This presentation of superlative adjectives includes revision of comparatives and *have got*.

1   Ask students to look at the pictures of the hotels and read the information about each of them. Ask them to tell you which they like and why. Here they could be

revising *have got*, but don't insist on this, as the main aim here is to generate interest in the theme and to take in some of the information about the hotels.

2   This exercise has been specially designed so that *all* the true sentences contain examples of superlative adjectives, thereby providing a means of highlighting the new structure. The false sentences contain examples of comparatives and *have got*.

Focus attention on the examples, pointing out the superlative example *the cheapest* but not going into detail at this stage. Students work in pairs to decide which sentences are true and which are false, and to correct the information in the false ones.

> **POSSIBLE PROBLEMS**
>
> 1   In sentence 4, make sure students are clear about which opposite of *old* students need to use (*new*).
>
> 2   You will have to draw attention to *the* in superlatives. It is common for students to omit this.
>
> 3   Point out that the superlative *the furthest* is irregular – the adjective is *far* and the comparative is *further*.
>
> 4   Draw students' attention to the prepositions in sentences 10 and 11: *the nearest to*, and *the furthest from*.

Check the answers with the whole class.

> **Answers**
> 3   Claridge's is the most expensive hotel.   ✔
> 4   The Mandarin Oriental is older than the Plaza.   ✘
>   **No, it isn't. It's newer.**
> 5   Claridge's is the oldest hotel.   ✔
> 6   The Plaza is the biggest hotel.   ✔
> 7   The Mandarin Oriental is smaller than Claridge's.   ✘
>   **No, it isn't. It's bigger.**
> 8   The Plaza has got a swimming pool. **No, it hasn't.** ✘
> 9   Claridge's is nearer the airport than the Mandarin. ✘
>   **No, it isn't.**
> 10 The Mandarin is the nearest to the airport.   ✔
> 11 The Plaza is the furthest from the airport.   ✔

Get students to work in pairs and focus on the six correct sentences. Ask your class what they notice about all these sentences. Students should highlight the *-est* endings in the short adjectives and *the most* form with longer adjectives, but be prepared to prompt them if necessary. (Do not go into a full explanation of the rules, as this is the focus of the *Grammar Spot* activity on p77.)

3   Check comprehension of *best* as the superlative of *good*. Get students to discuss which is the best hotel near where they live and to describe what it has got.

1   Students complete the superlative sentences and try to supply the rules. Prompt and guide them if they need it. Write the rules up on the board as students work them out, taking the opportunity to remind them of the comparative forms.

> **Answers**
> The Green Palace is the **cheapest** hotel in New York.
> The Four Seasons is the **most expensive**.
> –   *the . . .-est* is used with short adjectives such as *cheap*, (*cheaper*), *the cheapest*.
> –   *the most* is used with longer adjectives such as *expensive*, (*more expensive*), *the most expensive*.

2   Students focus on the irregular forms and the dictionary entry for *good*. Elicit what information the dictionary gives (phonetic script, word category, and irregular comparative and superlative forms). Students complete the irregular forms for *bad* and *far*, using their dictionaries if appropriate.

> **Answers**
> bad   **worse, the worst**   far   **further, the furthest**

Read the Grammar Reference 10.3 on p131 together in class, and/or ask students to read it at home. Encourage them to ask you questions about it.

The biggest and best!

This is another activity which integrates pronunciation work on stress and intonation.

1   Demonstrate the activity by reading the example aloud to the class. Then ask students to work on their own to complete the sentences.

T 10.4 Play the recording and ask your students to check their answers. Also tell them to listen carefully to the rhythm/stress and intonation of the sentences.

> **Answers and tapescript**
> 1   That house is very big.
>   Yes, **it's the biggest house** in the village.
> 2   Claridge's is a very expensive hotel.
>   Yes, **it's the most expensive hotel** in London.
> 3   Castle Combe is a very pretty village.
>   Yes, **it's the prettiest village** in England.
> 4   New York is a very cosmopolitan city.
>   Yes, **it's the most cosmopolitan city** in the world.
> 5   Tom Hanks is a very popular film star.
>   Yes, **he's the most popular film star** in America.

6 Miss Smith is a very funny teacher.
  Yes, **she's the funniest teacher** in our school.
7 Anna is a very intelligent student.
  Yes, **she's the most intelligent student** in the class.
8 This is a very easy exercise.
  Yes, **it's the easiest exercise** in the book.

2 **T 10.5** Now ask students to close their books. Play the first lines again, pausing after each one so that your students can produce the reply. You could do this in chorus with the whole class, or ask individuals to respond, or mix the two approaches.

Really work hard to encourage good (probably exaggerated) stress and intonation in the replies, with the main stress on the superlative adjective.

Student(s): *Yes, it's the biggest house in the village.*

Yes, it's the most expensive hotel in London.

The more you work on the stress and intonation, the more fun the activity becomes!

Talking about your class

This is a freer speaking activity, which should be good fun, provided you warn students to be careful not to offend other people! Give them enough time to describe one or two other people, but do not let the activity go on too long.

You could put some other cues on the board to prompt comparative and superlative sentences: *lives near to school/lives far from school*; *has a big bag*, etc.

3 Read the examples with students, then put them into small groups and ask them to make sentences about the other students.

  Get the class to give you comments about each other.

4 Students write the name of their favourite film star and then tell the rest of the class. Write the names of the stars on the board and keep a score for each one. Students work in pairs and compare the stars, e.g. *(Brad Pitt) is more popular than (Tom Cruise)*. Then get students to say who is the most popular star in the class.

Check it

5 Ask students to work in pairs or small groups to tick the correct sentence. Ask them to work quite quickly, then conduct a full class feedback on which are the correct answers. Try to get students to correct each other and explain any mistakes they hear.

Answers
1 Yesterday was hotter than today.
2 She's taller than her brother.
3 I'm the youngest in the class.
4 Last week was busier than this week.
5 He hasn't got any sisters.
6 Do you have any bread?
7 My homework is the worst in the class.
8 This exercise is the most difficult in the book.

ADDITIONAL MATERIAL

Workbook Unit 10
Exercises 7–9 These practise comparatives and superlatives together.

READING AND SPEAKING (SB p78)

Three musical cities

This activity is a jigsaw reading. This means that it should result in not only reading practice but also some freer speaking as in Unit 6.

The class divides into three groups and each group reads a different but similar text about a city and answers the questions. After this students from the different groups get together to exchange information about the city in their text. This means that they should get some speaking practice whilst their main attention is on the completion of the reading task.

The texts are about three cities which are famous for music – New Orleans, Vienna, and Liverpool. These were chosen because they all have a very strong link to music and are important tourist centres, but are different enough to make for interesting reading. The information comes from travel brochures but the texts have been simplified and rewritten to include examples of the grammar taught in this and previous units.

1 This exercise aims to generate some interest in the topic of musical cities and hopefully provide some motivation to read the texts.

  T 10.6 Tell students they are going to hear three types of music. Play the recording and get students to answer the questions in pairs.

Answers
Jazz – New Orleans
Classical music – Vienna
The Beatles – Liverpool

The recording contains extracts from the following music:
When The Saints Go Marching In (traditional) arranged by Tony Meehan (New Orleans)

Thunder and Lightning Polka by Johann Strauss Jnr played by the Royal Philharmonic Orchestra (Vienna)
Mersey Mania by Henry Marsh (Liverpool)

2 Pre-teach/check *bank* (of a river), *port*, *cousin*, *found* (a university), *trade centre*, *spices*, *slaves*, and *immigrants*. Students work in pairs and exchange what they know about the three cities. Get them to label the sentences NO (New Orleans), V (Vienna), or L (Liverpool). If students have problems with some of the sentences, tell them not to worry at this stage. Explain that they will be able to find the correct information from one of the texts or from the other students in the class.

3 Divide the class into three groups. Tell Group 1 to read about New Orleans, Group 2 to read about Vienna, and Group 3 to read about Liverpool. Students should read and check the answers to exercise 2 that relate to the city they are reading about. Allow dictionaries to be used to check new words.

Re-group the students, so that there is a Group 1, Group 2, and Group 3 student working together. Each group of three students should check the answers to exercise 2. Briefly check the answers with the whole class.

Answers
1 V   2 NO   3 V   4 L   5 NO   6 V   7 L   8 L

4 Students work individually. Ask them to read their text again and answer the questions about their city. Each group has the same questions to answer. When they have read the texts, they could either go through the questions on their own and then check with others from the same group, or work with a partner from the same group to answer the questions.

Check the answers with the students from each group separately. The main idea of these questions is to check understanding, therefore short answers are perfectly acceptable.

Answers
Group 1 – New Orleans
1 About 550,000.
2 The Mississippi River.
3 It's cosmopolitan. It has a famous Mardi Gras carnival every year.
4 1682 – The French named Louisiana after the French King, Louis XIV.
   1718 – They built New Orleans.
   1762 – Louis XV gave it to his cousin Carlos of Spain.
   1800 – City became French again until Napoleon sold it to the USA in 1803.
5 Louis Armstrong and Jelly Roll Morton.

6 Jazz.
7 Jazz.
8 • go by ship to Ireland ✘
   • see Sigmund Freud's house ✘
   • see a famous carnival ✔
   • walk round the French Quarter ✔
   • listen to a famous orchestra ✔
   • visit the homes of a famous rock group ✘

Group 2 – Vienna
1 over 1,500,000.
2 River Danube.
3 Because of its music, theatre, museums, and parks.
4 1365 – university opened.
   1558–1806 – was the centre of the Holy Roman Empire.
   18th and 19th centuries – became an important cultural centre for art and learning.
5 Sigmund Freud.
6 Classical music and opera.
7 Vienna Philharmonic and the State Opera House.
8 • go by ship to Ireland ✘
   • see Sigmund Freud's house ✔
   • see a famous carnival ✘
   • walk round the French Quarter ✘
   • listen to a famous orchestra ✔
   • visit the homes of a famous rock group ✘

Group 3 – Liverpool
1 nearly 500,000.
2 River Mersey.
3 People visit Liverpool to see the homes of the Beatles.
4 1207 – King John founded Liverpool.
   18th century – became an important trade centre for sugar, spices, and slaves.
5 The Beatles.
6 Rock/pop.
7 The Beatles.
8 • go by ship to Ireland ✔
   • see Sigmund Freud's house ✘
   • see a famous carnival ✘
   • walk round the French Quarter ✘
   • listen to a famous orchestra ✘
   • visit the homes of a famous rock group ✔

5 Tell each student to find partners from the other two groups and compare the cities, using their answers from exercise 4. Encourage students to exchange information in a meaningful way, using comparative and superlative forms and *have got* where possible. e.g.
Vienna has got the biggest population.
New Orleans and Vienna have got an orchestra, but Liverpool hasn't.
New Orleans is more cosmopolitan than Vienna or Liverpool.

However, do not stop students during the group work and insist on these forms as this will limit students' confidence.

Conduct a full class feedback and get information about all three cities, encouraging your students to compare and contrast. This way you might get some freer use of comparatives, superlatives and *have got*, but don't force this, just be pleased if it happens! The aim of this feedback is to encourage some fluency practice.

Your home town

6 Students write a short description of where they live, giving similar information as in exercise 4. Then they tell a partner or the rest of the class about it.

If you have time, you could get students to exchange their written descriptions and check grammar, spelling, etc., before moving on to the speaking phase. If time is short, you could set the writing activity for homework, check it (sympathetically!), and then do the speaking phase during the next lesson.

VOCABULARY AND PRONUNCIATION (SB p80)

Town and country words

1 Students work in pairs and put the words into the correct columns. They can use their dictionaries and/or they can ask you about words they don't know.

Answers

Town	Country	Both
cathedral	wood	park
port	farm	museum
factory	field	church
theatre	lake	bridge
night club	village	car park
	mountain	hill
	cottage	building
	river bank	
	tractor	

Go through the columns with the whole class. Ask individuals to read out what they have in their columns and see if the others agree. Be prepared for some debate about such things as *theatre* and *lake* which could go in the *Both* column. Correct pronunciation as you go.

2 This exercise aims to consolidate the vocabulary in exercise 1 and review superlative and comparative forms. Do this exercise quickly with the whole class. Ask students for suggestions and when you have established the correct answer and practised saying it, ask them to complete the sentences. Make sure students realize that numbers 2 and 5 require the same word, but that students should decide which one needs a capital letter.

Answers

1	mountain	4	port
2	Bridge bridge	5	Building building
3	lake	6	cathedral

3 This exercise gives more practice on phonetic transcription, again using words that students have already seen. Always encourage your students to consult the phonetic symbols chart on p143 when they do an exercise like this. Ask them to do it on their own and then check answers with a partner.

T 10.7 Play the recording and get students to check their answers. Play the recording again and get students to listen and repeat, looking at the phonetic transcription as they do so.

Answers and tapescript
wood
theatre
farm
village
factory
cottage
field
church

4 This is a fun activity to give further practice with the town and country vocabulary. Demonstrate the activity by getting students to say the examples in the Student's Book chorally and individually. Encourage them to deliver the sentences rhythmically. Give a new sentence with five or six examples to demonstrate 'list' intonation, e.g.

… and I saw a farm, some cows, a church, a cottage, a field, and a lake.

Get students to divide themselves into a 'country' and a 'town' group, according to which they prefer. If you have one group with a lot more students than the other, you may have to ask some students to switch. Get each set of students to play the game. The group that can continue the longest without forgetting a word is the winner.

ADDITIONAL MATERIAL

Workbook Unit 10

Exercise 10 This is a vocabulary exercise which introduces and revises compound nouns connected with town life, such as *town centre* and *railway station*.

Exercises 11 and 12 There are two writing exercises. The first introduces simple relative pronouns. The second provides a model text about London and gives guidance for students to write a similar piece about their own capital city.

Directions 2

The listening text and the pictures provide the context for the introduction of prepositions of movement.

1 **T 10.8** Briefly revise *left* and *right*. Focus attention on the map and get students to find Park Road. Play the recording and tell students to mark the route to the lake with a pencil (or a finger).

Now ask them to work with a partner to fill in the gaps. Play the recording again for a final check.

Answers and tapescript

Drive **along** Park Road and turn **right**. Go **under** the bridge and **past** the pub. Turn **left** up the hill, then drive **down** the hill to the river. **Turn right** after the farm and the lake is **on the right**. It takes twenty minutes.

2 Focus attention on the pictures of Norman and ask students to briefly describe the situation. Complete the first three sentences as a class, using the prepositions from the box (see Answers below). Students work in pairs to complete the rest of the text, using the information in the pictures.

T 10.9 Students listen to the recording and check.

Answers and tapescript

Norman drove **out of** the garage, **along** the road, and **under** the bridge.
Then he drove **past** the pub, **up** the hill, and **down** the hill.
Next he drove **over** the river, **through** the hedge, and **into** the lake!

T 10.9

Well, I drove out of the garage, along the road, and under the bridge. Then I drove past the pub, up the hill, and down the hill. But then I drove over the river, and then – it was terrible – I went through the hedge, and into the lake!

3 Get students to cover the text, look at the pictures, and tell Norman's story in pairs.

As an alternative or extension to students telling the story in the third person, it can be fun to ask them to pretend to be Norman. When you ask students to retell the story as Norman, encourage them to include some of these, rather than just read out the description in the first person. This practises natural stress and intonation. Ask one or two students to do this for the others.

4 Demonstrate the activity by giving some directions to a few places near your school and getting students to call out when they think they know the answer.

Students continue working in pairs. Go round and help and check as they do it.

Don't forget!

Word list
Remind your students of the Word list for this unit on p139. They could write in the translations, learn them at home, and/or write some of the words in their vocabulary notebook.

Pronunciation Book Unit 10

Video

There are two video sections that can supplement Units 9 and 10 of the Student's Book.

Report (Section 8) *Tea* This is a mini-documentary about the history of tea and its importance to the British people, in the past and present.

The following video section also revises some polite requests practised in Unit 9 of the Student's Book, but thematically you might prefer to use this section after Units 12 and 13.

Situation (Section 9) *The Phone Box* This is a short situation where Paola phones British Airways to book her flight home.

Present Continuous • *Whose?*
Clothes • Words that rhyme
In a clothes shop

Looking good!

Introduction to the unit

This is the first unit where students encounter the Present Continuous. The Present Simple was introduced and practised much earlier in *New Headway Elementary* because it is used far more frequently, but by this stage of the course students should be ready to compare and contrast the two present tenses.

The theme of this unit is describing people, and there is a lot of related vocabulary input. The unit also practises *Whose … ?* in conjunction with possessive pronouns. There is a song, *What a wonderful world*, by Louis Armstrong.

Language aims

Grammar – Present Continuous In this unit, we aim to teach the Present Continuous as though the present participle were just another adjective used after the verb *to be*, for example,
She's tall, pretty, hungry → *She's working, cooking, thinking.*

> **POSSIBLE PROBLEMS**
>
> The Present Continuous has no equivalent form in many other languages, which use the present tense to convey the two concepts of 'action which relates to all time' and 'activity happening now'. For example, in French, *il fume dix cigarettes par jour* (he smokes ten cigarettes a day) and *il fume en ce moment* (he is smoking now), the present tense *fume* expresses both ideas.
>
> Students not only confuse the two concepts of the Present Simple and the Present Continuous, they also confuse the forms. When they have seen the *am/is/are* in the Present Continuous, they tend to try to use it in the Present Simple.
>
> The use of Present Continuous for activities happening in the near future can seem strange, so the unit also highlights and practises this use.
>
> **Common mistakes**
> **She's come from Spain.*
> **She's coming from Spain.*
> **I'm come to school by bus.*
> **What does he doing?*
> **Does he wearing a suit?*

Whose is it? It's mine.

> **POSSIBLE PROBLEMS**
>
> The question *Whose … ?* and possessive pronouns present few problems of concept, but learners do confuse *who's* and *whose*. Possessive pronouns simply have to be learned. They are practised in this unit in conjunction with *Whose … ?* and there is also a complete overview of subject and object pronouns, and possessive adjectives and pronouns in the *Grammar Spot* on p85.

Vocabulary There is a lot of vocabulary to do with describing people – colours, clothes, adjectives. There is also an exercise on words that rhyme and further practice of the phonetic script.

Everyday English Language used in a clothes shop is introduced and practised, as is the use of *will* to express a spontaneous decision.

Workbook There is a section on the Present Continuous, and the Present Simple and the Present Continuous are further compared and contrasted. The spelling of the present participle is practised.

Whose … ? and possessive pronouns are further practised.

In the vocabulary section, some names for parts of the body are taught. In the writing section, there is more work on linking words, and students are invited to write about someone in their family.

Notes on the unit

STARTER (SB p82)

1   Ask students to look around the classroom and try to find the items of clothing. You might need to bring in pictures of the items that might not be present in the classroom, e.g. a suit, a hat.

Focus attention on the examples *trousers, jeans, shorts, shoes, trainers,* and *boots.* Ask students what they notice about these words (they are all plural in English).

Drill the pronunciation of the words and briefly revise colours. Ask students to make sentences such as *It's a white T-shirt, They're black shoes,* but avoid the Present Continuous at this stage.

2 | **NOTE**
    | Exercise 2 aims to give initial practice in the Present Continuous with just one simple sentence. Do *not* go into a full presentation of the tense at this stage.

Drill the examples in the Student's Book. Get students to give two or three examples in open pairs to practise the *I* and *you* forms. Students continue in closed pairs and then get a few students to tell the whole class about themselves and you.

DESCRIBING PEOPLE (SB p82)

Present Continuous

1   Pre-teach/check *pretty* and *fair/dark/grey* (hair). Explain the difference between *good-looking* (general), *handsome* (for men), and *pretty* (for girls/women). Focus attention on the photo of Becca and on the description of her. Elicit one or two other descriptions from the whole class and then drill the sentences around the class. Students continue in pairs.

Sample answers
1   Ruth, Cathy, and Jane are pretty. Cathy's got long, fair hair.
2   Nadia's got long, dark hair. She isn't very tall.
3   Rudi's got long, dark hair. He's good-looking.
4   Flora is tall. Toni's got short hair.
5   Angela is tall, and she's got long hair.
6   Juan isn't very tall. He's got short, dark hair.
7   Edna and Violet have got grey hair.
8   Miles has got fair hair and blue eyes. He's handsome.
9   Becca's got brown eyes and dark hair.

2   Pre-teach/check the verbs in the list. Use mime to demonstrate the verbs if necessary. Ask the questions for the examples in the Student's Book and get students to read the answers, *Toni's smiling* and *Angela's running.* Ask the students each of the questions in the list and get them to reply using the contracted form of the third person of the Present Continuous.
Drill the questions and answers. Students ask and answer the questions in the list in pairs.

Sample answers
1   Ruth and Cathy are laughing. Jane's smiling.
2   Naida's standing up/cooking.
3   Rudi's sitting down/playing.
4   Flora and Toni are standing up/talking. Toni's smiling.
5   Angela's running.
6   Juan's playing.
7   Edna and Violet are laughing/sitting down.
8   Miles is writing/smiling/sitting down.
9   Becca's eating.

3   Say the names of two or three people in the photos and get students to describe what they are wearing. Drill the sentences and then get students to continue in pairs. Get students to continue practising the *he/she* form by talking about the other students, e.g. *Giulia's wearing jeans and a black T-shirt.*

GRAMMAR SPOT

1   Read the notes with the whole class. Elicit other examples, by pointing to people and objects in the class, e.g. *He's tall. It's new. We're happy,* etc.

2   Read the notes with the whole class and then get students to complete the table, using contracted forms. Check the answers with the whole class.

Answers		
I	'm (am)	
You	're (are)	learning English.
He/She	's (is)	sitting in a classroom.
We	're (are)	listening to the teacher.
They	're (are)	

Name the tense and then get students to work out the negative and question forms. Get students to do this in pairs and then write up the answers on the board, or refer students to Grammar Reference 11.1 and 11.2 on p132.

Answers

Negatives

I	'm not	
You	aren't	
He/She	isn't	learning English.
We	aren't	sitting in a classroom.
They	aren't	listening to the teacher.

Questions

Am	I	
Are	you	
Is	he/she	learning English?
Are	we	sitting in a classroom?
Are	they	listening to the teacher?

3   Focus attention on the sentences. Get students to work out the difference between the two tenses. Make sure they understand that Present Simple describes things that are always true, or true for a long time, and that Present Continuous describes activities happening now and temporary activities. (Do not overload students by focusing on the use of Present Continuous for activities happening in the near future. This is covered later in the unit.)

You could put sentences on the board to discuss with the whole class, e.g.

Present Simple	**Present Continuous**
She usually wears jeans.	*She's wearing a dress today.*
He works in a bank.	*He's working in the garden today.*
They speak French.	*They're speaking English at the moment.*
I like music.	Not possible: **I'm liking music … .*

Read Grammar Reference 11.1 and 11.2 on p132 together in class, and/or ask students to read it at home. Encourage them to ask you questions about it.

PRACTICE (SB p83)

Who is it?

1   Make sure that students are clear what *Yes/No* questions are. Demonstrate the activity by drilling the question forms chorally and individually and correcting any mistakes.

Ask a student to think of someone in the room, and ask a few *Yes/No* questions yourself. Drill these questions as

much as necessary. When you feel students are ready, ask them to work in pairs. Remind them not to ask questions that are too personal!

2   This activity aims to practise the Present Continuous in a personalized way. Demonstrate the activity by giving two or three examples about yourself. Get students to work individually and write their answers.

Get students to work in pairs and exchange their answers. Monitor and check for correct use of the Present Continuous and for appropriate linking, e.g. *I'm not wearing a jacket.* If necessary, drill pronunciation before eliciting a range of answers from students.

Sample answers
2   I'm not wearing jeans, I'm wearing trousers.
3   I'm not standing up, I'm sitting down.
4   I'm not looking out of the window, I'm looking at my book.
5   It's raining.
6   The teacher isn't writing.
7   We're working hard.
8   I'm chewing gum.

Who's at the party?

3   **T 11.1** This activity aims to practise the difference between the two present tenses, first in a recognition exercise, then in a productive one. Pre-teach/check the following vocabulary items: *musician, rich, stories, cigar, pilot, upstairs.*

Read the instructions with the whole class. Students listen and write the names next to the correct people.

Answers and tapescript
From left to right:
Roz Sam Harry Mandy Fiona George

T 11.1

O = Oliver   M = Monica

O Oh dear! Monica, I don't know any of these people. Who are they?

M Don't worry Oliver. They're all very nice. Can you see that man over there? He's sitting down. That's Harry. He's a musician. He works in LA.

O Sorry, where?

M You know, LA. Los Angeles.

O Oh yeah.

M And he's talking to Mandy. She's wearing a red dress. She's very nice and very rich! She lives in a beautiful old house in the country.

O Rich, eh?

M Yes. Rich and married! Next to her is Fiona. She's drinking a glass of red wine. Fiona's my oldest friend, she and I were at school together.

O And what does Fiona do?

M She's a writer. She writes children's stories – they're not very good but . . . anyway, she's talking to George. He's laughing and smoking a cigar. He's a pilot. He travels the world, thousands of miles every week.

O And who are those two over there? They're dancing. Mmmm. They know each other very well.

M Oh, that's Roz and Sam. They're married. They live in the flat upstairs.

O So . . . er . . . that's Harry and Mandy and . . . er . . . it's no good, I can't remember all those names.

4 Focus attention on the table and on the names of the guests in the first column. Play the recording again as far as *He works in LA* and get students to read the example in the table.

Ask students to work in pairs to complete the table. Play the recording again to check before you provide the answers.

Answers

	Present Continuous	Present Simple
Mandy	She's wearing a red dress.	She lives in a beautiful old house.
Fiona	She's drinking a glass of red wine. She's talking to George.	She writes children's stories.
George	He's laughing and smoking a cigar.	He travels the world.
Roz and Sam	They're dancing.	They live in the flat upstairs.

SUGGESTION

You might want to get some further practice of the two present tenses from this exercise. You could ask questions such as the following:

Where is Harry sitting? Where does he work?
What is Mandy wearing? Where does she live?
What is Fiona drinking? What does she write?
What is George smoking? Where does he travel?
What are Roz and Sam doing? Where do they live?

You could begin by asking a few questions yourself, and then encourage students to ask and answer the other questions in open and/or closed pairs.

5 You will need to photocopy the pictures on p131 of the Teacher's Book, enough for half of the class to have picture A and the other half to have picture B. Students should be familiar with such information gap activities by now, but still be careful with instructions. Use L1 if necessary. You could set the activity up by doing one or two examples with the class first.

You may need to give students some vocabulary before the exercise, or, if the class is small enough, let them ask you for words when the need arises. (That way you won't give away clues as to what may be missing or different in the pictures beforehand!)

Answers
The ten differences in the pictures:
Picture A
Three people are dancing.
The girl standing up with fair hair is wearing a black dress.
The boy with the cap is eating a sandwich.
There's a boy taking a photo.
There's a girl wearing sunglasses.
There are two people kissing on the right.
There's a girl writing.
Two girls are sitting down and talking.
Two people next to the sofa are eating a sandwich.
There's a boy with short fair hair wearing trousers.

Picture B
Four people are dancing.
The girl standing up with fair hair is wearing a white dress.
The boy with the cap is drinking.
There's a boy using a camcorder.
There's a girl wearing glasses.
There are two people talking on the right.
There's a girl reading.
Two girls are standing up and talking.
Two people next to the sofa are eating a pizza.
There's a boy with short hair wearing shorts.

ADDITIONAL MATERIAL

Workbook Unit 11
Exercises 1–5 Present Continuous
Exercises 6–7 Present Continuous and Present Simple

A DAY IN THE PARK (SB p84)

Whose is it?

SUGGESTION

You might choose to introduce *Whose is it?* and possessive pronouns using the classroom situation and use the coursebook material for further practice and consolidation.

Take some personal possessions from the students and put them on the floor where everyone can see them. Hold something up and ask *Whose is this? Is it Pedro's? Is it Maria's?* The aim is to convey the concept of possession.

You could use the board and write up the question *Whose is this?*, pointing out that *whose* is not the same as *who's*. Then hold up a possession of your own, and ask *Whose is this?* Teach *It's mine*. Write this on the board. Then do the same for the other possessive pronouns, *yours, his, hers, ours,* and *theirs*.

1 Focus attention on the picture. Students work in pairs and locate the items in the scene. Drill the pronunciation of the words chorally and individually.

2 If you haven't presented *Whose?* using the classroom situation, do so now using the technique in the *Suggestion* above. Do not present all the possessive pronouns, as this can be done from the book. Just focus on *Whose is this?*, making sure students understand the concept by translating into L1 if possible.

T 11.2 Play the recording. Students listen to the questions and then complete the answers with *his, hers,* or *theirs.*

Answers
1 Whose is the baseball cap?   It's his.
2 Whose are the rollerblades?   They're hers.
3 Whose is the dog?   It's theirs.

Drill the questions and answers from the recording. Demonstrate the singular and plural question forms, using words from the box in exercise 1, e.g. *Whose is the bike? Whose are the sunglasses?* Students ask and answer questions about the other things in exercise 1.

Answers

Whose is the bike?	It's hers.
Whose is the football?	It's theirs.
Whose are the trainers?	They're his.
Whose are the sunglasses?	They're hers.
Whose is the radio?	It's his.
Whose is the skateboard?	It's his.
Whose is the umbrella?	It's his.
Whose are the flowers?	They're hers.

3 Get students to give you some objects that belong to them. Practise questions with *Whose?* in open pairs, making sure that the objects will generate each of the possessive pronouns in the box. Do the questions and answers as a class, with you giving models for repetition, drilling, and correction. Then ask students to continue the activity in pairs.

GRAMMAR SPOT

1 Make sure students understand the different categories in the table by putting simple sentences on the board and asking students to highlight the key word, e.g.
We speak English. (subject pronoun)
They are helping **us**. (object pronoun)
Our classroom is large. (possessive adjective)
Those book are **ours**. (possessive pronoun)

Answers

Subject	Object	Adjective	Pronoun
I	me	my	mine
You	you	**your**	**yours**
He	**him**	his	his
She	**her**	**her**	hers
We	use	our	**ours**
They	them	**their**	**theirs**

2 Read the notes with the whole class. Point out that there are two ways of asking the question, *whose + noun + is this*, or *whose + is this + noun*, and that possessive pronouns replace possessive adjectives + noun.

3 Highlight the difference between *Who's = Who is* and *Whose?* for possession. Tell students that the pronunciation is the same, but the meaning is different.

Read Grammar Reference 11.3 on p132 together in class, and/or ask students to read it at home. Encourage them to ask you questions about it.

PRACTICE (SB p85)

who's or whose?

1 Students work individually and choose the correct word. Get students to compare with a partner before checking the answers with the whole class.

Answers
1 your
2 Our, theirs
3 their, ours
4 My, hers
5 Who's, your
6 mine, yours
7 Whose, his
8 Who's
9 Whose, our

2 **T 11.3** Read the instructions. Students shout out 1 if they think the word is *Whose … ?* and 2 if they think it is *Who's … ?* This is not an easy exercise, so take it slowly, and if a lot of students find it difficult, repeat each sentence as often as necessary.

Answers and tapescript

T 11.3
1 Who's on the phone? **2**
2 I'm going to the pub. Who's coming? **2**
3 Wow! Look at that sports car. Whose is it? **1**
4 Whose dictionary is this? It's not mine. **1**
5 There are books all over the floor. Whose are they? **1**
6 Who's the most intelligent in our class? **2**
7 Who's got my book? **2**
8 Do you know whose jacket this is? **1**

What a mess!

> **NOTE**
> This exercise introduces the use of the Present Continuous to refer to arrangements in the near future. You might decide that this use merits a full presentation from you, but you could also decide to downplay it. Students are introduced to the *going to* future in Unit 12. The area of future forms and the concepts that they express in English is very complex, and we do not suggest that you explore it at this level.
>
> It is not such a leap for students to be told that the Present Continuous can be used to describe activities happening in the near future, even though in their own language this concept may be expressed by the equivalent of the Present Simple. You can also mention that to express an arrangement in the near future, the Present Continuous usually needs a future time reference, e.g. *I'm doing my homework (now)* versus *I'm doing my homework tonight.*

3 **T 11.4** Students listen and complete the conversation. Check the answers.

> **Answers and tapescript**
> **A** **Whose** is this tennis racket?
> **B** It's **mine**.
> **A** What's it doing here?
> **B** I'm **playing** tennis this afternoon.

Read the information in the Caution Box as a class. Use L1 to translate and explain if you can.

4 **T 11.4** Play the recording of the conversation again. Get students to listen and repeat. (It can be good fun to practise the intonation of an exasperated person tidying up!)

Students work in pairs to make similar dialogues. Do the first couple as an example with the whole class.

> **Answers**
> 1 Whose are these football boots?
>   They're John's.
>   What are they doing here?
>   He's playing football later.
> 2 Whose are these ballet shoes?
>   They're Mary's.
>   What are they doing here?
>   She's going dancing tonight.
> 3 Whose is this suitcase?
>   It's mine.
>   What's it doing here?
>   I'm going on holiday tomorrow.
> 4 Whose is this coat?
>   It's Jane's.
>   What's it doing here?
>   She's going for a walk soon.

> 5 Whose is this plane ticket?
>   It's Jo's.
>   What's it doing here?
>   She's flying to Rome this afternoon.
> 6 Whose are all these glasses?
>   They're ours.
>   What are they doing here?
>   We're having a party tonight.

Follow up the activity by getting students to tell the class what they are doing at the following times: *this afternoon, tonight, tomorrow, later, soon.*

Check it

5 Students work individually and correct the mistakes and then check their answers in pairs. Then check the answers with the whole class.

> **Answers**
> 1 Alice is tall and she's got long, black **hair**.
> 2 **Whose** boots are these?
> 3 I'm wearing **jeans**.
> 4 Look at Roger. He's **standing** next to Jeremy.
> 5 He **works** in a bank. He's the manager.
> 6 What's **Suzie** drinking?
> 7 **Who's** that man in the garden?
> 8 Where **are** you going tonight?
> 9 What **are you doing** after school today?

ADDITIONAL MATERIAL

Workbook Unit 11
Exercise 8 Auxiliary verbs
Exercises 9 and 10 *Whose … ?* and possessive pronouns
Exercise 11 This is an error-correction exercise based on the target language of the unit.

LISTENING AND SPEAKING (SB p86)

What a wonderful world!

> **SUGGESTION**
> You might want to start this activity by asking your students what they know about Louis Armstrong. (He was mentioned in Unit 10 in the text about New Orleans.) He was a very famous American jazz musician, with the nickname 'Satchmo'. He was born in 1901 in New Orleans and gained recognition for his trumpet playing with the *Hot Five* and *Hot Seven* in the 1920s. His pure tone, skill at improvisation, quirky voice, and appearances in films all contributed to his becoming a legend of the jazz world. He died in 1971. Louis Armstrong's song 'What a wonderful world!' has been chosen because of the language of description it contains and the examples of the Present Continuous.

1 Look out of the window and give a brief description of what you can see. If possible, include examples of the Present Continuous to describe what people are doing.

Get students to look out of the window and describe what they can see (from a different vantage spot if possible!) Encourage them to be as detailed as possible and include colours and other adjectives in their description.

> **NOTE**
> If you have a large group, you will have to choose just three or four students to do this activity. With a smaller group, you could do this as a pairwork activity, with Student A describing the scene and Student B with his/her back to the window and listening.
> If you have a classroom with no windows, you can still do this activity by getting students to imagine the scene.

2 Do the first two collocations with the whole class as an example – *shake hands* and *babies cry*. Students continue the activity in pairs. If students have access to dictionaries, encourage them to use them. If students do not find the collocations as a separate dictionary entry, encourage them to look at any example sentences for the words as these may help.

Check the answers with the whole class.

> **Answers**
> shake hands
> babies cry
> sunny day
> starry night
> blue skies
> red roses
> white clouds
> green trees
> flowers bloom
> colours of the rainbow

Students use the phrases to talk about the photos. Encourage them to do this in a meaningful way, rather than just pointing and saying the phrases, e.g. *There are two people smiling and shaking hands. The sun is shining and there are some white clouds in the sky.*

3 Get students to work in pairs and try and complete the lines from the song, using the words from exercise 2 where they can.

4 **T 11.5** Play the recording. Students check their answers and complete the song with any words they couldn't guess.

> **Answers and tapescript**
> **What a wonderful world!**
> I see **trees** of green
> Red **roses** too
> I see them **bloom** for me and you
> And I think to myself
> what a wonderful world.
> I see **skies** of blue
> and **clouds** of white
> the bright **sunny** day
> and the dark **starry** night
> and I think to myself
> what a wonderful world
> The **colours** of the rainbow
> so pretty in the sky
> are also on the **faces**
> of the people going by.
> I see friends shaking **hands**
> saying 'How do you do?'
> They're really saying
> 'I **love** you.'
> I hear **babies** cry
> I watch them grow.
> They'll **learn** much more
> than you'll ever know
> and I think to myself
> what a wonderful world.
> Yes, I think to myself
> what a wonderful world.

You could point out that the way of describing the things in the song differs from how they would be described in normal spoken English, e.g. *I see trees of green* would be *I (can) see green trees.* Similarly, *How do you do?* has the meaning of *How are you?* in the song. Explain that songs and poetry often use a different form of expression, but don't go into too much detail as this may spoil the enjoyment of having listened to and understood the song.

What do you think?

Give some examples of the things that you think are wonderful. Be as open as you can (without embarrassing yourself or the class!). This helps students to see their teacher as a real person and also encourages them to talk about themselves more openly.

Students write their lists and then compare in pairs. Elicit a few interesting or surprising examples in a short feedback session with the whole class.

Words that rhyme

> **SUGGESTION**
> You could do this exercise as it is in the book, or you could put the words in their columns on the board and ask students to do the exercise in pairs or small groups. This makes a nice warmer to do at the beginning of a lesson, as the whole class is focused on the board, and students don't have their 'noses' in the book.
>
> **POSSIBLE PROBLEMS**
> Students find the different pronunciations of the spelling *ea* difficult.
> *mean* /iː/
> *near* /ɪə/
> *wear* /eə/
> The following words often cause problems, too.
> *laugh* (*gh* pronounced as /f/)
> *bought* (silent *gh*)
> *half* (silent *l*)

1 The aim of this exercise is to show students once again that English spelling is not phonetic, and so the same sound can be spelled in different ways. Most or all of the vocabulary should be known, but check comprehension before students start matching.

Students work in pairs or small groups to match the words that rhyme. Do one or two as a class as an example. Again the pronunciation in the book and on the cassette recording are based on English RP. If, as a native speaker teacher, your accent differs (and some of the pairs don't rhyme for you) then you can point this out to your students.

Students check their answers.

Answers			
red	said	white	night
hat	that	near	beer
kissed	list	they	pay
green	mean	hair	wear
laugh	half	rose	knows
whose	shoes	ours	flowers
short	bought		

Ask students to practise the words in rhyming pairs. Do this first as a class so that you can monitor pronunciation. Correct mistakes very carefully! Then students can practise the words again in pairs.

2 Students categorize two of the words according to the vowel sound. Check first that they know the symbols. They can use the phonetic symbols chart on p143. Note that the symbols are in three groups – single sounds, long sounds, and diphthongs.

T 11.6 Students listen and check.

Answers			
Vowels			
1	/e/	red	said
2	/æ/	hat	that
3	/ɪ/	kissed	list
4	/iː/	green	mean
5	/ɑː/	laugh	half
6	/uː/	whose	shoes
7	/ɔː/	short	bought
Diphthongs			
1	/aɪ/	white	night
2	/ɪə/	near	beer
3	/eɪ/	they	pay
4	/eə/	hair	wear
5	/əʊ/	rose	knows
6	/aʊ/	ours	flowers

3 Students work in pairs and think of more words to add to the lists. If students have access to dictionaries, they could check their suggestions as they go along. Build up a set of answers on the board.

Sample answers		
Vowels		
1	/e/	bread, head, when, again, ten
2	/æ/	ham, cat, sat, stamp, map
3	/ɪ/	fish, give, lived, his, it
4	/iː/	meat, feet, leave, see, be
5	/ɑː/	heart, part, start, dark, card
6	/uː/	boot, suit, you, true, blue
7	/ɔː/	ball, door, caught, floor, or
Diphthongs		
1	/aɪ/	buy, light, right, shy, die
2	/ɪə/	here, dear, clear, real, hear
3	/eɪ/	say, way, main, game, shake
4	/eə/	where, fair, care, pear, rare
5	/əʊ/	clothes, soap, hope, no, show
6	/aʊ/	hour, shower, now, how, cow

Tongue twisters

4 **T 11.7** Read the instructions with the whole class. Check comprehension of the vocabulary in the tongue twisters and then play the recording. Students listen and repeat.

Students work in pairs and say the tongue twisters to each other. Make sure students try and say them quickly, rather than read each word off the page.

5 Students learn two of the tongue twisters and say them to the rest of the class. You could introduce a little light-hearted competition and get students to vote for the 'tongue twister champion'. Allow students to 'get their own back' by asking you to say a tongue twister from their language! If you have a multilingual group, just choose one or two examples from the languages represented by the class.

EVERYDAY ENGLISH (SB p89)

In a clothes shop

> **SUGGESTION**
> The final activity in this section works best if you have some props! Try to bring in some clothes so that students can actually try them on.

1 Students look at the lines of a conversation in a clothes shop and decide who says them.

You could perhaps do this as a class so that you can sort out any unknown vocabulary. Point out that *I'm afraid* can also mean *I'm sorry*, as it does in this exercise. This is the first time that students may have come across the use of *will* for spontaneous decisions.

> **Answers**
> a **SA** Can I help you?
> b **C** Oh yes. I like that one much better. Can I try it on?
> c **SA** £39.99. How do you want to pay?
> d **C** Yes, please. I'm looking for a shirt to go with my new suit.
> e **C** Blue.
> f **SA** Yes, of course. The changing rooms are over there.
> g **C** OK. I'll take the white. How much is it?
> h **C** Can I pay by credit card?
> i **SA** What colour are you looking for?
> j **C** No, it isn't the right blue.
> k **C** No, it's a bit too big. Have you got a smaller size?
> l **SA** That's the last blue one we've got, I'm afraid. But we've got it in white.
> m **SA** Well, what about this one? It's a bit darker blue.
> n **SA** What about this one? Do you like this?
> o **SA** Is the size OK?
> p **SA** Credit card's fine. Thank you very much.

2 Students try to match some of the lines in the conversation. Get them to practise any sets of lines that work but not to recreate the whole conversation at this stage.

3 Students work in pairs and try to put all the lines of the conversation in the correct order.

T 11.8 Students listen and check their order against the recording. They might find other lines that match, so do go through and check their alternatives with them after they have listened to the recording.

> **Answers and tapescript**
> **SA = shop assistant   C = customer**
> **SA** Can I help you?
> **C** Yes, please. I'm looking for a shirt to go with my new suit.
> **SA** What colour are you looking for?
> **C** Blue.
> **SA** What about this one? Do you like this?
> **C** No, it isn't the right blue.
> **SA** Well, what about his one? It's a bit darker blue.
> **C** Oh yes. I like that one much better. Can I try it on?
> **SA** Yes, of course. The changing rooms are over there.
> *(pause)*
> Is the size OK?
> **C** No, it's a bit too big. Have you got a smaller size?
> **SA** That's the last blue one we've got, I'm afraid. But we've got it in white.
> **C** OK. I'll take the white. How much is it?
> **SA** £39.99. How do you want to pay?
> **C** Can I pay by credit card?
> **SA** Credit card's fine. Thank you very much.

4 Students practise the conversation with a partner and then make similar improvised conversations. Use the props! Some interesting dialogues might ensue!

Don't forget!

Workbook Unit 11
Exercise 12 Vocabulary of parts of the body
Exercises 13 and 14 There is a writing exercise on linking words and students are invited to write about a member of their family.

Word list
Remind your students of the Word list for this unit on p140. They could write in the translations, learn them at home, and/or write some of the words in their vocabulary notebook.

Pronunciation Book Unit 11

Video
This unit can be supplemented by the following video section.
Situation (Section 11) *The Dinner Party* Paola and David go to dinner at their friends' house.

12

going to future
Infinitive of purpose
The weather • Making suggestions

Life's an adventure!

Introduction to the unit

The theme of this unit is planning the future. We focus on the *going to* future for plans and intentions. We do not at the same time introduce and contrast the Future Simple with *will* (this rather complex distinction is for a later stage of learning), but in the *Everyday English* section we do focus on *shall* for suggestions and revise *will* for immediate decisions. The second presentation in the unit is the infinitive of purpose, which is relatively simple to operate in English but is often realized differently in other languages. The skills work includes a jigsaw reading about dangerous sports – sky-diving and motor racing. This highlights the theme of adventure and provides opportunities to revise the grammar not only of this unit but also of previous units (Past Simple and comparatives/superlatives). It is worth noting that the theme of dangerous sports is taken up in the *Headway Elementary* Video, where there is a short documentary about two climbers, but they don't climb mountains, they climb buildings!

Language aims

Grammar – *going to* The learning of the *going to* future is facilitated by the fact that students already know the present forms of the verb *to be*, both on its own and as part of the Present Continuous, which they met in the previous unit, Unit 11. These are, of course, intrinsic parts of this structure. Also, as this is the first future they have encountered (apart from the Present Continuous with future meaning touched on briefly in Unit 11), the problem of when to use it in relation to other future forms (always an area of difficulty for students) is deferred for the time being, and they can simply concentrate on this one. The two uses of *going to* are introduced in the unit: plans and intentions, such as *I'm going to be a photographer*, and making predictions based on present evidence, such as *It's going to rain./He's going to fall*.

POSSIBLE PROBLEMS

1 With the verbs *go* and *come* we often avoid using the full *going to* future form, and just use the Present Continuous.

   She's going to go to Rome next week. → *She's going to Rome next week.*

2 The Present Continuous can be used for future arrangements and is often interchangeable with the *going to* future.

   I'm going to see the doctor tomorrow./I'm seeing the doctor tomorrow.

The infinitive of purpose The infinitive of purpose answers the question *why* in place of *because I wanted to*, e.g. *Why did you go to the shops? Because I wanted to buy a newspaper./To buy a newspaper.*

There is often a problem for learners when they attempt to translate this item from their own language and insert *for* which is wrong in English.

Common mistakes
I went to the shops for to buy a newspaper.
I went to the shops for buy a newspaper.
I went to the shops for buying a newspaper.

Vocabulary Vocabulary to do with weather is introduced, such as *It's sunny/windy/rainy*. The question for description *What ... like?* is presented and practised in dialogues, but only in connection with weather: *What's the weather like?*

Everyday English Two of the most common functional exponents for asking for and making suggestions are introduced:
What shall we do?
Let's go to the cinema.

Workbook There are exercises to consolidate the uses of *going to* and the infinitive of purpose. All of the auxiliary verbs covered so far – *am/is/are* and *do/does/did* – are brought together and practised.

The vocabulary section focuses on word stress and phonetic transcription of a range of words students are already familiar with.

There is also an exercise on the prepositions *from, like, than*.

The writing syllabus continues with work on writing postcards, and provides an opportunity to bring together *going to* with other tenses.

Notes on the unit

STARTER (SB p90)

1 Focus attention on the *I'm going to Florida* and *I went to Florida*. Establish the overall time reference by asking *past, present, or future?* about each sentence. Students should recognize *went* as the past of *go* but make sure that they realize *going to* refers to the future. (Do not go into a full presentation of the tense at this stage.)

Pre-teach/check the meaning of *retire*. Students work in pairs and make sentences using the time references in the second box. Check the answers with the whole class.

Answers
I'm going to Florida soon/next month/in a year's time/when I retire.

I went to Florida when I was a student/two years ago.

2 Demonstrate the activity by giving similar sentences about yourself, e.g. *I'm going to (London) soon. I went to (South America) when I was a student*, etc. Drill the sentences in the Student's Book and then get students to continue the activity in pairs.

Elicit any interesting or surprising examples in a short feedback session with the whole class.

FUTURE PLANS (SB p90)

going to

1 The context for the presentation of *going to* is future plans not only of a young girl but also of an older woman who is about to retire.

Ask your students to look at the photographs of Rosie and her teacher Miss Bishop. Elicit a few suggestions about what their future plans might be.

Pre-teach/check the meaning of *grow up, retire, open a school* (meaning establish a new one), and *TV star*.

POSSIBLE PROBLEM
The *when* clauses with *grow up* and *retire* require the Present Simple. Sometimes students find it strange that the Present Simple is used to talk about future events; they might want to say *When I will grow up ....* However, try not to go into this at this stage.

Make it clear that students are going to read about Rosie's and Miss Bishop's future plans, therefore what they are looking at is a future tense. Put students into pairs to discuss the sentences and put R or MB according to who they think is speaking. Tell them that sometimes Rosie and Miss Bishop both have the same plan, so they must write R and MB next to the sentence. (The sentences have been selected so that there are some surprises.)

T 12.1 Play the recording of both Rosie and Miss Bishop right through, asking students to listen carefully and check if they are right. At the end ask *Were all your answers right? Were there any surprises?*

Answers and tapescript
R	1	I'm going to be a ballet dancer.
R, MB	2	I'm going to travel all over the world.
R, MB	3	I'm going to learn Russian.
MB	4	I'm going to learn to drive.
R	5	I'm going to open a school.
R	6	I'm not going to marry until I'm thirty-five.
MB	7	I'm not going to wear skirts and blouses.
MB	8	I'm going to wear jeans and T-shirts all the time.
MB	9	I'm going to write a book.
MB	10	I'm going to become a TV star.

T 12.1

Rosie (aged 11)
When I grow up I'm going to be a ballet dancer. I love dancing. I go dancing three times a week. I'm going to travel all over the world and I'm going to learn French and Russian because I want to dance in Paris and Moscow. I'm not going to marry until I'm thirty-five and then I'm going to have two children. First, I'd like a girl and then a boy – but maybe I can't plan that! I'm going to work until I'm 75. I'm going to teach dancing and I'm going to open a dance school. It's all very exciting.

Miss Bishop (aged 59)
When I retire ...? ... er ... well ... er ... two things. First, I'm going to learn Russian – I can already speak French and German, and I want to learn another language. And second, I'm going to learn to drive. It's terrible that I'm 59 and I can't drive – no time to learn. Then I'm going to buy a car and travel all over the world. Also I'm not going to wear boring clothes any more, I hate the skirts and blouses I wear every day for school. I'm going to wear jeans and T-shirts all the time. And when I return from my travels I'm going to write a book and go on TV to talk about it. I'm going to become a TV star!

2 This exercise moves from first person to third person, still practising positive and negative sentences only. First ask individuals to give you some of Rosie's and Miss Bishop's plans. Focus on the pronunciation of *going to*: /'gəʊɪŋtə/ or /'gəʊɪŋtʊ/. Practise it in isolation first, and then as part of a full sentence, drilling the examples in the book.

Now put your students into pairs, one to tell the other about Rosie's plans, and the other about Miss Bishop's focusing on the plans they have in common, using *They're both going to ...* . Monitor as they do this, checking for correct use and pronunciation of *going to*.

Answers
Rosie
Rosie's going to be a ballet dancer.
Rosie's going to open a school.
Rosie isn't going to marry until she's thirty-five.

Miss Bishop
Miss Bishop's going to learn to drive.
Miss Bishop's going to write a book.
Miss Bishop isn't going to wear skirts and blouses.
Miss Bishop's going to wear jeans and T-shirts all the time.
Miss Bishop's going to become a TV star.

The two plans that are the same
They're both going to travel all over the world.
They're both going to learn Russian.

3 **T 12.2** Now we focus on the formation and pronunciation of the question, which should not cause your students too much difficulty because they are already familiar with the Present Continuous.

Play the recording and ask students to repeat the questions and answers. Encourage them to use falling intonation for *wh-* questions.

GRAMMAR SPOT

Highlight that the form of *going to* builds on what students already know by getting the class to chorus first the positive and then the negative forms of the verb *to be*. (Conjugating verbs may be deemed 'old-fashioned' in these communicative days, but it is an effective way of consolidating grammatical forms!)

1 Read the notes with the whole class and then get students to complete the table using contracted forms. Check the answers with the whole class.

Answers

I	'm	
You	're	
He/She	's	going to leave tomorrow.
We	're	
They	're	

Get students to work out the question and negative forms in pairs, and then write the answers on the board or refer students to the Grammar Reference on p133.

Answers
Negatives

I	'm not	
You	aren't	
He/She	isn't	going to leave tomorrow.
We	aren't	
They	aren't	

Questions

Am	I	
Are	you	
Is	he/she	going to leave tomorrow?
Are	we	
Are	they	

This may be a good opportunity to draw students' attention again to the two realizations of the negative of *to be*. Remind them that this is possible in all persons except the first person singular.

2 Focus attention on the uses of the Present Continuous for future and *going to*. Establish that there is little difference between the two sentences.

Read Grammar Reference 12.1 on p133 together in class, and/or ask students to read it at home. Encourage them to ask you questions about it.

PRACTICE (SB p91)

Questions about Rosie

1 Students work in pairs to form the questions about Rosie and then match the answers.

Answers and tapescript
1 e Why is she going to learn French and Russian? Because she wants to dance in Paris and Moscow.
2 d When is she going to marry? Not until she's thirty-five.
3 b How many children is she going to have? Two.
4 a How long is she going to work? Until she's seventy-five.
5 c What is she going to teach? Dancing.

2 **T 12.3** Play the recording and get students to check their answers. Then ask them to practise saying the questions and answers in pairs. Go round and help and check as they do this. If students have problems with the falling intonation of the *wh-* questions, get them to listen and repeat the questions from the recording and then continue asking and answering in pairs.

Questions about you

3 Now we move away from Rosie and Miss Bishop and get students to talk about themselves. Drill the example in the Student's Book individually and chorally. Get one or two students to demonstrate question 2 in open pairs. Then get students to work in closed pairs, asking and answering the rest of the questions. Go round and monitor as they do this, checking for correct use and pronunciation of the *Yes/No* questions.

4 Ask students to tell the class about themselves and their partner, thereby practising third person singular and first person singular and plural.

I'm going to sneeze!

Here we introduce the second use of *going to*, when we can see now that something is sure to happen in the future. Read the Caution Box with the whole class. If possible and necessary, use L1 to explain.

5 Ask students to look at the pictures and write a sentence for each picture using *going to* with *it, you, I*, etc. If students have access to dictionaries, get them to look up new words, or they can ask you. Students can work in pairs so that they can help each other with vocabulary.

Check through the answers with the class as a whole. Ask individuals to read a sentence aloud.

> **Answers**
> 1 It's **going to rain**.
> 2 You're **going to be late**.
> 3 I'm **going to sneeze**.
> 4 They're **going to have a baby**.
> 5 She's **going to win the race**.
> 6 He's **going to jump**.
> 7 He's **going to fall**.
> 8 They're **going to kiss**.

6 Students work on their own or in pairs to fill the gaps, using sentences from exercise 5.

T 12.4 Play the recording and get students to check their answers. There are some useful little expressions included in the sentences: *Look at the time! Oh dear! Bless you!* Illustrate the meaning of these when you go through the exercise and get the class to repeat them. It can also be interesting and fun to discuss what is said in the students' own language(s) when someone sneezes, and to express disgust, e.g. *Yuk!* in sentence 7.

They can then practise saying the sentences with a partner and have fun practising the stress and intonation in the expressions.

> **Answers and tapescript**
> 1 Take an umbrella. **It's going to rain.**
> 2 Look at the time! **You're going to be late** for the meeting.
> 3 Anna's running very fast. **She's going to win the race.**
> 4 Look! Jack's on the wall. **He's going to fall.**
> 5 Look at that man! **He's going to jump.**
> 6 **They're going to have a baby.** It's due next month.
> 7 There's my sister and her boyfriend! Yuk! **They're going to kiss.**
> 8 'Oh dear. **I'm going to sneeze.** Aaattishooo!'
>   'Bless you!'

ADDITIONAL MATERIAL

Workbook Unit 12
Exercises 1–5 These consolidate and practise all aspects of the *going to* future.

I WANT TO TRAVEL THE WORLD (SB p92)

Infinitive of purpose

1 The aim of this activity is to set the scene and check the vocabulary needed for the presentation dialogue in exercise 2.

First ask your students to look at the photographs on p93 and ask them which places they recognize. The photographs will also help to check some of the vocabulary needed for the matching exercise. Briefly check the pronunciation of the names of the places, focusing on *Moscow* /ˈmɒskəʊ/, *Egypt* /ˈiːdʒɪpt/, and *Kenya* /ˈkenjə/ in particular.

Students work in pairs to match a country or city with an activity, and a photograph if possible. Then check quickly through the exercise with the whole class.

> **Answers**
> Holland – see the tulips (pic 4)
> Spain – watch flamenco dancing (pic 7)
> Moscow – walk in Red Square (pic 9)
> Egypt – visit the pyramids (pic 2)
> Kenya – take photographs of the lions (pic 5)
> India – visit the Taj Mahal (pic 6)
> China – walk along the Great Wall (pic 1)
> Japan – see Mount Fuji (pic 3)
> the USA – fly over the Grand Canyon (pic 10)
> Rio – sunbathe on Copacabana beach (pic 8)

2 In this activity, students meet Miss Bishop again. She is now planning all the places she will visit on her travels.

Go through the dialogue with the whole class. Ask one student to read Miss Bishop's lines and another Harold's. See if they can complete Miss Bishop's final line.

T 12.5 Play the recording for your students, not only to check the line, but also to familiarize them with the stress and intonation in the dialogue.

Answers and tapescript
MB = Miss Bishop   H = Harold

MB	First I'm going to Holland.
H	Why?
MB	To see the tulips, of course!
H	Oh yes! How wonderful! Where are you going after that?
MB	Well, then I'm going to Spain to **watch flamenco dancing**.

GRAMMAR SPOT

1   Read through the notes with the class (if you have not done so earlier) and highlight the use of *going/coming* rather than *going to go/going to come*.

2   Focus attention on the sentences and get students to decide if they mean the same.

Answer
Yes, the sentences do mean the same.

Explain, in L1 if possible, that the infinitive can be used in answer to a *Why ... ?* question and focus on the example in the Student's Book.

Read Grammar Reference 12.2 on p133 together in class, and/or ask students to read it at home. Encourage them to ask you questions about it.

PRACTICE (SB p93)

Roleplay

1   This is a controlled practice roleplay, where students work in pairs and take the roles of Miss Bishop and Harold, and ask and answer questions about the places on p92. Do the example in the book in open pairs across

the class to illustrate the activity. Then put your students into closed pairs to complete it.

2   This is an extension of the previous activity, so you could move on to the next activity if you are short of time.

Put students into groups of four so that the activity can be completed quite quickly. Ask them to take turns to tell part of Miss Bishop's planned journey. Remind them to use the adverbs *first, then, next, after that, finally*.

Sample answer
Student 1: First she's going to Holland to see the tulips. Then she's going to Spain to watch flamenco dancing.
Student 2: Next she's going to Moscow to walk in Red Square, then to Egypt to visit the pyramids, and after that to Kenya to take photographs of the lions.
Student 3: After that she's going to India to see the Taj Mahal and then to China to walk along the Great Wall, and to Japan to see Mount Fuji.
Student 4: Then she's going to the USA to fly over the Grand Canyon, and finally to Rio to sunbathe on Copacabana beach.

Why and *When?*

3   This activity personalizes the infinitive of purpose. It also moves away from practising the structure with *going to*, and revises the Past Simple.

You could introduce the activity by just going through the examples in the Student's Book, but it is much more interesting if *you* say some names of places *you* visited in the past and then get students to ask you why you went there and when, for example:

Teacher: *I went to Madrid.*
Student(s): *Why did you go to Madrid?*
Teacher: *To visit a friend and to practise my Spanish.*
Student(s): *When did you go?*
Teacher: *Eighteen months ago.*

Ask students to write down the names of some places they visited in the past – countries, cities, villages, or any places of interest. Then put them into pairs to ask each other questions about the places. Let this go on for as long as students are interested if you have time.

Round the activity off by asking one or two individuals to give feedback to the class about their partner.

4   This activity follows the same pattern as exercise 3, but focuses on the future. Remind students of the expressions of future time that they can use, e.g. *soon, next week/month/year, in a few weeks' time*, etc. Again, you can use the examples in the Student's Book or give examples about places *you* are going to visit.

Students work in pairs and ask each other questions about the places. Ask one or two individuals to give feedback to the class about their partner.

Check it

5 This exercise brings together the key structures from this unit. Ask your students to do it on their own as quickly as possible, then check their answers with a partner before you conduct feedback with the whole class.

> **Answers**
> 1 It's going to rain.
> 2 Are you going to wash your hair this evening?
> 3 She's going to have a baby.
> 4 I'm going to the Post Office to buy some stamps.
> 5 I'm going home early this evening.
> 6 I opened the window to get some fresh air.

ADDITIONAL MATERIAL

Workbook Unit 12
Exercises 6 and 7 These consolidate and practise the infinitive of purpose.

READING AND SPEAKING (SB p94)

Living dangerously

1 This activity pre-teaches some of the collocations that appear in the texts. Get students to work in pairs and match the verbs with the nouns or phrases. Check the answers with the whole class.

> **Answers**
> have an accident   feel sick   get top marks
> win a race   float in water

2 This activity is to set the scene for the reading task and hopefully motivate students to read about the dangerous sports.

First, ask your students to work on their own and number the list according to which sports they think are the most dangerous. Make it clear that *1* is the *most* dangerous. Obviously, there are no right or wrong answers to this.

Students compare their ideas with a partner. Encourage them to give reasons for their choices.

Get students to compare their ideas with the whole class. Again, encourage them to justify their answers (with luck some free speaking might result if there is disagreement across the group!). Finally, establish with everyone where *motor racing* and *sky-diving* came on their lists.

3 Focus attention on the photos of Clem and Sue. Establish who does which sport (Clem = sky-diving and Sue = motor racing). Ask students which sport they would most like to try and why. Ask if anyone does either of these sports and to briefly describe their reasons and/or any experiences they had doing the sport.

Then divide the class into two groups. Tell Group A to read about Clem and Group B to read about Sue. Students should read and answer the questions about their person. Each group has the same questions to work on. If they have access to dictionaries, allow students to check new words. Otherwise, they can ask you for help or ask other students in their group.

Students check their answers with others from the same group. Then check the answers with Group A students and Group B students separately.

> **Answers**
> **Clem Quinn**
> 1 He tried to fly by jumping off the garden shed.
> 2 He worked as a taxi driver.
> 3 He did a parachute jump and loved it.
> 4 Because the world looks so good – you can see blue sky, green fields, and white clouds. You float through the air and it's like floating in water. The views are fantastic. You can forget all your worries.
> 5 No, he says it's safer than football.
> 6 Yes, he's a full-time teacher of sky-diving.
> 7 He's going to do a sky-dive with 100 people from six planes.
> 8 Never.
> 9   5 – Clem's age when he jumped off the garden shed
>   6 – the number of planes he's going to use for his record dive
>   20 – the number of years ago that he did his first jump
> 100 – the number of people who are going to do the record dive with Clem
>
> **Sue Glass**
> 1 She had a car accident so she didn't like driving.
> 2 She worked in a car company.
> 3 She met Julian Swayland. He drove her around Brands Hatch racing circuit and she loved it.
> 4 Because she loves the excitement of motor racing.
> 5 Yes, and she says she's always very frightened. She felt sick before a race because she was so nervous.
> 6 No, but she's going to teach other people to drive.
> 7 She's going to open a driving school next year.
> 8 She stopped a year ago.
> 9   5 – the number of men on the motor racing course with Sue
>   6 – the number of years ago that she met Julian Swayland
>   20 – the number of men she beat in her first championship race
> 100 – the speed she drove around corners at the racing circuit

4 Tell each student to find a partner from the other group and to compare Clem and Sue, using their answers from exercise 3. Encourage them to exchange information in a meaningful way, rather than just read their answers, e.g.

A *Clem tried to fly by jumping off the garden shed. What about Sue?*
B *She had a car accident so she didn't like driving. What job did Clem do?*
A *He was a taxi driver. And Sue?*
B *She worked in a car company.*

Interviews

1 Put students back into the A and B groups they were in for the reading task. Tell students that the As are Clem and the Bs are Sue. Ask the As to get together in small groups to prepare the questions they are going to ask about Sue, and the Bs to get together in small groups to prepare the questions they are going to ask about Clem. Make sure students understand they have to use a range of tenses in the questions.

Check the answers with Group A and B students separately.

> **Answers**
> **Group A**
> 1 Why didn't you like driving?
> 2 Why did Julian Swayland take you to Brands Hatch?
> 3 Why did you do well on the motor racing course?
> 4 Why did you stop motor racing?
> 5 What are you going to do next year?
>
> **Group B**
> 1 What did you do when you were five?
> 2 When did you do your first parachute jump?
> 3 Why did you move to the country?
> 4 Why do you love sky-diving?
> 5 What are you going to do next July?

2 Students work with a partner from the other group and interview each other. Make sure they work with a different partner from the reading stage and that they answer as either Clem or Sue. Monitor and help where necessary.

Finally, ask a couple of pairs to act out their interview to the whole class. It would be a great idea to tape some of the roleplays if possible and play them back to the whole class for them to comment on and correct. Students often find this very productive and satisfying.

ADDITIONAL MATERIAL

Video
Report (Section 10) This is a short documentary about two climbers, but they don't climb mountains, they climb buildings. The documentary shows them climbing Coventry Cathedral.

VOCABULARY AND SPEAKING (SB p96)

The weather

> **NOTE**
> Before the lesson, you need to photocopy the World Weather Reports on p132 of this book to give to Student B for the information gap activity.

1 Ask your students to look at the weather symbols. Elicit words for symbols students already know and then get them to continue working in pairs to match the remaining symbols and words. If students have access to dictionaries, get them to look up words they don't know.
Go through the answers with the class.

> **Answers**
> cloudy, foggy, sunny, rainy, windy, snowy

The next part of this exercise is to practise which *pairs* of adjectives *commonly* go together to describe weather. This will vary in different countries according to the climate, for example it can be *warm and windy* in many climates but is only rarely so in Britain.

Ask your class to give you their ideas about British weather. (Everyone always has something to say about British weather!)

> **CULTURAL NOTES**
> 1 Despite London's reputation, the last big fog/smog (smoke + fog) was in 1957 when the Clean Air Act was passed!
> 2 There are lots of jokes about British weather. Can your students understand this one?
> *If you don't like English weather, wait ten minutes!*

You could have a mini-discussion comparing which pairs they think will often go together in Britain and which for the climate of their own country.

> **Sample answers** (for Britain)
> | | |
> |---|---|
> | cool and cloudy | cold and windy |
> | cool and rainy | warm and sunny |
> | cool and windy | hot and sunny |
> | cold and cloudy | cold and foggy |
> | dry and cloudy | cold and rainy |
> | wet and windy | cold and snowy |
>
> Also you often hear the pairs *warm and dry, cold and wet* together.

2 **T 12.6** Get students to look out of the window at the weather conditions. Either play the recording or model the questions yourself.

POSSIBLE PROBLEM

What … like? for descriptions always creates some difficulty because of the different use of *like*. You need to make two things very clear to your students:

1 It has nothing to do with the verb *like*. The Caution Box will help you do this.

2 The answer does *not* contain the word *like*.
  What's the weather like? It's sunny.
  NOT *It's like sunny.*

Ask your students to listen and write in the weather for today, yesterday, and tomorrow. Check their answers.

Answers and tapescript
A What's the weather like today?
B It's **snowy** and **it's very cold**.
A What was it like yesterday?
B Oh, it was **cold** and **cloudy**.
A What's it going to be like tomorrow?
B I think it's going to be **warmer**.

Read through the Caution Box with the students (see *Possible problem* above).

Practise the questions and answers in open pairs. Encourage falling intonation in the *wh-* questions.

3 This is an information gap activity. Ask your students to work in pairs. Tell Student A to look at the World Weather information on p96 of the Student's Book and give Student B the information you have photocopied from p132 of the Teacher's Book. (It is repeated to help you save paper when photocopying.)

Briefly check the pronunciation of the cities, focusing in particular on *Edinburgh* /ˈedɪnbrə/ and *Los Angeles* /lɒsˈændʒəlɪz/. Illustrate the activity by doing the first questions and answers about Athens and Berlin across the class. This is a good time to feed in the modifier *quite*, if you feel your students can cope with it. (Make sure they realize that this is *yesterday's* weather and therefore they need to use *was* in the questions and answers.)

Student A *What was the weather like in Athens?*
Student B *It was sunny and (quite) warm. 18 degrees.*

Get students to continue the activity in closed pairs. Go round and check as they do it.

Check the answers with the whole class. Get students to read out their answers as complete sentences, e.g. *It was sunny and (quite) warm in Athens yesterday. 18 degrees.*

Answers
World weather: noon yesterday

		°C	It was:
Athens	S	18	sunny and warm
Berlin	R	7	wet/rainy and cold
Bombay	R	31	rainy and hot
Edinburgh	C	5	cloudy and cold
Geneva	C	12	cloudy and cool
Hong Kong	S	29	sunny and hot
Lisbon	C	19	cloudy and warm
London	R	10	wet/rainy and cool
Los Angeles	Fg	21	foggy and warm
Luxor	S	40	sunny and very hot
Milan	Fg	19	foggy and warm
Moscow	Sn	−1	snowy and very cold
Oslo	Sn	2	snowy and cold

S = sunny	C = cloudy	Fg = foggy
R = rainy	Sn = snowy	

4 Get students to answer the questions about the weather report in pairs before checking with the whole class.

Answers
Luxor was the hottest. (Ask your students if they know where this is. It's in Egypt.)
Moscow was the coldest.
The month is in fact March. (Encourage a bit of discussion about this – it could be other months, but clearly, in Europe anyway, the season is either winter or early spring.)

ADDITIONAL MATERIAL

Workbook
Exercise 13 Writing postcards fits nicely after this vocabulary as it includes information about the weather. It could be done in class or for homework.

EVERYDAY ENGLISH (SB p97)

Making suggestions

NOTES
In order not to overload students, we have restricted the exponents in this section to: *shall* to ask for suggestions and make suggestions, and *Let's* to make a suggestion for everyone.
We also revise *will* for immediate decisions, which was introduced in the previous unit.

1 Focus attention on the two examples and then elicit a few more activities for good weather (*go for a walk, play tennis, gardening,* etc.) and some for bad weather (*read a book, do a jigsaw, play chess,* etc.) Students continue the two lists on their own and then compare their lists with a partner's. Ask for some feedback from the whole class and tell students that they will need their lists later.

2 **T 12.7** Tell students that they are going to hear the beginnings of two conversations, one for good weather and one for bad. Ask them to read and listen at the same time and complete B's suggestions.

> **Answers and tapescript**
> 1 **A** It's a lovely day! What shall we do?
>   **B** Let's **play tennis**!
> 2 **A** It's raining again! What shall we do?
>   **B** Let's stay **at home** and **watch a video**.

Then get students to listen and repeat in chorus. First focus on the question, and then practise the answer. Encourage good stress and intonation.

What shall we do?   /wɒt ʃəl wi duː/
Let's play tennis.   /lets pleɪ tenɪs/

Ask students to practise the conversations in pairs.

Read through the Caution Box with the whole class. In a monolingual class, you could ask students to translate the sentences.

3 Ask your students to work in pairs. Ask them first to find the 'good weather' lines and then the 'bad weather' lines. Then ask them to put each set in order to complete the conversations from exercise 2.

T 12.8 Play the recording and get students to check their answers. Play the recording again and get students to repeat, encouraging good stress and intonation. Get students to practise the conversations in closed pairs.

> **Answers and tapescript**
> 1 **A** It's a lovely day! What shall we do?
>   **B** Let's play tennis!
>   **A** Oh no! It's too hot to play tennis.
>   **B** Well, let's go to the beach.
>   **A** OK. I'll get my swimming costume.
> 2 **A** It's raining again! What shall we do?
>   **B** Let's stay at home and watch a video.
>   **A** Oh no! We watched a video last night.
>   **B** Well, let's go to the cinema.
>   **A** OK. Which film do you want to see?

4 Students continue to work in pairs. Ask them to look at the lists they made in exercise 1. Demonstrate the activity by asking for examples of a good weather and a bad weather activity and building the dialogues with the whole class. Get students to continue in pairs, using the activities in their lists. Monitor and check.

To round off the activity, you could either ask a couple of pairs to do their dialogues for the whole class, or record a few dialogues and play them for the class to correct any mistakes in the language and the pronunciation.

Don't forget!

Workbook Unit 12

Exercises 8 and 9 These bring together all the auxiliary verbs covered so far.

Exercises 10 and 11 These revise many items of vocabulary covered so far. They focus on word stress and phonetic transcription.

Exercise 12 Prepositions *from*, *like*, and *than*.

Word list

Remind your students of the Word list for this unit on p140. They could write in the translations, learn them at home, and/or write some of the words in their vocabulary notebook.

Pronunciation Book Unit 12

Video

There are two video sections that can supplement Units 11 and 12 of the Student's Book.

Report (Section 10) Climbers (You may have done this already after the reading.) It is a mini-documentary about people who climb buildings.

Situation (Section 11) The Dinner Party This is a short situation where Paola and David go to dinner at their friends' house.

> **EXTRA IDEAS UNITS 9–12**
> On pp133–134 of the Teacher's Book there are two additional activities – a reading text and a song.
>
> If you have time and feel that your students would benefit from it, you can photocopy it and use it in class. The reading exercise revises all the units so far, particularly Units 9–12. It could also be done for homework. The answers are on p155.
>
> You will find the song after the tapescript for Unit 12 on the Class Cassette/CD. Students choose the correct lines to complete the song, then listen and check their answers.

13

Question forms • Adverbs and adjectives
Describing feelings • Catching a train

How terribly clever!

Introduction to the unit

Question forms are the main target language of this unit. This is not a particularly new language area, as question forms have been introduced and practised throughout the book, but focusing on question forms allows a lot of language areas, especially tenses, to be pulled together and revised.

The theme of the unit is general knowledge, and reading stories. In the reading and listening section, students read a simplified story taken from the *Oxford Bookworms* series of readers. If you haven't already encouraged your students to read outside the coursebook, now is the time to start! Reading is one of the easiest, cheapest, and most pleasurable ways of learning a foreign language and there is a big range of simplified stories available in series of readers such as the *Oxford Bookworms*.

Language aims

Grammar – question forms All the *wh-* questions (*when, where, who, what, why, which*) except *whose*, and questions with *how* + adjective (e.g. *How old … ?*) and *how* + adverb (e.g. *How far … ?*) are revised. *What* + noun (*What languages … ?/What sort of … ?*) is also practised.

We 'drop in' three subject questions, *Who won … ?*, *What happens … ?* and *What happened … ?* in the quiz in the first presentation. The first of these is 'dropped in' in case students want to make such a question in exercise 3, where they are asked to think up some general knowledge questions of their own. The second two are 'dropped in' because they are needed to talk about stories in the *Reading and listening* section. We suggest that you do not embark on a detailed presentation of the difference between subject and object question forms. If students wonder (very sensibly) why *do/does/did* is not used in these questions, try to satisfy them with a quick explanation. Put on the board the sentences *Joe likes Betty. Betty likes Tim.* Ask these questions: *Who likes Betty? (Joe does.) Who does Betty like? (She likes Tim.)* to show them that the first question refers to the subject of the sentence, while the second one asks about the object of the sentence. Then tell them not to worry about it at this stage! In our experience, it would not further students to go too deeply into it at this level, or at all, unless they ask about it.

Adverbs and adjectives There are exercises to highlight the difference between adjectives and adverbs, and regular and irregular adverbs are presented and practised.

Vocabulary The vocabulary section focuses on describing feelings and highlights adjectives with both *-ed* and *-ing* endings. Students often find these confusing and so choose the wrong form.
Common mistakes
**I'm interesting in sport.*
**I was very boring.* (when the student meant to say *I was very bored!*)
**The problem is very worried.*

Everyday English The language used when catching a train is practised. This picks up on the stories in the *Reading and listening* section.

Workbook Question words are further consolidated and the question *Which one … ?* is introduced and practised.
There is further practice on adverbs and adjectives.
Noun and adjective suffixes are introduced, and *-ed* and *-ing* adjectives (*interested/interesting*) are further practised.
In the writing section, adjectives and adverbs are further practised, and students are invited to write a fairy story.

Notes on the unit

STARTER (SB p98)

This activity provides a quick review of the question words students have already met, without making them form complete questions. It also acts as a preview to the focus on stories later in the unit.

1 Demonstrate the activity with the whole class by asking students to match *When ... ?* and *Where ... ?* with the appropriate answer (*When ... ?* – 1991, *Where ... ?* – *Paris*). Students work in pairs and continue the activity. Check the answers with the whole class.

> **Answers**
>
> When ... ? – 1991.   Which ... ? – The red ones.
> Where ... ? – Paris.   How ... ? – By plane.
> What ... ? – Some roses.   How much ... ? – £25.
> Who ... ? – John.   How many ... ? – Six.
> Why ... ? – Because I love him.

2 Students look at the answers again and say what type of story it is (a love story). You could encourage students to make up a short story. Introduce Mary.

Sample story: *In 1991 Mary went to Paris by plane with John. He bought her six red roses because he loved her. The roses cost £25.*

A QUIZ (SB p98)

Question words

1 Students work in groups to answer the general knowledge quiz. Encourage discussion if/when students disagree about the answers. Elicit a range of answers to the quiz questions but do not confirm or reject students' ideas at this stage.

2 **T 13.1** Students listen and check their answers.

> **Answers and tapescript**
>
> 1 When did the first man walk on the moon?
>   In 1969.
> 2 Where are the Andes mountains?
>   In South America.
> 3 Who did Mother Teresa look after?
>   Poor people in Calcutta.
> 4 Who won the last World Cup?
>   France in 1998 (*sample answer*).
> 5 How many American states are there?
>   50.
> 6 How much does an African elephant weigh?
>   5–7 tonnes.
> 7 How far is it from London to New York?
>   6,000 kilometres.
> 8 How old was Princess Diana when she died?
>   36.
> 9 What languages do Swiss people speak?
>   German, French, Italian, and Romansch.
> 10 What did Marconi invent in 1901?
>   The radio.
> 11 What sort of music did Louis Armstrong play?
>   Jazz.
> 12 What happens at the end of *Romeo and Juliet*?
>   Romeo and Juliet kill themselves.
> 13 What happened in Europe in 1939?
>   The Second World War started.
> 14 Why do birds migrate?
>   Because the winter is cold.
> 15 Which was the first country to have TV?
>   Britain.
> 16 Which language has the most words?
>   English.

Play some of the questions again and ask students to focus on the intonation of the questions. Ask them whether the voice rises or falls at the end (the voices falls because these are all questions with a question word). If necessary, highlight this on the board by writing up the first two questions and adding the stress marks and intonation arrows:

When did the first man walk on the moon?

Where are the Andes mountains?

Drill the questions chorally and individually.

GRAMMAR SPOT

1 Ask students to underline the question words in the quiz. Remind them that some question words consist of two words. Check the answers.

> **Answers**
>
> 1 When ... ?   9 What ... ?
> 2 Where ... ?   10 What ... ?
> 3 Who ... ?   11 What ... ?
> 4 Who ... ?   12 What ... ?
> 5 How many ... ? 13 What ... ?
> 6 How much ... ? 14 Why ... ?
> 7 How far ... ?   15 Which ... ?
> 8 How old ... ?   16 Which ... ?

2 This exercise extends the focus on question formation to include *Yes/No* questions. Read the example with the whole class and then get students to continue making the questions working on their own. Tell them to use contracted forms where possible and not to write the answers at this stage. Students who finish early can check in pairs. Check the answers with the whole class.

> **Answers**
> 1 What's she wearing?
>   Is she wearing jeans?
> 2 Where does she work?
>   Does she work in the bank?
> 3 When's he leaving?
>   Is he leaving tomorrow?
> 4 Who did you visit?
>   Did you visit your aunt?
> 5 How did you come?
>   Did you come by taxi?
> 6 Why are they going to have a party?
>   Are they going to have a party?

3 Elicit the short answers for the two types of question in number 1 (*Jeans.* and *Yes, she is./No, she isn't.*) Students continue writing the answers, giving both a positive and negative answer to the *Yes/No* questions.

Check the answers with the whole class.

> **Answers**
> 1 Jeans.
>   Yes, she is /No, she isn't.
> 2 In the bank.
>   Yes, she does./No, she doesn't.
> 3 Tomorrow.
>   Yes, he is./No, he isn't.
> 4 My aunt.
>   Yes, I did./No I didn't.
> 5 By taxi.
>   Yes, I did./No I didn't.
> 6 Because it's her birthday. *(sample answer)*
>   Yes, they are./No they aren't.

Read Grammar Reference 13.1 on p133 together in class, and/or ask students to read it at home. Encourage them to ask you questions about it.

3 Students work in groups to write some more general knowledge questions. Allow adequate time for this. It might take students a while to get started. Go round the groups to ensure that the questions are well formed.

When they have a reasonable number of questions, ask the groups to put the questions to the rest of the class. You could make this activity into a team game and allocate points if time allows.

PRACTICE (SB p99)

Questions and answers

1 Demonstrate the activity by getting students to give you the correct question and answer, matching the question word and answer in A and C and choosing the correct question from B. (*Where did you go? To the shops.*) Explain that students will have to use some of the questions in B more than once. Students continue the activity, working in pairs.

Ask students for their answers before giving them the correct versions. This will allow you to see where students are going wrong.

> **Answers**
> Where did you go? To the shops.
> What did you buy? A new jacket.
> When did you go? This morning.
> Who did you go with? A friend from work.
> Why did you go? To buy some new clothes.
> Which one did you buy? The black, leather one.
> How did you go? We drove.
> How much did you pay? £120.99.
> How many did you buy? Only one.

If students have made a lot of mistakes, go back over the question words and how they relate to the answers. Then drill the questions and answers in open pairs, getting students to repeat in closed pairs if necessary.

> **POSSIBLE PROBLEM**
> If students get confused by the use of *one* in *Which one … ?*, *The black leather one* and *Only one*, explain that we say *Which one … ?* and *The black leather one* to avoid repeating the word *jacket*, and that *Only one* refers to the number one. This point is further practised in exercise 4 in the Workbook.

Listening and pronunciation

2 **T 13.2** Students listen and tick the sentence they hear. Let students check in pairs before you give the answers.

> **Answers and tapescript**
> 1 Why do you want to go?
> 2 Who is she?
> 3 Where's he staying?
> 4 Why didn't they come?
> 5 How old was she?
> 6 Does he play the guitar?
> 7 Where did you go at the weekend?

Asking about you

3 Demonstrate the activity by getting students to put the words in number 1 in the correct order (*Do you like learning English?*). Students continue the activity in pairs.

Check the answers with the whole class.

> **Answers**
> 2 What did you do last night?
> 3 How many languages does your mother speak?
> 4 When did you last go shopping?
> 5 Which football team do you support?
> 6 Did you come to school by car today?
> 7 How much do you weigh?
> 8 Who do you usually sit next to in class?
> 9 Why do you want to learn English?

4 Drill the questions around the class. Make sure that students use the correct intonation – falling on the *wh*-questions and rising on the *Yes/No* questions.

In pairs, students ask and answer the questions about themselves. Remind them that they can use short answers where appropriate. Monitor and check for correct intonation and for acceptable short answers.

> **Sample answers**
> 1 Yes, I do.
> 2 I went to the cinema.
> 3 Two (Spanish and French).
> 4 A week ago.
> 5 Manchester United.
> 6 No, I came by bus.
> 7 60 kilos.
> 8 Roberto.
> 9 Because I need it for my job.

ADDITIONAL MATERIAL

Workbook Unit 13
Exercises 1–5 Question forms including *What (sort)?*, *How (old)?*, *Which (one)?*

DO IT CAREFULLY! (SB p100)

Adverbs and adjectives

1 Focus on the first pair of sentences as an example. Elicit the answers (*bad* – adjective, *badly* – adverb). Students then work in pairs. Check the answers with the whole class.

> **Answers**
> 1 *bad* – adjective
>   *badly* – adverb
> 2 *carefully* – adverb
>   *careful* – adjective

> 3 *easy* – adjective
>   *easily* – adverb
> 4 *well* – adverb (point out that *well* is the irregular adverb of *good*)
>   *good* – adjective
> 5 *hard* – adjective
>   *hard* – adverb (This question is difficult, as *hard* is irregular.)

GRAMMAR SPOT

1 Read the sentences and the explanation about adjectives and adverbs as a class.

2 If necessary, put some adjectives that have regular adverbs on the board, e.g. *quick, bad, careful*. Include an example of an adjective ending in *-y*, e.g. *easy*. Elicit the adverbs and get students to tell you the rule.

> **Answers**
> We make regular adverbs by adding *-ly* to the adjective. If the adjective ends in *-y*, it changes to *-ily*.

3 Ask students to look back at exercise 1 and find the irregular adverbs. Check the answers.

> **Answers**
> *well* and *hard* are irregular.

Read Grammar Reference 13.2 on p133 together in class, and/or ask students to read it at home. Encourage them to ask you questions about it.

2 This activity focuses on adverbs that collocate with common verbs and phrases. Elicit adverbs that can go with *get up* as an example (*get up slowly/quietly/early/quickly*).

Students work in pairs and continue the activity. Remind them to decide which adverbs in the box are irregular. Check the answers with the whole class.

> **Answers**
> get up slowly/quietly/early/quickly
> walk slowly/quietly/fast/quickly/carefully
> work slowly/quietly/carefully/hard/fast/quickly
> run slowly/fast/quickly
> speak slowly/quietly/fast/quickly
> speak English slowly/fluently/fast/quickly
> pass the exam easily
> do your homework slowly/carefully/easily/fast/quickly
>
> *hard* and *fast* are irregular.

Order of adjectives/adverbs

1 Students put the word in brackets in the correct place in the sentences, changing the adjective to an adverb if necessary. Tell them that sometimes more than one answer is possible. Students can work in pairs, or alone and then check with a partner.

POSSIBLE PROBLEM

We do not overtly give the rules for the order of adverbs (front position, mid position, end position), because the rules are rather complicated. We do not suggest that you try to go into them at this stage. You could perhaps point out that adverbs usually follow the verb and object if there is one, whereas adjectives go before the noun (unlike many other languages). Otherwise let students see how they get on without rules, and simply correct any mistakes.

Answers
1 We had a holiday in Spain, but unfortunately we had **terrible** weather.
2 Maria dances **well**.
3 When I saw the accident, I phoned the police **immediately** (or I **immediately** phoned . . .).
4 Don't worry. Justin is a **careful** driver.
5 Jean-Pierre is a **typical** Frenchman. He loves food, wine, and rugby.
6 Please speak **slowly**. I can't understand you.
7 We had an **easy** test today.
8 We all passed **easily**.
9 You speak **good** English./You speak English **well**.

Telling a story

2 Focus on sentence 1 as an example with the whole class. Elicit a range of endings that will fit with the adverb *fortunately*, e.g. *I had a umbrella./we were inside./the rain didn't last long.*

Students continue working in pairs. Monitor and check if their answers fit with the adverbs given. Where possible, elicit a range of answers for each sentence that highlight the meaning of the adverb.

Answers
1 Fortunately, I had a umbrella./we were inside./the rain didn't last long.
2 Unfortunately, I couldn't go./I was ill./I was on holiday.
3 . . . suddenly the phone rang./I heard a loud noise./the dog started to bark.
4 Immediately, I called the police.

If you want to double-check that students have understood the adverbs, explain or translate them. You could get them to look up the definitions in dictionaries.

3 Ask students to look at the picture and describe what they can see.

T 13.3 Students listen to the story and number the adverbs in the correct order. Check the answers.

Answers and tapescript
8 quickly   3 carefully
4 quietly   1 suddenly
2 slowly   7 fortunately
5 immediately   6 really

T 13.3 It was about two o'clock in the morning, and . . . suddenly I woke up. I heard a noise. I got out of bed and went slowly downstairs. There was a light on in the living room. I listened carefully. I could hear two men speaking very quietly. 'Burglars!' I thought. 'Two burglars!' Immediately I ran back upstairs and phoned the police. I was really frightened. Fortunately the police arrived quickly. They opened the front door and went into the living room. Then they came upstairs to find me. 'It's all right now, sir,' they explained. 'We turned the television off for you!'

---

4 In pairs, students retell the story either one sentence at a time each, or one student first, then the other. Remind them to use the order of adverbs to help them.

Check it

5 Students work in pairs to correct the mistakes.

Answers
1 Where does Anna's sister live?
2 The children came into the classroom noisily.
3 What does *whistle* mean?
4 I always work hard.
5 Can you help me, please?
6 When is Peter going on holiday?

ADDITIONAL MATERIAL

Workbook Unit 13
Exercises 6 and 7 Adverbs

Describing feelings

1 Demonstrate the activity by getting students to find the correct picture for *bored* (5). Students match the rest of the feelings to the pictures.

Check the answers with the whole class.

Answers

bored	5	excited	3
tired	1	annoyed	2
worried	6	interested	4

Drill the pronunciation of the feelings, making sure that students pronounce *bored* and *tired* as one syllable – /bɔːd/, /taɪəd/.

2 Demonstrate the activity by getting students to find the correct reason for *bored* (*I am bored because I have nothing to do.*). Students continue the activity in pairs. Then check the answers with the whole class.

Answers
I am tired because I worked very hard today.
I am worried because I can't find my keys.
I am excited because I'm going on holiday tomorrow.
I am annoyed because I want to go to the party but I can't.
I am interested because we have a good teacher.

Focus attention on the Caution Box. Read the notes with the whole class. Using L1 if possible, explain that adjectives ending in -*ed* often describe a person's feeling or reactions, and that adjectives ending in -*ing* often describe the person or thing that provokes those feelings or reactions.

3 Focus on the pair of sentences in number 1 as an example (*Life in New York is very **exciting**. The football fans were very **excited**.*) Students complete the rest.

Check the answers with the whole class.

Answers
2 The marathon runners were very **tired**.
  That game of tennis was very **tiring**.
3 The child's behaviour was really **annoying**.
  The teacher was **annoyed** when nobody did the homework.
4 The news is very **worrying**.
  Everybody was very **worried** when they heard the news.

4 Drill the pronunciation of the pairs of adjectives in exercise 3, making sure students can clearly distinguish the -*ing* and -*ed* forms. Drill the example in the Student's Book chorally and individually.

Continue the activity by asking the following questions and getting students to respond with a suitable adjective in the correct form (sample answers are given in brackets). Elicit a range of answers by asking several students the same question.
Did you enjoy the last film you saw? (*Yes, it was interesting.*)

Why don't you run six kilometres every morning? (*Because it's tiring.*)
How do you feel after the lesson? (*A bit tired.*)
How do you feel before an exam? (*Very worried.*)
How do you feel if your friend is late? (*A bit annoyed.*)
Do you like football? (*No, it's very boring.*)
Do you like learning English? (*Yes, it's interesting, but a bit tiring.*)

ADDITIONAL MATERIAL

Workbook Unit 13
Exercises 8 and 9 Adjective suffixes, and -*ed*/-*ing* adjectives

READING AND LISTENING (SB p102)

A story in a story

Notice that in many of the exercises in this section, a lot of the questions are in the Present Simple, not the Past Simple. This use of the Present Simple is called the Historic Present, and it is common when talking about stories, films, etc. We do not suggest that you point this out to students, and don't worry too much if students want to reply using the Past Simple.

1 Demonstrate the activity by telling the class who told you stories when you were a child and what your favourite story was. Then get the students to continue talking about stories in pairs or small groups.

2 Focus attention on the first picture. Discuss the questions as a class. Of course, students won't know the answers for sure, but they can speculate.

Sample answer
The woman and the children are part of the same family. Perhaps the woman is the children's mother. The young man doesn't know the family.

3 **SUGGESTION**
We suggest that students read and listen at the same time to discourage them from worrying too much about unknown vocabulary. However, if you think that your students will be put off by coming across words they don't recognize, you could pre-teach/check the following items: *whistle, countryside, sheep, field, grass, behave, lake, save, ridiculous*.

As an alternative approach, you could ask students to read in silence, deal with any vocabulary queries they have, and then play the recording afterwards.

T 13.4 Students read and listen to part one of the story. Get them to compare the ideas they had about the characters in exercise 2.

4 Students answer the questions in pairs or small groups. (Question 7 revises *-ed/-ing* adjectives.) Check the answers with the whole class.

> **Answers**
> 1 The people on the train are three young children and their aunt, and a young man.
> 2 Cyril asks questions about sheep and grass in a field that he can see.
> 3 She tells the children a story because the man looks annoyed and she wants the children to be quiet.
> 4 The story is about a beautiful, good little girl who fell into a lake. People in the village saved her.
> 5 No, the children don't like the story.
> 6 The young man agrees with the children and he says that the aunt's story is ridiculous.
> 7 **The aunt:** tired, worried, boring
> **The children:** noisy, badly-behaved, tired, bored, annoying
> **The young man:** quiet, tired, annoyed

5 Focus attention on the pictures of Bertha. Work as a class and get students to predict what happens to Bertha from the pictures. Pre-teach/check key vocabulary from part two of the story: *well behaved, medals, king, palace, woods, wolf*. Accept any interpretation that students give at this stage, so that they can compare their ideas with the actual story.

6 **T 13.5** Students read and listen to part two and compare their version from exercise 5.

7 Check students understand the meaning of *moral* (important message or lesson) and also the use of *pay* (have a good result) in question 4. Students work in pairs and answer the questions.

> **Answers**
> 1 Both stories are about very good children, but in the aunt's story the good little girl survives, but in the young man's story she doesn't.
> 2 No, she doesn't, because it shows that to be very good does not always have a good result.
> 3 Yes, they do, because they like the idea of being good having a bad result.
> 4 It doesn't always pay to be good.

8 Students retell the story of Bertha working from the pictures on p103. Remind them to use the Past Simple tense to do this, but don't worry if they switch to the Present. Encourage them to add in any details they think relevant. (You could do this activity at the beginning of the next lesson if you think students have had enough of the story.)

Language work

This section revises adjectives and adverbs, and question words. If you are short of time, it could be done quickly in class or set for homework.

1 Elicit examples of adjectives and adverbs from paragraph 1 of the story about Bertha (adjectives – *long, little, well behaved, late, dirty, untidy, rude*; adverbs – *hard*). Students continue in pairs to find adjectives and adverbs from the story. (If time is short, you could get students to work in groups and focus on just one paragraph of the story, before exchanging answers with the rest of the class.) Remind them that adjectives can be in comparative or superlative forms.

> **Answers**
> **Paragraph 2**
> Adjectives: bored, pretty, smaller, young, good, late, polite, best
> Adverbs: horribly
> **Paragraph 3**
> Adjectives: young, good, best, clean, white, big, hungry, lovely
> Adverbs: —
> **Paragraph 4**
> Adjectives: young, heavy
> Adverbs: quickly, quietly, fast, easily
> **Paragraph 5**
> Adjectives: terrible, best
> Adverbs: —

2 Students write questions using the question words in the box. Go round and check that students have formed the questions correctly.

> **Sample questions**
> How many medals did Bertha win?
> What did the medals say?
> Why did Bertha go to the King's palace?
> Where did Bertha walk to get to the palace?
> How did the wolf move towards Bertha?
> What did the wolf do?

Students ask and answer questions across the class.

Catching a train

> **NOTE**
> You will need to photocopy the information on train times on p135 of the Teacher's Book.

1 Read the introduction as a class. (Bristol is a port in the south-west of England and Bristol Temple Meads is its main station. Oxford is a city in south central England.) If you have a map of Britain in your classroom it would be a nice idea to show your students where Oxford is in relation to Bristol.

Read the Caution Box with the whole class. If necessary, put a few times on the board to help students practise the 24-hour clock:

0645 = oh six forty-five
1219 = twelve nineteen
0835 = oh eight thirty-five
1127 = eleven twenty-seven

T 13.6 Students listen and complete the timetable. Check the answers.

Answers and tapescript

DEPARTURE TIME	ARRIVAL TIME
from Oxford	at Bristol Temple Meads
0816	**0946**
0945	**1114**
1040	**1208**

T 13.6
Trains from Oxford to Bristol Temple Meads. Monday to Friday.
Here are the departure times from Oxford and arrival times in Bristol.
0816 arriving 0946
0945 arriving 1114
1040 arriving 1208
11 . . .

2 **T 13.7** Students listen to the conversation and complete it. Play it once through first, then in sections so students have time to write. Check the answers.

Answers and tapescript
A = Ann B = clerk
A Good morning. (1) **Can you tell me** the times of trains (2) **from** Bristol (3) **back to** Oxford, please?
B Afternoon, evening? When (4) **do you want to come back**?
A About five o'clock this afternoon.
B About (5) **five o'clock**. Right. Let's have a look. There's a train that (6) **leaves at** 5.28, then there isn't (7) **another one** until 6.50.

A And (8) **what time do they** get in?
B The 5.28 gets into Oxford at 6.54 and the 6.50 (9) **gets in at 8.10**.
A Thanks a lot.

Students practise the conversation in pairs. If students have problems, let them listen to the recording and repeat the conversation, before practising again in pairs.

3 Explain that Ann is now at the ticket office. Students work in pairs to put the conversation in the right order.

T 13.8 Students listen and check.

Answers and tapescript
A = Ann C = clerk (2)
A Hello. A return to Bristol, please.
C Day return or period return?
A A day return.
C How do you want to pay?
A Cash, please.
C That's eighteen pounds.
A Here's a twenty-pound note.
C Here's your change and your ticket.
A Thank you. Which platform is it?
C You want platform 1 over there.
A OK, thanks very much. Goodbye.

Students practise the conversation in pairs. If students have problems, let them listen to the recording and repeat the conversation, before practising again in pairs.

4 Hand out the photocopied information on the train journeys from Oxford. Students work in pairs: A is the passenger and B is the clerk. A decides on a destination, asks for information about times, and then buys a ticket.

Get students to change roles after they have practised one full conversation.

Don't forget!

Workbook Unit 13
Exercise 10 Students read a fairy story. They are then invited to write a story of their own.

Word list
Remind your students of the Word list for this unit on p141. They could write in the translations, learn them at home, and/or write some of the words in their vocabulary notebook.

Pronunciation Book Unit 13

Video
This unit can be supplemented by the following video section, if you haven't already used it.
Situation (Section 9) *The Phone Box* This is a short situation where Paola phones British Airways to book her flight home.

14

Present Perfect + *ever, never, yet,* and *just*
At the airport

Introduction to the unit

This unit introduces one of the most difficult tenses for students of English to learn. The Present Perfect is one of the most commonly used tenses in English, especially spoken English, but its presentation has been deferred until Unit 14. This is because until students have understood the concept that the Past Simple refers to the definite past, they will not be able to grasp the idea that the Present Perfect refers to the indefinite past.

The theme of this unit is 'in my life', and various people's experiences in life are explored. There is a jigsaw reading activity where students read about three people who are 100 years old. This gives further exposure to and practice in the Present Perfect contrasted with the Past Simple, and also provides a springboard for discussing life and experiences. There is also a *Listening* section with the song *Leaving on a jet plane*. This links into the *Everyday English* section – *At the airport*.

Language aims

Grammar – Present Perfect In this unit, we introduce one of the main uses of the Present Perfect, that is, to refer to an experience some time in one's life. We also focus on another use (to refer to the present result of a past action) with the adverbs *yet* and *just.* We do not introduce at all the third main use of the Present Perfect, which is to refer to unfinished past (*I have been a teacher for ten years*), nor do we teach the Present Perfect Continuous.

The aim of this unit is to provide an introduction to the Present Perfect, but do not expect your students to master the area quickly! It takes a long time (and a lot of mistakes, correction, and re-teaching) before students feel confident with this tense.

> **POSSIBLE PROBLEMS**
> The Present Perfect tense presents students with problems mainly because a similar form of auxiliary verb *have* + past participle exists in many European languages, but it is used in a very different way. In English, the Present Perfect expresses the concept of an action happening at an indefinite time *before now,* and so it cannot be used when a definite time is given. The following sentences are examples of incorrect usage.
> **Common mistakes**
> **I have seen him last week.*
> **When have you been to the States?*
> **Did you ever try Chinese food?*
> **In my life I went to most countries in Europe, but I never went to Greece.*
>
> Note that American English can use the Past Simple with *just* and *yet.*
> *Did you do your homework yet? I just did it.*

Vocabulary There is no self-standing vocabulary section in this unit, but a lot of general vocabulary is recycled and extended through the structural input.

Everyday English Language useful in situations at an airport is introduced and practised.

Workbook The Present Perfect is further practised in contrast with Past Simple. The time expressions *ever* and *never, ago* and *last week, yet* and *just,* and *ever* or *ago* are consolidated with the appropriate tense. The difference between *been* and *gone* is presented.

In the Vocabulary section, phrasal verbs are revised or introduced.

The writing syllabus concludes with a focus on writing a thank-you letter.

Notes on the unit

STARTER (SB p106)

This section is a fun way of getting students into the topic of places people have visited.

1 Focus attention on first two flags and elicit the names of the corresponding countries. Students continue matching the countries and flags.

Check the answers with the whole class. If students have problems with the pronunciation of the countries, drill them chorally and individually.

Answers

1	Germany	7	Greece
2	Italy	8	Great Britain
3	Spain	9	the USA
4	France	10	Hungary
5	Brazil	11	Australia
6	Japan	12	Canada

2 Tell students the countries you have been to. Students then tick off the countries they have visited.

IN MY LIFE (SB p106)

Present Perfect + *ever* and *never*

POSSIBLE PROBLEMS

1 Students find the difference between *He's been to the States* and *He's gone to the States* quite confusing. This is dealt with in exercise 8 of the Workbook. We do not suggest that you attempt to sort this out at this stage of the presentation.

2 Students have already seen a Present Perfect form with the structure *have got*, but we do not suggest that you mention this at all. It would be very confusing for students, as *have got* expresses an essentially present-time concept.

1 **T 14.1** Students read and listen to the sentences. Remember that they will probably never have seen the Present Perfect tense before, and *been* will be unfamiliar. Using L1 if possible, explain that *been* is the past participle of the verb *to be*, and sometimes *to go*, and that *have been* is an example of the Present Perfect tense. Don't try to do a full presentation at this stage, but just explain that the sentences refer to the idea of 'some time in your life'.

Ask students to repeat the sentences on the recording (whether they are true for them or not). Do this chorally and individually, and correct mistakes carefully.

Now ask students to make similar sentences, saying which countries they have/haven't been to. Demonstrate this yourself first with true information about the countries you have visited. Then elicit examples from the whole class, so you can check students' accuracy in the use and pronunciation of the structure. Students continue the activity in groups. Monitor and check.

2 **T 14.2** This activity introduces the question form. Students read and listen to the conversation. They can practise saying each sentence, either after the recording or with you modelling each one. This exercise highlights the 'experience' use of the Present Perfect, and shows it in contrast to the Past Simple. Draw students' attention to the question form of the Present Perfect, then to *When did you go?* and ask what tense this is (Past Simple). Just name the tenses at this stage and do not try to explain the different uses. (These are given in the *Grammar Spot* on p107.)

Get students to ask you questions about countries you have been to, following the model in exercise 2. Encourage them to ask *When did you go?* and tell them.

Students continue in open pairs asking and answering about countries they have been to, and when. This might sound repetitive and laborious, but remember you are introducing students to a very new concept with the Present Perfect tense and they need practice with forming questions, answers, and negatives.

3 Students write down the names of four cities, and in pairs make similar conversations. Go round and check as they do this. Monitor for accuracy in the use and pronunciation of the two tenses.

4 This practises the third person singular for the first time, so students will need to make the change from *have* to *has*. Focus attention on the examples to highlight this and on the contracted form *'s = has*. Drill the examples chorally and individually. Ask three or four students to talk about their partner.

GRAMMAR SPOT

1 Read the notes with the whole class. Highlight the use of *ever* with the Present Perfect in the question form to mean 'at any time on your life'. Stress that we do not use *ever* in the answer.

2 Read the notes with the whole class. Highlight the use of the Past Simple to say exactly when something happened. Elicit other past time references that can be used with the Past Simple, e.g. *last month*, *a long time ago*, *yesterday*, etc.

3 Read the notes with the whole class and get students to complete the table. Check the answers.

Answers

	Positive	Negative	
I/You/We/They	**have**	**haven't**	been to Paris.
He/She/It	**has**	**hasn't**	

4 Students complete the sentences with *ever* or *never*. Check the answers.

Answers
Has he **ever** been to London?
He's **never** been to London.

If your students have a similar tense form in their language, and if you can use L1, you might like to make a brief comparison between the way L1 and English use the auxiliary verb *have* + past participle. Be careful, however! Keep it short, and as simple as possible, because it would be very easy to overload students with too much information at this early stage of their exposure to the Present Perfect.

Read Grammar Reference 14.1 on p134 together in class, and/or ask students to read it at home. Encourage them to ask you questions about it.

PRACTICE (SB p107)

Past participles

1 Remind students of the term 'past participle' and give an example: infinitive – *be*, past participle – *been*. Tell students that they will often be able to guess which infinitive a past participle comes from and focus on the example in the Student's Book *eaten* – *eat*.

Students write in the infinitives for the rest of the verbs. All the verbs are used in exercises that come later in this unit and they are very common verbs when talking about experiences. Get students to check in pairs before checking with the whole class.

Answers

eaten	**eat**	made	**make**	given	**give**
seen	**see**	taken	**take**	won	**win**
met	**meet**	driven	**drive**	had	**have**
drunk	**drink**	cooked	**cook**	stayed	**stay**
flown	**fly**	bought	**buy**	done	**do**

2 Ask students to look at the selection of verbs and decide which two are regular. Check the answers.

Answers
The two regular verbs are *cook* and *stay*.

3 Elicit the Past Simple forms of *eat* (*ate*) and *see* (*saw*) and get students to continue the list in pairs.

4 Refer students to the list of irregular verbs on p142 and get them to check their answers.

The life of Ryan

1 Focus attention on the photo of Ryan and elicit some basic information about him. Pre-teach/check the vocabulary in the list, especially: *foreign*, *company*, *jumbo jet*, *play*, *tractor*, *competition*.

Also check the following items from the recording: *first class/business class*, *politician*, *farm*, *lottery*.

T 14.3 Focus attention on the questionnaire and the column that relates to Ryan. Students listen and tick the things Ryan has done.

Ask students to check in pairs before they give you the answers.

Answers and tapescript
lived in a foreign country	✔
worked for a big company	✔
stayed in an expensive hotel	✗
flown in a jumbo jet	✔
cooked a meal for ten (or more) people	✗
met a famous person	✗
seen a play by Shakespeare	✔
driven a tractor	✔
been to hospital	✗
won a competition	✗

T 14.3 Yes, I've lived in a foreign country. In Japan, actually. I lived in Osaka for a year. I enjoyed it very much. I loved the food. And, yes, I have worked for a big company. I worked for Nissan, the car company, that's why I was in Japan. That was two years ago, then I got another job. Have I stayed in an expensive hotel? No, never – only cheap hotels for me, I'm afraid, but I have flown in a jumbo jet – four or five times, actually. Oh, I've never cooked a meal for a lot of people. I love food but I don't like cooking, sometimes I cook for me and my girlfriend but she likes it better if we go out for a meal! And I've never met a famous person – oh, just a minute, well not met but I've seen . . . er . . . I saw a famous politician at the airport once – oh, who was it? I can't remember his name. Er . . . I've only seen one Shakespeare play, when I was at school, we saw *Romeo and Juliet*. It was OK. I've driven a tractor though, I had a holiday job on a farm when I was 17. I enjoyed that. Good news – I've never been to hospital. I was born in hospital, of course, but that's different. Bad news – I've never won a competition. I do the lottery every week but I've never, ever won a thing!

2 First ask students to go through the questionnaire to produce some sentences about Ryan. This is to further practise the third person singular. Get some positive sentences first, then some negative ones. Drill them around the class, correcting carefully.

Read the instructions for this exercise. Ask for the positive sentences in the Present Perfect again. This time, where possible, you will ask follow-up questions in the Past Simple, which students will answer in the Past Simple. (You might want to play the recording again before you do this to remind students of the information about Ryan.) Although these questions and answers practise the Past Simple, you are also indirectly helping students with the Present Perfect, because you are showing them when the Present Perfect *isn't* applicable.

Follow-up questions (and the students' answers)
(Note that not all the Present Perfect sentences which students might produce from the questionnaire have a possible follow-up question in the Past Simple.)

Which city did he live in? (Osaka.)
Did he enjoy it? (Yes, he did.)
Did he like the food? (Yes, he did.)
What sort of company did he work for? (A car company.)
When did he work there? (Two years ago.)
Who did he see at the airport? (A famous politician.)
What play did he see? (*Romeo and Juliet.*)
When did he see *Romeo and Juliet*? (When he was at school.)
When did he drive a tractor? (When he worked on a farm.)
When did he work on a farm? (When he was seventeen.)
Where was he born? (In hospital.)

3 This activity gives further practice in the question forms. Drill the example questions in the Student's Book. Make sure students use rising intonation on the *Yes/No* questions in the Present Perfect and falling intonation on the *wh-* questions in the Past Simple. Students ask you the rest of the questions. Make sure they remember to include *ever* in the Present Perfect questions. Answer their questions.

4 Students ask a partner the same questions. Monitor and check for correct pronunciation and formation of the questions.

Students tell the class about their partner. Encourage them to give follow-up information in the Past Simple where appropriate, e.g. *Elena has flown in a jumbo jet. She flew from London to New York five years ago.*

ADDITIONAL MATERIAL

Workbook Unit 14
Exercises 1 and 2 Present Perfect and Past Simple
Exercise 3 and 4 Time expressions *ever* and *never*, and *ago* and *last week*

Present Perfect + *yet* and *just*

SUGGESTIONS

1 The concepts expressed by *yet* and *just* are very subtle and they are realized by different structures in different languages. We do not ask any questions in the *Grammar Spot* that test concept (only form), because the language required would be more complex than the target item itself. Students should be able to get the meaning through context and use, but you can check comprehension of the two adverbs by translating into L1. Get them to look up the adverbs in dictionaries.

2 It might be a good idea to do exercise 8 in the Workbook on *been* versus *gone* before you do the presentation of Present Perfect + *yet* and *just*. This clarifies the difference of meaning between *been* and *gone* as the two past participles of *to go*.

1 Read the introduction and the list as a class. Check that students understand *honeymoon* (a holiday after two people get married). Ask students what they know about places and activities in the list. Refer them to the photos of places and activities in London and use the background information below if necessary.

London
Buckingham Palace – London home of the British king/queen, built in 1703 for the Duke of Buckingham, but bought by George III in 1762. It was reconstructed in 1821–36 and a new front was added in 1913.
the Houses of Parliament – the building where the UK legislative assembly meets which incorporates sections of the medieval Palace of Westminster.
The London Eye – a huge Ferris wheel next to the Thames and near the Houses of Parliament.
Hyde Park – one of the largest open spaces in London which includes a boating lake called the Serpentine.
Harrods – the famous department store in Knightsbridge (London's luxury shopping area) where it is said that you can buy anything!
the Crown Jewels in the Tower of London – the crown, jewels, etc. that the British king/queen wears for ceremonies are housed in the Tower of London and both are popular tourist attractions.
double-decker bus – a bus with two levels. In London, these are red and have become a symbol of the city.

2 **T 14.4** Read the instructions as a class. Students listen to the recording and put a tick next to the things Marilyn and Rod have done.

Answers and tapescript

go to Buckingham Palace	✔
see the Houses of Parliament	✔
have a boat ride on the River Thames	✔
go on the London Eye	✔
walk in Hyde Park	
go shopping in Harrods	
see the Crown Jewels in the Tower of London	
travel on a double-decker bus	✔
go to the theatre	

T 14.4

M = Marilyn   J = Judy

M We're having a great time!

J Tell me about it! What have you done so far?

M Well, we've been to Buckingham Palace. That was the first thing we did. It's right in the centre of London! We went inside and looked around.

J Have you seen the Houses of Parliament yet?

M Yeah, we have. We've just had a boat ride on the River Thames and we went right past the Houses of Parliament. We saw Big Ben! Then we went on the London Eye. That's the big wheel near Big Ben. That was this morning. This afternoon we're going to take a taxi to Hyde Park and then go shopping in Harrods. Tomorrow morning we're going to see the Crown Jewels in the Tower of London.

J Wow! You're busy! And what about those big red buses? Have you travelled on a double-decker bus yet?

M Oh, yeah we took one when we went to Buckingham Palace. We sat upstairs. You get a great view of the city.

J Tomorrow's your last night. What are you going to do on your last night?

M Well, we're going to the theatre, but we haven't decided what to see yet.

J Oh, you're so lucky! Give my love to Rod!

M Yeah. Bye, Judy. See you soon!

GRAMMAR SPOT

POSSIBLE PROBLEMS

1 Remember that these questions focus on the form of *yet* and *just*, not the concept, because any questions that tested students' understanding of these items would be more complex than the items themselves. You need to make sure, probably via translation if possible, that students have understood them. Explain that *(not) yet* means *(not) before now* whereas *just* means *a short time before now*, using examples from the text or putting examples on the board.

2 Be prepared to prompt and help with the questions in the *Grammar Spot*, as students may find them hard.

Look at the questions in the *Grammar Spot* as a class.

1 Get students to think about which words they need to complete the gapped sentences. If necessary, refer them back to exercise 1 for the correct information and the past participles. Check the answers.

Answers

1 Have you **seen** the Crown Jewels yet?
2 We **haven't** been to the theatre yet.
3 We've just **had** a boat ride on the Thames.

Focus on the use of *yet* and *just* in the sentences and check comprehension (see *Possible problems* above).

2 Elicit the answers to the questions about the position of *yet* and *just*.

Answers

yet comes at the end of a sentence.
just comes before the past participle.

---

3 Allow students time to work out the rules for the use of *yet*. Then check the answer.

Answer

We can use *yet* only in questions and negative sentences, not in positive sentences.

Read Grammar Reference 14.2 on p134 together in class, and/or ask students to read it at home. Encourage them to ask you questions about it.

3 Refer students back to the list in exercise 1 on p108. Elicit the past participle of each of the verbs in the list, making sure students give *been* as the participle of *go*. Remind students that the ticks refer to things that Marilyn and Rod *have* done. Drill the examples in the Student's Book and elicit one or two more examples.

Students continue working in pairs, saying what Marilyn and Rod have and haven't done. Monitor and check for the correct form of the Present Perfect and the correct position of *yet*.

T 14.4 Play the recording again so that students can check their answers. Then check the answers with the whole class.

PRACTICE (SB p109)

I've just done it

1 Students haven't practised Present Perfect questions with *yet* or answers with *just*, so now's the time to do it! Drill the question and answer in the Student's Book, making sure students imitate the rising intonation on the question and the falling intonation on the answer. Students give one or two more examples in open pairs. Remind students that they will need to use different pronouns in their answers (*it/him/her/one*) and point out that some questions can have more than one answer.

Students continue working in closed pairs. Then check the answers with the whole class.

Answers
2 Have you done the shopping yet?
   Yes, I've just done it.
3 Have you washed your hair yet?
   Yes, I've just done/washed it.
4 Have you cleaned the car yet?
   Yes, I've just done/cleaned it.
5 Have you made the dinner yet?
   Yes, I've just made it.
6 Have you met the new student yet?
   Yes, I've just met him/her.
7 Have you had a coffee yet?
   Yes, I've just had one.
8 Have you given your homework to the teacher yet?
   Yes, I've just given it to her/him.
9 Have you finished the exercise yet?
   Yes, I've just finished it.

Check it

2 This exercise revises the grammar just covered in the unit. Students work in pairs to choose the correct sentence. Then check the answers with the whole class.

Answers
1 I saw John yesterday.
2 *(Note: both are possible here – 'Did you ever eat . . .' is common in American English.)*
3 Donna won £5,000 last month.
4 I've never drunk champagne.
5 Tom has never been to America.
6 Has your sister had the baby yet?
7 I haven't finished my homework yet.
8 Has she just bought a new car?

ADDITIONAL MATERIAL

Workbook Unit 14
Exercise 5 *yet*
Exercise 6 *yet* and *just*
Exercise 7 Check it
Exercise 8 *been* or *gone?*

READING AND SPEAKING (SB p110)

How to live to be 100

1 Demonstrate the activity by telling the class about the oldest person you know and a little about their lifestyle. Students work in pairs to answer the questions.

   Get a few students to tell the rest of the class about the person they know in a brief feedback session.

2 This exercise pre-teaches some of the important vocabulary in the texts. If students have access to dictionaries, they can look up the new words. Alternatively, get students to work in pairs or small groups to help each other categorize the vocabulary.

   Then check the answers with the whole class, giving a brief description of the illnesses if necessary. You could translate in a monolingual class.

Answers

Jobs	Illnesses
ambulance driver	pneumonia
engineer	heart attack
secretary	lung cancer
dressmaker	rheumatic fever

3 Get students to read the introduction. They should understand *centenarian* from the context, but if students ask, explain that it means a person who is 100 years old or older. Elicit students' reactions to the facts in the introduction and get them to compare with their own country. (If you have a multilingual group, you could get students to do this stage in pairs and then feed back to the whole class.) If students don't know the facts for their own country, encourage them to talk about previous generations of their own family and families they know.

4 Divide the class into groups of three. Get students to choose one of the texts and read about their character. If they have access to dictionaries, they can check any unknown vocabulary or they can ask you.

Get students to read through the questions and check they understand them. Pre-teach/check *give up smoking cigarettes* in question 6. Students answer the questions. They should be able to do this fairly easily, but if you feel they need to check with you before comparing the characters, put them in the same text groups and go through the answers.

Answers

Joyce Bews
1 She was a dressmaker.
2 She lives in Portsmouth.
3 She has been to Australia, America, and Spain.
4 She married, but she didn't have any children.
5 No, her husband died 10 weeks after they were married.
6 She gave up smoking cigarettes when she was 65 because her husband died of lung cancer.
7 Her husband died of lung cancer only 10 weeks after they married. Her niece is 75. Her youngest brother has just died, aged 90.
8 Only once. She had pneumonia when she was 20.
9 She likes fruit.
10 She doesn't like doing exercise.

Tommy Harrison
1 He was an engineer.
2 He lives in Bristol.
3 He has only been abroad once, to France during the War.
4 He married, but he didn't have any children.
5 No, his wife died 14 years ago.
6 He gave up smoking cigarettes 40 years ago and changed to a pipe.
7 His wife, Maude, died 14 years ago. His father lived until he was 99.
8 Only once. He had rheumatic fever just before the First World War.
9 He likes English breakfast – bacon, eggs, toast, and marmalade.
10 He likes dancing and swimming.

Alice Patterson-Smythe
1 She was an ambulance driver and a school secretary.
2 She lives in Norfolk.
3 She has been to Japan and America.
4 She married, and she had three children.
5 No, her husband died 25 years ago.
6 She gave up smoking cigarettes when she was 68 because she had a heart attack.
7 She has three children, six grandchildren and 11 great-grandchildren. Her grandson is a millionaire. He took her on his aeroplane to visit Tokyo, Los Angeles, and Miami. Her mother was 95 when she died.
8 She had a heart attack when she was 68.
9 She likes fruit and vegetables.
10 She likes golf and Latin American dancing.

5 Run through the pronunciation of the proper names in the texts that students might have problems with (*Maude* /mɔːd/, *Joyce* /dʒɔɪs/, *Portsmouth* /ˈpɔːtsməθ/, *Norfolk* /ˈnɔːfək/. Tell students they are going to work in their groups and compare the three people. Show them how they can do this in a meaningful way, rather than just read off their answers in order, e.g.
A Tommy was an engineer. What about Joyce and Alice?
B Joyce was a dressmaker.
C And Alice worked as an ambulance driver and a school secretary.

Remind students that they will need to use the Present Perfect, Past Simple, and Present Simple tenses in their answers. Students compare the three people in groups. Monitor and check how students manage with the different tenses, but don't expect them to get everything right. You can note down and give feedback on common errors, but bear in mind that the main focus is the information exchange through reading and speaking, not grammar accuracy.

What do you think?

Discuss the questions as a class.

Sample answers to first question
The three people have lived so long because . . .
they have exercised.
they have eaten well.
they haven't been ill very often.
they have given up smoking cigarettes.
they have stayed active.
they are from families who have lived a long time.

Ask students if they would like to live to be 100. Encourage them to give reasons why or why not.

LISTENING (SB p112)

Leaving on a jet plane

1 Ask students to mask the words of the song and to look at the picture. Get them to predict what the song might be about and accept any suggestions at this stage.

T 14.5 Ask students to close their books and listen to the song. Play the recording through once and then establish the general topic (the singer is leaving the person he/she loves and going to fly to another place). Get students to check if their predictions were correct.

2 Students open their books. Get them to read the words. Check students understand that *morn'* in line 5 is short for *morning, lonesome* in line 8 is often used in American English to mean *lonely, babe* in line 15 is a way of addressing the person you love, and that *There's* is used instead of *There are* in line 16 to help the number of syllables fit the line. Highlight that this is an example of a song 'bending' the rules of grammar.

Students work in pairs to decide which word is better in each gap. Remind them to look at the context, rhyme and also to think about grammar!

3 Play the recording again and get students to check their answers.

Answers and tapescript
All my (1) **bags** are packed, I'm ready to go
I'm standing here outside your (2) **door**,
I (3) **hate** to wake you up to say goodbye,
But the dawn is breaking,
It's early morn',
The taxi's (4) **waiting**,
He's blowing his (5) **horn**,
Already I'm so lonesome
I could (6) **die**.

Chorus
So kiss me and (7) **smile** for me,
(8) **Tell** me that you'll wait for me,
(9) **Hold** me like you'll never let me go,
'Cos I'm leaving on a jet plane,
I don't know when I'll be back again,
Oh babe, I hate to go.

There's so (10) **many** times I've let you down,
So many times I've (11) **played** around,
I tell you now
They don't mean a thing.
Every (12) **place** I go, I'll think of you,
Every song I sing, I'll sing for you,
When I (13) **come** back,
I'll wear your wedding (14) **ring**.

Chorus

If students want to hear the song again, play the recording and encourage them to sing along. If you have time and students seem keen, you could get them to talk about saying goodbye and any experiences they have had (e.g. leaving home to get married/go to university, leaving a job/company, leaving a person you love, etc.)

At the airport

1 Students read the sentences and then put them in the correct order, working in pairs or small groups.

Check the answers with the whole class.

Answers
5   You wait in the departure lounge.
7   You board the plane.
2   You get a trolley for your luggage.
1   You arrive at the airport.
3   You check in your luggage and get a boarding pass.
4   You go through passport control.
6   You check the departures board for your gate number.

---

2 **T 14.6** Focus attention on the chart and check students understand the headings. Tell students to listen carefully and complete the chart with the missing information. Play the recording and get students to check in pairs. If necessary, play the recording again to let students complete their answers.

Check the answers with the whole class.

Answers

Flight Number	Destination	Gate number	Remark
BA 516	Geneva	4	LAST CALL
SK 832	**Frankfurt**	–	DELAYED **one hour**
AF 472	**Amsterdam**	17	NOW BOARDING GATE **17**
LH 309	**Miami**	32	NOW BOARDING GATE **32**
VS 876	**New York**	–	WAIT IN LOUNGE

T 14.6
British Airways flight BA 516 to Geneva boarding at gate 4, last call. Flight BA 516 to Geneva, last call. Scandinavian Airlines flight SK 832 to Frankfurt is delayed one hour. Flight SK 832 to Frankfurt, delayed one hour. Air France flight 472 to Amsterdam is now boarding at gate 17. Flight AF 472 to Amsterdam, now boarding, gate 17.
Lufthansa flight 309 to Miami is now boarding at gate 32. Flight LH 309 to Miami, now boarding, gate 32. Virgin Airlines flight to New York, VS 876 to New York. Please wait in the departure lounge until a further announcement. Thank you. Passengers are reminded to keep their hand luggage with them at all times.

---

3 Students read the conversations in exercise 4 through quickly and decide who the people are and where they are. Get students to compare in pairs before checking the answers with the whole class.

Answers

1 Two passengers in the departure lounge
2 Check-in assistant and passenger at the check-in desk
3 Rod and Marilyn meeting Marilyn's sister, Judy, in the arrival hall
4 Boyfriend/Girlfriend talking to girlfriend/boyfriend at the departure gate

4 Students complete the conversations with the correct question. Get students to check in pairs.

T 14.7 Play the recording and get students to check their answers.

Answers and tapescript
1 A Listen! . . . BA516 to Geneva. That's our flight.
  B **Did the announcement say gate 4 or 14?**
  A I couldn't hear. I think it said 4.
  B Look! There it is on the departure board. It *is* gate 4.
  A OK. Come on! Let's go.

2 A Can I have your ticket, please?
  B Yes, of course.
  A Thank you. How many suitcases have you got?
  B Just one.
  A And **have you got much hand luggage**?
  B Just this bag.
  A That's fine.
  B Oh . . . can I have a seat next to the window?
  A Yes, that's OK. Here's your boarding pass. Have a nice flight!

3 A Rod! Marilyn! Over here!
  B Hi! Judy! Great to see you!
  A It's great to see you too. You look terrific! **Did you have a good honeymoon?**
  B Fantastic. Everything was fantastic.
  A Well, you haven't missed anything here. Nothing much has happened at all!

4 A There's my flight. It's time to go.
  B Oh no! It's been a wonderful two weeks. I can't believe it's over.
  A I know. **When can we see each other again?**
  B Soon, I hope. I'll write every day.
  A I'll phone too. Goodbye.
  B Goodbye. Give my love to your family.

Students practise the conversations with a partner. If necessary, play the recording again and get students to repeat before practising in pairs.

5 Give students time to decide their roles for each conversation. Encourage them to modify the information in the conversations where possible, e.g.
conversation 1 – different flight numbers, destinations, and gate numbers
conversation 2 – different number of suitcases and lots of hand luggage

conversation 3 – different people, e.g. friends meeting other friends after a holiday, husband meeting wife after a business trip
conversation 4 – different people saying goodbye, e.g. two business colleagues, two teenagers

Be prepared to feed in the language students might need for the characters and contexts they choose. Get students to act out one conversation each for the whole class. If possible, record the conversations and then play them back for students to comment on and correct.

Don't forget!

Workbook Unit 14
Exercise 9 Vocabulary – phrasal verbs
Exercise 10 The writing syllabus concludes with a focus on writing a thank-you letter. The context reintroduces a character from Unit 2 of the Student's Book, Dorita, who is writing a thank-you letter to her flatmates. Students are then invited to write a thank-you letter to someone who has looked after them.

Word list
Remind your students of the Word list for this unit on p141. They could write in the translations, learn them at home, and/or write some of the words in their vocabulary notebook.

Video
There are two video sections that can supplement this unit.
Report (Section 4) *Heathrow Airport* If you haven't already used this section after Unit 6, this section links in thematically with the end of Unit 14.
Situation (Section 12) *Cappuccino* Paola spends her last day with David in Bath, before going back to Italy.

Pronunciation Book Unit 14

EXTRA IDEAS UNITS 13–14

On pp136–7 of the Teacher's Book there are two additional activities: a reading text and a song. If you have time and feel that your students would benefit from them, you can photocopy them and use them in class. The reading exercise revises Units 13–14 and could also be done for homework. Activities to exploit the reading are provided, and the answers are on p156.

You will find the song after Unit 14 on the Class Cassette/CD. Students decide what is missing from several words which end in *-in'*, then listen and complete the songs with the words they hear.

Photocopiable material

Unit 2 **Practice 1** (SB p13)
Identity card for Student A

Surname	_Binchey_
First name	
Country	_Ireland_
Job	
Address	_82, Hill Road, Dublin_
Phone number	
Age	_47_
Married?	

Surname	_Binchey_
First name	
Country	_Ireland_
Job	
Address	_82, Hill Road, Dublin_
Phone number	
Age	_47_
Married?	

Surname	_Binchey_
First name	
Country	_Ireland_
Job	
Address	_82, Hill Road, Dublin_
Phone number	
Age	_47_
Married?	

Surname	_Binchey_
First name	
Country	_Ireland_
Job	
Address	_82, Hill Road, Dublin_
Phone number	
Age	_47_
Married?	

Unit 2 **Practice 4** (SB p13)
Identity card for Students A and B

Student A

Name	
Country/town	
Age	
Job	
Phone number	
Married?	

Student B

Name	
Country/town	
Age	
Job	
Phone number	
Married?	

Student A

Name	
Country/town	
Age	
Job	
Phone number	
Married?	

Student B

Name	
Country/town	
Age	
Job	
Phone number	
Married?	

Extra ideas Units 1–4 Revision

Reading

1   A magazine called *Weekend* interviewed a politician, Roberta Tomlinson. Read about her.

2   Complete the questions or answers in the interview with Roberta Tomlinson.

   1   **A** What's your name?
      B Roberta Tomlinson.

   2   **A** _____ ?
      B T – O – M – L – I – N – S – O – N.

   3   **A** Where are you from?
      B _____ .

   4   **A** _____ ?
      B I'm forty-three.

   5   **A** Are you married?
      B _____ .

   6   **A** _____ ?
      B Andrew.

   7   **A** What does your husband do?
      B _____ .

   8   **A** Do you have any children?
      B _____ .

   9   **A** _____ ?
      B Yes. I have two brothers.

  10   **A** Do you enjoy your work?
      B _____ ,

  11   **A** _____ ?
      B Because I meet a lot of people.

  12   **A** Where do you live?
      B _____ .

  13   **A** Do you have a garden?
      B _____ .

  14   **A** _____
         in your free time?
      B Having friends for dinner, going to the theatre, and listening to music.

Meet ...
Roberta Tomlinson

Me and my family

I'm from Glasgow, in Scotland, and I'm forty-three years old. I'm married, and my husband's name is Andrew. He's a teacher in a school for blind children. We have three children – two boys and a girl. I have two brothers. They still live in Scotland.

Me and my work

I'm a Member of Parliament, so I work in London for part of the week and in Scotland for the rest. I enjoy my work very much. I like it because I meet a lot of people and it is my job to help them. I work about fifty or sixty hours a week.

Me and my home

We have a flat in London, but my home is Glasgow, and we have a large house there. There are about twelve rooms, and the house is like a hotel. So many people come and go! We have a garden where we grow fruit and vegetables.

Me and my free time

Well, I have very little free time, but when I can, I like having friends for dinner. We sit, eat, drink, and talk for hours! I also enjoy the theatre, and I love the Edinburgh Festival, which takes place in August. I like all kinds of music but especially folk music.

Song

Complete the song with the words you hear.

Colours
DONOVAN LEITCH

(1) _____ is the colour of my true love's hair
(2) _____ when we rise
(3) _____ when we rise
That's the time, that's the time (4) _____

(5) _____ is the colour of the sparklin' corn
(6) _____ when we rise
(7) _____ when we rise
That's the time, that's the time I love the best

Mellow is the feelin' that I get
When I see her mm-hmm
When I see her uh-huh
That's the time, that's the time (8) _____

Freedom is a (9) _____ I rarely use
Without thinkin' mm-hmm
Without thinkin' mm-hmm
Of the (10) _____ when I've been loved

Complete the song with the words you hear.

Colours
DONOVAN LEITCH

(1) _____ is the colour of my true love's hair
(2) _____ when we rise
(3) _____ when we rise
That's the time, that's the time (4) _____

(5) _____ is the colour of the sparklin' corn
(6) _____ when we rise
(7) _____ when we rise
That's the time, that's the time I love the best

Mellow is the feelin' that I get
When I see her mm-hmm
When I see her uh-huh
That's the time, that's the time (8) _____

Freedom is a (9) _____ I rarely use
Without thinkin' mm-hmm
Without thinkin' mm-hmm
Of the (10) _____ when I've been loved

Unit 5 **Practice 1 and 2** (SB p37)

Student A

Student B

Alternative to roleplay

A = Interviewer   B = Alexandra or Lukas

A Hello, _____ ! Can I _____ you a few questions?

B Yes, of course.

A First of all, how old _____ you?

B I'm _____ .

A And do you _____ to school?

B Yes, I …

A And _____ do you live?

B I live in … with …

A _____ you born in _____?

B No, I _____ . I …

A That's interesting. And were you special when you _____ very young?

B Well, perhaps. You see I could …

A I can't believe it! Tell me, do you _____ much free time?

B No, I _____ , because I …

A Oh! And do you _____ to different countries?

B Yes, last year I …

A Thank you very much. That's all very interesting. Good luck in the future!

Alternative to roleplay

A = Interviewer   B = Alexandra or Lukas

A Hello, _____ ! Can I _____ you a few questions?

B Yes, of course.

A First of all, how old _____ you?

B I'm _____ .

A And do you _____ to school?

B Yes, I …

A And _____ do you live?

B I live in … with …

A _____ you born in _____?

B No, I _____ . I …

A That's interesting. And were you special when you _____ very young?

B Well, perhaps. You see I could …

A I can't believe it! Tell me, do you _____ much free time?

B No, I _____ , because I …

A Oh! And do you _____ to different countries?

B Yes, last year I …

A Thank you very much. That's all very interesting. Good luck in the future!

Alternative to roleplay

A = Interviewer   B = Alexandra or Lukas

A Hello, _____ ! Can I _____ you a few questions?

B Yes, of course.

A First of all, how old _____ you?

B I'm _____ .

A And do you _____ to school?

B Yes, I …

A And _____ do you live?

B I live in … with …

A _____ you born in _____?

B No, I _____ . I …

A That's interesting. And were you special when you _____ very young?

B Well, perhaps. You see I could …

A I can't believe it! Tell me, do you _____ much free time?

B No, I _____ , because I …

A Oh! And do you _____ to different countries?

B Yes, last year I …

A Thank you very much. That's all very interesting. Good luck in the future!

Alternative to roleplay

A = Interviewer   B = Alexandra or Lukas

A Hello, _____ ! Can I _____ you a few questions?

B Yes, of course.

A First of all, how old _____ you?

B I'm _____ .

A And do you _____ to school?

B Yes, I …

A And _____ do you live?

B I live in … with …

A _____ you born in _____?

B No, I _____ . I …

A That's interesting. And were you special when you _____ very young?

B Well, perhaps. You see I could …

A I can't believe it! Tell me, do you _____ much free time?

B No, I _____ , because I …

A Oh! And do you _____ to different countries?

B Yes, last year I …

A Thank you very much. That's all very interesting. Good luck in the future!

Student A

Did you know that ...

... Vincent van Gogh sold only two of his paintings while he was alive.

... the actress Shirley Temple was a millionaire before she was ten.

... Shakespeare spelled his name in eleven different ways.

... in 1979 it snowed in the Sahara Desert.

... King Louis XIV of France had a bath only three times in his life.

... the American President George Washington grew marijuana in his garden.

Student A

Did you know that ...

... Vincent van Gogh sold only two of his paintings while he was alive.

... the actress Shirley Temple was a millionaire before she was ten.

... Shakespeare spelled his name in eleven different ways.

... in 1979 it snowed in the Sahara Desert.

... King Louis XIV of France had a bath only three times in his life.

... the American President George Washington grew marijuana in his garden.

Student B

Did you know that ...

... it took 1,700 years to build the Great Wall of China.

... King Henry VIII of England had six wives.

... Walt Disney used his own voice for the character of Mickey Mouse.

... Shakespeare and the Spanish novelist Cervantes both died on the same day, 23 April 1616.

... King Francis I of France bought the painting *The Mona Lisa* to put in his bathroom.

... when Shakespeare was alive, there were no actresses, only male actors.

Student B

Did you know that ...

... it took 1,700 years to build the Great Wall of China.

... King Henry VIII of England had six wives.

... Walt Disney used his own voice for the character of Mickey Mouse.

... Shakespeare and the Spanish novelist Cervantes both died on the same day, 23 April 1616.

... King Francis I of France bought the painting *The Mona Lisa* to put in his bathroom.

... when Shakespeare was alive, there were no actresses, only male actors.

Extra ideas Units 5–8 Revision

Reading and speaking

1 Work in groups. How good is your memory? Answer the questions.
   1 When is your parents' wedding anniversary?
   2 What did you have to eat last night?
   3 Where were you ten days ago? What did you do that day?
   4 Where were the Olympic Games in 1996?
   5 When was your mother born?
   6 How many phone numbers can you remember?

2 Read the newspaper article about Dominic O'Leary, the man with the best memory in the world.

3 Answer the questions.
   1 What are some of the things Dominic can remember?
   2 How did he become world champion?
   3 Was he good at school? Why not?
   4 What did his teachers say about him?
   5 When did he start to improve his memory? What did he see?
   6 Why isn't he popular with casino managers?
   7 How many clubs did he visit with the interviewers?
   8 How many clubs did he play in? Why?
   9 What do you think of Dominic's suggestions for a good memory?

   Try his ideas to remember some words in English!

4 Here are the answers to some questions. Write in the questions.
   1 _____ ?
     Wednesday.
   2 _____ ?
     Last October.
   3 _____ ?
     Eight hundred pounds a day.
   4 _____ ?
     She's a clothes designer.
   5 _____ ?
     Seven hundred and fifty pounds.
   6 _____ ?
     He likes number games, crosswords, writing music, and playing the piano.

5 There are a lot of numbers in the article. What do these numbers refer to?
   Example
   1876   *April 21, 1876 was a Wednesday.*
   1 35   3 £1,000   5 £1,250
   2 34   4 7   6 5

WORLD CHAMPION MEMORY MAN

THIS IS DOMINIC O'LEARY, the man with the best memory in the world. He can tell you the day of any date in any year. What day was April 21, 1876? 'Wednesday,' says Dominic. He can remember the teams and the scores of every football match in every World Cup. And he became world champion memory man when he remembered the order of thirty-five packs of playing cards!

At school, Dominic was a pupil who couldn't remember his lessons. 'My maths and English teachers said I was stupid because I could never remember what they taught me.' But four years ago he saw a programme on television which showed people how to improve their memory, and last October he became world champion. 'I remembered the order of thirty-five packs of cards,' said Dominic. 'It was quite easy.'

Dominic, 34, can earn £800 a day on European TV programmes. He lives with his wife, Alison, a clothes designer, in a small village near Bath, and he is the manager of an office cleaning company.

WINNING

Casino managers don't want Dominic to visit their casinos, because he can remember every card. 'I played as a professional gambler for a few months, and I won £1,000 a night, but then the managers asked me to leave.'

We went with Dominic to seven clubs in London and Brighton. He started with £500, and four hours later, he had £1,250 in his pocket. He won £750.

He played in just three clubs for four hours. The other four clubs knew his face and didn't want him to play.

In his free time, Dominic loves number games and crosswords, writing music, and playing the piano. He says children can learn to improve their memory from the age of five. 'Then they can do anything,' says Dominic.

HOW TO IMPROVE YOUR MEMORY
Dominic says anyone can have a good memory. These are his suggestions.

1 When you go to bed, remember everything you did that day.
2 Remember things in pictures, not words. 'Words are difficult to remember, but pictures are easy.' For example, if you want to remember the name Kate, think of a cat. For the number 8814, think of two snowmen, a tree and a bird.
3 If you forget something, remember where you were when you *could* remember it.

Song

Choose the correct words to complete the song. Listen and check.

Stevie Wonder
I Just Called To Say I Love You

• •

No New Year's (1)_____ to   *Day/Eve*
  celebrate,
No chocolate covered candy
  (2)_____ to give away,   *smiles/hearts*
No first of spring, no song to
  (3)_____ ,   *play/sing*
In fact here's just another
  ordinary (4)_____ .   *day/time*

No April rain, no (5)_____   *flowers/colours*
  bloom,
No (6)_____ Saturday   *wedding/birthday*
  within the month of June.
But what it is is something
  (7)_____ ,   *blue/true*
Made up of these three
  (8)_____ that I must say   *lines/words*
  to you

Chorus

I just called to say I love you
I just called to say how much
  I (9)_____   *care/know*
I just called to say I love you,
And I (10)_____ it from the   *mean/give*
  bottom of my heart.

No summers high, no   *warm/hot*
  (11)_____ July
No harvest (12)_____ to   *sun/moon*
  light one tender August night
No autumn breeze, no falling
  (13)_____   *leaf/leaves*
Not even time for birds to
  (14)_____ to southern skies   *fly/go*

No Libra sun, no hallowe'en
No giving (15)_____ to all
  the Christmas joy you bring   *thanks/presents*
But what it is, though old, so new
To fill your (16)_____ like
  no three words could ever do.   *heart/time*

Chorus

Choose the correct words to complete the song. Listen and check.

Stevie Wonder
I Just Called To Say I Love You

• •

No New Year's (1)_____ to   *Day/Eve*
  celebrate,
No chocolate covered candy
  (2)_____ to give away,   *smiles/hearts*
No first of spring, no song to
  (3)_____ ,   *play/sing*
In fact here's just another
  ordinary (4)_____ .   *day/time*

No April rain, no (5)_____   *flowers/colours*
  bloom,
No (6)_____ Saturday   *wedding/birthday*
  within the month of June.
But what it is is something
  (7)_____ ,   *blue/true*
Made up of these three
  (8)_____ that I must say   *lines/words*
  to you

Chorus

I just called to say I love you
I just called to say how much
  I (9)_____   *care/know*
I just called to say I love you,
And I (10)_____ it from the   *mean/give*
  bottom of my heart.

No summers high, no   *warm/hot*
  (11)_____ July
No harvest (12)_____ to   *sun/moon*
  light one tender August night
No autumn breeze, no falling
  (13)_____   *leaf/leaves*
Not even time for birds to
  (14)_____ to southern skies   *fly/go*

No Libra sun, no hallowe'en
No giving (15)_____ to all
  the Christmas joy you bring   *thanks/presents*
But what it is, though old, so new
To fill your (16)_____ like
  no three words could ever do.   *heart/time*

Chorus

Millionaire A

4 houses

30 cars – 10 Jaguars,
10 Porsches, and
10 Ferraris

100 Arab horses

5 boats

8 gold watches

50 gold and
diamond rings

10 servants

50 million dollars

Millionaire B

5 houses – two in
France, one in Miami,
one in the Caribbean,
and a castle in Scotland

50 cars –
10 Lamborghinis,
15 Mercedes-Benz,
and 25 Rolls-Royces

275 Arab horses

12 boats

18 gold watches

80 platinum and
diamond rings

25 servants

150 million dollars

Millionaire A

4 houses

30 cars – 10 Jaguars,
10 Porsches, and
10 Ferraris

100 Arab horses

5 boats

8 gold watches

50 gold and
diamond rings

10 servants

50 million dollars

Millionaire B

5 houses – two in
France, one in Miami,
one in the Caribbean,
and a castle in Scotland

50 cars –
10 Lamborghinis,
15 Mercedes-Benz,
and 25 Rolls-Royces

275 Arab horses

12 boats

18 gold watches

80 platinum and
diamond rings

25 servants

150 million dollars

Millionaire A

4 houses

30 cars – 10 Jaguars,
10 Porsches, and
10 Ferraris

100 Arab horses

5 boats

8 gold watches

50 gold and
diamond rings

10 servants

50 million dollars

Millionaire B

5 houses – two in
France, one in Miami,
one in the Caribbean,
and a castle in Scotland

50 cars –
10 Lamborghinis,
15 Mercedes-Benz,
and 25 Rolls-Royces

275 Arab horses

12 boats

18 gold watches

80 platinum and
diamond rings

25 servants

150 million dollars

Millionaire A

4 houses

30 cars – 10 Jaguars,
10 Porsches, and
10 Ferraris

100 Arab horses

5 boats

8 gold watches

50 gold and
diamond rings

10 servants

50 million dollars

Millionaire B

5 houses – two in
France, one in Miami,
one in the Caribbean,
and a castle in Scotland

50 cars –
10 Lamborghinis,
15 Mercedes-Benz,
and 25 Rolls-Royces

275 Arab horses

12 boats

18 gold watches

80 platinum and
diamond rings

25 servants

150 million dollars

Unit 12 **The weather 3** (SB p96)

WORLD WEATHER: NOON YESTERDAY

		°C
Athens	S	18
Berlin	___	___
Bombay	R	31
Edinburgh	___	___
Geneva	C	12
Hong Kong	___	___
Lisbon	C	19
London	___	___
Los Angeles	Fg	21
Luxor	___	___
Milan	Fg	19
Moscow	___	___
Oslo	Sn	2

S = sunny
Fg = foggy
Sn = snowy
C = cloudy
R = rainy

WORLD WEATHER: NOON YESTERDAY

		°C
Athens	S	18
Berlin	___	___
Bombay	R	31
Edinburgh	___	___
Geneva	C	12
Hong Kong	___	___
Lisbon	C	19
London	___	___
Los Angeles	Fg	21
Luxor	___	___
Milan	Fg	19
Moscow	___	___
Oslo	Sn	2

S = sunny
Fg = foggy
Sn = snowy
C = cloudy
R = rainy

WORLD WEATHER: NOON YESTERDAY

		°C
Athens	S	18
Berlin	___	___
Bombay	R	31
Edinburgh	___	___
Geneva	C	12
Hong Kong	___	___
Lisbon	C	19
London	___	___
Los Angeles	Fg	21
Luxor	___	___
Milan	Fg	19
Moscow	___	___
Oslo	Sn	2

S = sunny
Fg = foggy
Sn = snowy
C = cloudy
R = rainy

WORLD WEATHER: NOON YESTERDAY

		°C
Athens	S	18
Berlin	___	___
Bombay	R	31
Edinburgh	___	___
Geneva	C	12
Hong Kong	___	___
Lisbon	C	19
London	___	___
Los Angeles	Fg	21
Luxor	___	___
Milan	Fg	19
Moscow	___	___
Oslo	Sn	2

S = sunny
Fg = foggy
Sn = snowy
C = cloudy
R = rainy

Extra ideas Units 9–12 Revision

Vocabulary

The following words are either flowers or colours. Put them into the correct column. If you have a dictionary, use it to check new words.

tulip   pink   orange   daffodil   grey

rose   red   gold   white   snowdrop

yellow   primrose   brown

Flowers	Colours

The Garden that Moved House!

Artist Verena Devoy loves gardening. It is her passion. Until three days ago she lived in a lovely little thatched cottage in a village near Cambridge. She spent ten years and thousands of pounds to make her garden there beautiful. She had flowers and plants for every season of the year.

In autumn, big orange chrysanthemums grew next to the gold of the trees and bushes. In winter, little white snowdrops grew in the grass and under the trees. In spring there were bright yellow daffodils all over her front lawn and tulips and primroses next to the path. And summer! Summer was the prettiest season of all! She bought hundreds of roses to fill every part of the garden: she bought climbing roses to put round the windows and doors, pink roses for the front garden, and red and white roses for the back. A lot of people came to the village especially to see Verena's garden. It was more beautiful than the park.

Then last summer she decided that she would like to move to a bigger house. It was easy to sell her beautiful cottage. Mr and Mrs Grey from London came to see it. **'We fell in love with it immediately,** especially the garden – we couldn't believe the colours of the roses. We wanted to move from London because we didn't have a garden there.'

Of course Mr and Mrs Grey bought the cottage and at the end of the summer they moved from London. They arrived at the cottage.

'There was no garden! There was a brown field with some stones and rocks. There weren't any flowers or trees and there wasn't any grass! It looked terrible! We couldn't believe our eyes!'

But it was true! Verena Devoy loved her garden so much that she took it with her when she left. Five large lorries carried all the flowers, trees, and plants to her new house five miles away. It cost £1,000! She says:

'I've got a much bigger garden now and I'm going to make it even more beautiful than my first garden. I'm going to plant all the flowers and trees again and this time I'm going to have a pond with some goldfish.'

And Mr and Mrs Grey? What do they say? 'She can't do this! We bought the garden with the house! We're going to see our solicitor!'

Reading

Read the text and answer the questions. If you have a dictionary, use it to help with new words.

1 What is Verena's job? What is her hobby?
2 Why did she spend thousands of pounds?
3 Which was the most colourful season in her garden?
4 Why did Verena want to move?
5 Did Mr and Mrs Grey like the cottage when they first saw it?
6 Why were they shocked when they arrived at the cottage?
7 How much did Verena pay to move her garden?
8 What are her plans for her new garden?
9 What are Mr and Mrs Grey going to do?

Language work

1 Here are some answers. Complete the questions.

1 How much **did she spend to make her garden beautiful?**
   Thousands of pounds.

2 Which was _____?
   Summer. Because of all the roses.

3 Why _____?
   To see Verena's garden.

4 Was _____?
   Yes, it was. Very easy.

5 Why _____?
   Because they wanted to have a garden.

6 When _____?
   At the end of the summer.

7 What _____ like?
   It looked terrible. There weren't any flowers, just stones and rocks.

8 Has Verena _____ now?
   Yes, she has. It's much bigger.

9 What _____?
   She's going to make it even more beautiful and she's going to have a pond.

10 Who _____?
   Their solicitor.

2 Find examples of the following in the text. <u>Underline</u> them.

1 The present and past of *have got*
2 a comparative sentence
3 a superlative sentence
4 three irregular past tenses
5 three sentences about the future
6 an infinitive of purpose
7 a sentence with *some*
8 a sentence with *any*

Song

Complete each verse with a line from the box. Listen and check.

Wonderful Tonight

Eric Clapton

Verse 1

a	You look wonderful tonight.'
b	Then brushes her long blond hair
c	'Do I look all right?'
d	She's wondering what clothes to wear

It's late in the evening

1 _____

She puts on her make-up

2 _____

And then she asks me,

3 _____

And I say 'Yes,

4 _____

Verse 2

e	And then she asks me,
f	We go to a party
g	And I say 'Yes,
h	This beautiful lady

5 _____

And everyone turns to see

6 _____

That's walking around with me.

7 _____

'Do you feel all right?'

8 _____

I feel wonderful tonight.'

Verse 3

i	How much I love you
j	Because I see
k	And the wonder of it all

I feel wonderful

9 _____

The lovelight in your eyes

10 _____

Is that you just don't realize

11 _____

Verse 4

l	So I give her the car keys,
m	I say 'My darling,
n	It's time to go home now
o	And then I tell her

12 _____

And I've got an aching head

13 _____

She helps me to bed

14 _____

As I turn out the light

15 _____

You were wonderful tonight.'

Unit 13 Catching a train 4 (SB p105)

DEPARTURE TIME from Oxford	ARRIVAL TIME at London Paddington
0858	0951
0915	1010
0921	1031
1745	1844
1815	1915
1825	1932
Day return	£15.50
Period return	£22.50

DEPARTURE TIME from Oxford	ARRIVAL TIME at London Paddington
0858	0951
0915	1010
0921	1031
1745	1844
1815	1915
1825	1932
Day return	£15.50
Period return	£22.50

DEPARTURE TIME from Oxford	ARRIVAL TIME at Stratford-upon-Avon
0912	1018
1023	1127
1218	1325
1746	1904
1857	2031
1945	2110
Day return	£17.50
Period return	£25.50

DEPARTURE TIME from Oxford	ARRIVAL TIME at Stratford-upon-Avon
0912	1018
1023	1127
1218	1325
1746	1904
1857	2031
1945	2110
Day return	£17.50
Period return	£25.50

DEPARTURE TIME from Oxford	ARRIVAL TIME at Reading
0739	0808
0815	0838
0920	0943
1630	1715
1645	1709
1720	1754
Day return	£8.50
Period return	£15.50

DEPARTURE TIME from Oxford	ARRIVAL TIME at Reading
0739	0808
0815	0838
0920	0943
1630	1715
1645	1709
1720	1754
Day return	£8.50
Period return	£15.50

Extra ideas Units 13–14 Revision

Answer the questions.
- What films have you seen recently?
- What's your favourite film?
- Who are your favourite films stars?

Reading

1 Read the text about Liza Minnelli and choose the correct words.

2 Answer the questions about Liza Minnelli.
1 When was she born?
2 Who was her mother?
3 What happened to Liza in 1951?
4 Which studio did her mother and father work for?
5 How old was she when she first appeared in a film?
6 How many awards has she won?
7 When did she make her first album?
8 Has she had an easy life? Why/Why not?

Language work

1 Put the words in the right order to form a question.

1 children mother many did her how have

_____ ?

Three.

2 job what father's was her

_____ ?

He was a film director.

3 times did marry how mother her many

_____ ?

Five times.

4 1973 win what in she did

_____ ?

An Oscar.

5 films many she has how made?

_____ ?

More than fifteen.

6 did make *Stepping Out* she when

_____ ?

In 1991.

2 Find five verbs in the Past Simple, and five in the Present Perfect.

Liza Minnelli

Actress, Singer, Dancer...

Liza Minnelli was born on March 12, 1946, in Hollywood, California. She is the oldest of her mother's three children. Her mother, of course, was Judy Garland and her father was the film director, Vincente Minnelli. He was the second of Miss Garland's five husbands. In 1951, Liza's parents (1) *have divorced/divorced.*

Liza spent most of her childhood in Hollywood, and she often visited her mother's or father's film sets at the MGM Studios. She was (2) *interesting/interested* in everything to do with films, but she especially loved dancers such as Fred Astaire, Gene Kelly, and Cyd Charisse. 'I learned all their dances,' Liza Minnelli said in an interview in 1972, 'and I went home and practised them all in front of the mirror.' When she was only two and a half years old she (3) *has appeared/appeared* in her first movie, called *In the Good Old Summertime*, and five years later she danced on the stage of the Palace Theatre in New York.

She knew that she wanted to be a professional actress when she saw a musical on Broadway in 1960. 'The kids on stage looked fantastic,' she said 'so I (4) *immediately/immediate* decided to go to drama school.'

Liza has worked (5) *hard/hardly* all her life and has won many awards. She won her first award when she was nineteen for her performance in a musical called *Flora, the Red Menace*, and since then she has won five more. She won an Oscar in 1973 as Sally Bowles in *Cabaret*. She has made more than fifteen films and recorded eight albums. She made her first album, *Liza! Liza!* in 1963.

Liza has had an (6) *excited/exciting* life, but it has not always been (7) *easy/easily* for her. She has been married three times, but the marriages have (8) *never/ever* lasted very long. She was an alcoholic for many years and has also had problems with drugs. In 1984 she went to the Betty Ford Center in California and she has also had problems with her health. Her fans were very (9) *worried/worrying* about her in the 1990s because she (10) *has has/had* an operation on her hip in 1994 and one on her throat in 1997.

But Liza's career hasn't ended (11) *yet/ever*. In 1991, she made a film called *Stepping Out*, which was (12) *on/about* a group of people who find happiness and a purpose in life through dancing. This is a mirror of Liza Minnelli's life because she's now planning to appear on Broadway again in her new show *Minnelli on Minnelli*.

Song

1 Look at the underlined words and decide what's missing.
2 Listen and complete the song with the words you hear.

Summertime and the <u>livin'</u> is
(1) _____

Fish <u>are jumpin'</u> and the cotton is
(2) _____

Oh your Daddy's (3) _____ and
your ma is <u>good-lookin'</u>

So hush little baby, don't you
(4) _____ .

One of these (5) _____
you<u>'re goin'</u> to rise up singing

Then you'll spread your wings and
you'll take the (6) _____

But till that morning there's a <u>nothin'</u>
can harm you

With daddy and mammy <u>standin'</u> by.

Song

1 Look at the underlined words and decide what's missing.
2 Listen and complete the song with the words you hear.

Summertime and the <u>livin'</u> is
(1) _____

Fish <u>are jumpin'</u> and the cotton is
(2) _____

Oh your Daddy's (3) _____ and
your ma is <u>good-lookin'</u>

So hush little baby, don't you
(4) _____ .

One of these (5) _____
you<u>'re goin'</u> to rise up singing

Then you'll spread your wings and
you'll take the (6) _____

But till that morning there's a <u>nothin'</u>
can harm you

With daddy and mammy <u>standin'</u> by.

Stop and check 1

Correct the mistakes

Each sentence has a mistake. Find it and correct it.

Example
Antonia is ~~Italiana~~.   **Antonia is Italian.**

1   London is a city very big.
2   My mother works in a hotel is a receptionist.
3   My father watch TV in the evening.
4   He's like watching football.
5   On Sundays we go in a restaurant.
6   Hans is businessman.
7   You family is very nice.
8   I like listen to music.
9   Our school have a lot of students.
10   The childrens go to school near here.
11   We have the dinner at 7.00.
12   Buses in London are reds.
13   My brother no have a job.
14   Do you want a ice-cream?
15   Is near here, my flat.

[15]

Word order

Put the words in the correct order.

Example
Madrid   Jorge   from   comes.   **Jorge comes from Madrid.**

1   policeman   from   is   John   a   New York

_____

2   married   sister   is   your?

_____

3   mountains   sister   skiing   goes   the   in   my

_____

4   isn't   coffee   nice   English   very

_____

5   your   what   name   teacher's   is?

_____

6   surname   how   spell   do   your   you?

_____

7   often   weekends   go   I   at   swimming

_____

[7]

Choose the correct sentence

One sentence is correct. Which one?

Example
Where she from?   ✗
Where does she from?   ✗
Where is she from?   ✓

1   a   Sally is a nice girl, and I like.
    b   Sally is a nice girl, and I like her.
    c   Sally is a nice girl, and I like him.
2   a   He has 27 years old.
    b   He's 27 years.
    c   He's 27.
3   a   Peter works with his father.
    b   Peter works with he's father.
    c   Peter works with him father.
4   a   Sally and Tim live in Madrid. They're flat is lovely.
    b   Sally and Tim live in Madrid. Their flat is lovely.
    c   Sally and Tim live in Madrid. There flat is lovely.
5   a   She lives in a house or a flat?
    b   Does she lives in a house or a flat?
    c   Does she live in a house or a flat?
6   a   I don't like going to discos.
    b   I don't like go to discos.
    c   I no like going to discos.
7   a   How many languages you speak?
    b   How many languages do you speak?
    c   How many languages does you speak?
8   a   My brother work in a bank.
    b   My brother he works in a bank.
    c   My brother works in a bank.

[8]

Questions

1   Match a line in A with a line in B to make questions.

A	B
What	do you go to bed?
Where	languages do you speak?
What time	is a cup of coffee and a sandwich?
Who	do you usually sit next to?
How much	do you do at weekends?
How many	do you go on holiday?

[5]

2 Here are the answers to some questions. Write the questions. Use the words in brackets.

Example
What do you do? (you/do) I'm a hairdresser.

a _____?
(Peter / start work) At 8.00.

b _____?
(Sylvie and Jacques / come) From France.

c _____?
(your wife's) Jackie.

d _____?
(you / have) Three. Two girls and a boy.

e _____?
(you / like / gardening)
Yes, I do. I grow a lot of vegetables.

[5]

Prepositions

Complete the text with the prepositions in the box.

| at in about after for with by to on after |

Example
James lives _____in_____ a small flat.

James lives (1)_____ Cambridge. He lives (2)_____ two other boys who are students (3)_____ Cambridge University. They work hard during the week, but (4)_____ weekends they invite a lot of friends to their house. They cook a meal (5)_____ their friends, and then they go out (6)_____ the pub (7)_____ a drink, or they stay (8)_____ home and listen (9)_____ music.
James has two jobs. (10)_____ Mondays, Tuesdays, and Wednesdays he works (11)_____ a hospital, where he helps to look (12)_____ children who are ill. He goes to the hospital (13)_____ bus. He starts (14)_____ ten o'clock and works until quarter (15)_____ five. On Thursdays and Fridays he works (16)_____ home. He has a computer (17)_____ his bedroom and he writes stories. (18)_____ the evening, one of the boys cooks a meal. (19)_____ dinner they look in the newspaper to see what's on TV or they talk (20)_____ their day. They usually go to bed at about midnight.

[20]

Vocabulary

Put the words in the correct column. There are five words for each column.

| egg menu scientist favourite tuna accountant
collect hotel cake island want deliver letter
easy expensive chicken journalist dictionary
sell friendly interpreter magazine orange pub
beach nurse office newspaper busy listen |

Things to read	Professions	Things to eat	Places	Verbs	Adjectives
		egg			

[30]

am / is / do / does (not)

Complete the sentences with the verbs in the box.

| am/'m not is/isn't are/aren't does/doesn't do/don't |

Example
I _'m not_____ English.

1 Vienna _____ in Austria.
2 Where _____ you from?
3 I _____ on holiday. I'm at work.
4 My teacher _____ very funny.
5 What time _____ the bank open?
6 My sister _____ eat meat because she _____ like it.
7 I _____ hungry. How much _____ a tuna sandwich?
8 Where _____ you usually go on holiday?
9 Daddy, we _____ want to go to bed. We _____ tired.
10 Learning English_____ boring! It's interesting!

[10]

TOTAL [100]

TRANSLATE

Translate the sentences into your language. Translate the *ideas*, not word by word.

1 I am a student.
_____

2 My sister is a teacher.
_____

3 She isn't at home. She's at work.
_____

4 I live in a flat.
_____

5 My mother works in a bank.
_____

6 I don't smoke.
_____

7 My father doesn't like rock music.
_____

8 What do you do at weekends?
_____

9 John's flat is in the centre of town.
_____

10 Can I have a cup of coffee, please?

Stop and check 2

½ term Progress test

Correct the mistakes

Each sentence has a mistake. Find it and correct it.

Example

~~Where you live?~~ *Where do you live?*

1 There no is a supermarket.
2 Look at this pictures.
3 Is a bank near here?
4 I arrive at Heathrow airport at ten o'clock last night.
5 She could to speak three languages when she was ten.
6 Where did you went last night?
7 The plant is in front the window.
8 I don't can go out because I have a lot of homework.
9 In the kitchen is a table.
10 I was to the cinema last weekend.
11 Who are these people over there?
12 I buyed a new video.
13 Did you watch the football on TV last evening?
14 Italian people is very artistic.
15 I like cities because I can to go to the theatre.

[15]

Past Simple

Complete the text with the Past Simple form of the verbs in brackets. There are regular and irregular verbs.

Example

Leonardo da Vinci ___lived___ (live) in Italy in the fifteenth and sixteenth century.

He was a student in Florence, where he (1)_____ (study) painting, sculpture and design. He (2)_____ (begin) a lot of paintings, but he (3)_____ (not finish) many of them. His picture of the Mona Lisa is the most famous portrait in the world.

Leonardo (4)_____ (be) interested in many things. He (5)_____ (want) to know about everything he saw. He examined the human body. He (6)_____ (think) that the sun (7)_____ (not go) round the earth. He (8)_____ (write) music. He designed a flying machine 400 years before the first one flew. Many people (9)_____ (not understand) his ideas. It is difficult to think that one man (10)_____ (can) do so much.

[20]

Irregular verbs

Write the Past Simple form of these irregular verbs.

1 give _____
2 leave _____
3 sell _____
4 speak _____
5 lose _____
6 make _____
7 break _____
8 meet _____
9 win _____
10 take _____

[10]

can/ could/ was/ were (not)

Complete the sentences with the verbs in the box.

can	can't	was	wasn't	were	weren't	could	couldn't

Example

I ___can't___ drive. I'm only 14 years old.

1 Our teacher _____ at school last week because she _____ ill.
2 Leonardo _____ a student in Florence. He _____ draw, write music, and design buildings.
3 We _____ see the Mona Lisa in the Louvre in Paris.
4 'Where _____ you last night? You _____ at home. I phoned you, but there _____ no answer.'
5 'I _____ get into my flat because I lost my keys. I _____ at a friend's house.'

[10]

Questions and negatives

Write the statements as questions and negatives.

Example

He can swim. *Can he swim?*
         He can't swim.

1 There's a good restaurant in this town. _____
   _____
2 There are some eggs in the fridge. _____
   _____
3 You can speak French. _____
   _____

4 He was born in 1985.   _____
                               _____
5 She could play the piano   _____
   when she was three.   _____
6 They were in class last week. _____
                               _____
7 Your parents studied   _____
   German at school.   _____
8 The students went to the   _____
   theatre last night.   _____

                                        | 16 |

some/ any/ a/ an

Complete the sentences with *some*, *any*, *a*, or *an*.

Example
Heathrow is _____an_____ international airport.

1 Did Charles Dickens have _____ children?
2 I bought _____ newspaper and _____ magazines.
3 Jane lives in _____ old house in France.
4 There are _____ trees in my garden, but there aren't _____ flowers.
5 Do you have _____ books by Gabriel García Márquez?
6 There are _____ letters for you on the table.

                                        | 8 |

Vocabulary – connections

Match a line in A with a line in B.

A	B
birthday	kitchen
Easter Day	second
computer	operator
2nd	plane
telephone	egg
fridge	wedding
son	present
season	Internet
Congratulations!	war
ticket	sun
chemist	month
soldier	aspirin

                                        | 11 |

Vocabulary – opposites

Match a word in A with its opposite in B.

A	B
hot	rich
clean	far
win	under
old	left
near	cold
before	lose
happy	finish
poor	after
on	sad
begin	dirty
right	modern

                                        | 10 |

                              TOTAL | 100 |

TRANSLATE

Translate the sentences into your language. Translate the *ideas*, not word by word.

1 Is there a chemist near here?
   _____

2 There are two books on the table.
   _____

3 There are some flowers in the living room.
   _____

4 Are there any glasses?
   _____

5 I can ski, but I can't swim.
   _____

6 I couldn't go to the party last night.
   _____

7 I was ill.
   _____

8 Where were you born?
   _____

9 I was born in Mexico.
   _____

10 She started work when she was twelve.
   _____

11 He didn't like his first job.
   _____

12 Where did you go on holiday last year?
   _____

Stop and check 3

UNITS 9–12

Correct the mistakes

There is a mistake in each sentence. Find it and correct it.

Example

~~Where you live?~~ **Where do you live?**

1 It's very hot today – do you like something to drink?
2 Peter's got a lot of books because he'd like reading.
3 How many children do you got?
4 How many money has he got?
5 Who's is that new car?
6 I'm go home now because it's late.
7 Last night I went to a café for to meet my friends.
8 We're going have a test next week.
9 I'm wear my old clothes because I'm going to clean the car.
10 Pierre is French, he's coming from Paris.
11 What you doing tonight?
12 My sister is more old than me.
13 I think is going to rain.
14 Your house is bigger than my.
15 Who is the most rich person in the world?

| | 15 |

Questions and answers

Match a question in A with an answer in B.

A	B
Where does your sister work?	Yes, of course. What can I do for you?
Whose is this coat?	Yes. I think he's very nice.
How many cats have you got?	To buy some toothpaste.
How much did your bike cost?	To Turkey.
Could you help me, please?	In a bank.
Would you like some more to eat?	I stayed at home.
Do you like Henry?	Three.
Where are you going on holiday?	It's Jane's.
Why are you going to the chemist's?	£195.
What did you do last night?	Her name's Mrs Taylor.
Who's the new teacher?	No, thanks. I'm full.

| | 10 |

Comparatives and superlatives

Complete the chart.

Adjective	Comparative	Superlative
big	_____	_____
_____	more beautiful	_____
_____	_____	worst
exciting	_____	_____
noisy	_____	_____

| | 10 |

Comparing hotels

1 Look at the information about the two hotels. Write five sentences about the hotels using the comparative forms of the adjectives in the box.

Example

The Ritz is a better hotel than The Strand.

good	big	expensive	near	far	modern

	The Strand	The Ritz
Number of stars	★★★	★★★★
Number of rooms	102	55
Price	£80–£100	£120–£140
How many minutes to the sea?	10 minutes	15 minutes
How many minutes to the town centre?	20 minutes	8 minutes
Old or new?	New–1990	Old–1870

a _____
b _____
c _____
d _____
e _____

| | 10 |

2 Look at the information about The Star Hotel. Write five more sentences, comparing the three hotels. Use the superlative form of the adjectives.

Example

The Star is the best hotel.

© Oxford University Press   **Photocopiable**

	The Star
Number of stars	★★★★★
Number of rooms	45
Price	£150–£175
How many minutes to the sea?	1 minute
How many minutes to the town centre?	15 minutes
Old or new?	Old–1920

a _____
b _____
c _____
d _____
e _____

[ ] 10

some/ any/ a

Complete the sentences with *some*, *any*, or *a*.

Example

I don't have ___any___ brothers or sisters.

1 Would you like _____ cup of tea?
2 You have _____ lovely pictures on the walls!
3 Is there _____ water in the fridge?
4 Can I have _____ grapes, please?
5 I'd like _____ hamburger and _____ chips, please.
6 Do you want _____ sandwich?
7 The shop doesn't have _____ potatoes, peas, or bread.
8 There are _____ eggs in the cupboard, but there isn't _____ sugar.

[ ] 10

Present Simple and Continuous

Complete the sentences with the correct form of the verbs in brackets.

Example

I often ___watch___ (watch) TV in the evenings, but tonight ___I'm going___ (go) to the cinema.

1 Pierre _____ (smoke) twenty cigarettes a day, but he _____ (not smoke) now because he's in class.
2 Alice and Peter _____ (look) for a new house. They _____ (not like) living in London.
3 I always _____ (wear) nice clothes for work. Today I _____ (wear) a blue jacket and skirt.
4 'Why _____ you _____ (go) to bed? It's only 10.00.' 'I always _____ (go) to bed early.
5 Jane _____ (work) in a bank, but today she's at home. She _____ (write) letters.

[ ] 10

going to

Complete the sentences with *going to*. Use a verb and a place or person from the boxes.

Example

I'm going to do my homework in the living room.

buy	write	see	borrow	have

my friend	Florida	library	theatre	baker's

1 Peter _____ some bread at _____ .
2 I _____ some books from _____ .
3 We _____ a play at _____ .
4 They _____ a holiday in _____ .
5 I _____ a letter to _____ .

[ ] 10

Vocabulary

Put the words in the correct column.

wine fruit a dress a suit mushrooms milk a shirt cheese beer rice a jumper water juice shorts meat

Clothes shop	Food	Drinks
a dress		

[ ] 15

[TOTAL] 100

TRANSLATE

Translate the sentences into your language. Translate the *ideas*, not word by word.

1 I like Coke. I'd like a Coke.
_____

2 There is some bread on the table. There isn't any coffee.
_____

3 You're older than me, but Tim is the oldest in the class.
_____

4 My sister has got three children.
_____

5 I usually wear jeans, but today I'm wearing a suit.
_____

6 'Whose is this book?' 'It's mine.'
_____

7 We're going to have a party.
_____

8 I went into London to buy some books.
_____

Stop and check 4

Correct the mistakes

There is a mistake in each sentence. Find it and correct it.

Example
We ~~was~~ in Paris last year.   **We were in Paris last year.**

1 Why you want to learn Portuguese?
2 She hasn't never been to Madrid.
3 I've wrote to her three times and she hasn't answered yet.
4 I didn't enjoy the film. It was very bored.
5 How many times you been to Greece?
6 I'm very exciting about my holiday.
7 The students worked very hardly.
8 Say me when you want to stop for lunch.
9 What sort books do you like reading?
10 Did you ever been to Ireland?

| 10 |

Questions and tenses

Ask questions about the statements.

Example
John went to New York.   When **did he go** ?

1 Anna's tired.
   Why _____ ?
2 I don't go to work by car.
   How _____ you _____ ?
3 This pen isn't mine.
   Whose _____ ?
4 I met a famous actress.
   Who _____ you _____ ?
5 Sarah's bought a new car.
   What sort _____ ?
6 We saw Bill yesterday.
   Where _____ you _____ ?
7 Sue's watching television.
   What _____ ?
8 They're going on holiday.
   Where _____ ?
9 Peter's left the party.
   Why _____ ?
10 She drank a lot of wine.
   How much _____ ?

| 20 |

Past Simple and Present Perfect

1 <u>Underline</u> the correct tense.

Example
I *saw/have seen* Jill yesterday.

1 I *met/have met* Anna ten years ago.
2 My sister *did never go/has never been* to France.
3 I'm sorry. I *didn't finish/haven't finished* my work yet.
4 I *ate/have eaten* a lot of ice-cream when I was a child.
5 They *climbed/have climbed* Everest in 1953.

| 5 |

2 Put the verb in brackets in the correct form, the Present Simple or the Present Perfect.

Example
I travelled (travel) by plane for the first time last year.

1 We _____ (go) to Paris two years ago.
2 _____ you ever _____ (eat) Japanese food?
3 I _____ never _____ (be) to hospital.
4 Where _____ you _____ (live) when you were a student?
5 I can't give you your book back, because I _____ (not read) it yet.

| 10 |

Adverb or adjective?

<u>Underline</u> the correct form.

Example
I'm driving *careful/<u>carefully</u>* because it is raining.

1 Our village is always very *quiet/quietly*. Nothing happens.
2 Please speak more *slow/slowly*. I can't understand you.
3 She's a very *good/well* driver.
4 He doesn't drive very *good/well*.
5 My grandparents are very strong and *healthy/healthily* for their age.

| 5 |

Word order

Put the words in the correct order.

Example

letter you yet have written?
Have you written the letter yet?

1 many got you how cousins have?

_____

2 Rome they just have in arrived

_____

3 well speak you very English

_____

4 quickly road along man the walked the

_____

5 by play a have Shakespeare seen ever you?

_____

6 exam students the yesterday a had difficult

_____

7 carefully work you did your check?

_____

8 exercise this do please quickly

_____

9 people going many invite party how are
  to to your you?

_____

10 up is because she tired she got early

_____

| | 10 |

Auxiliaries

Complete the sentences with an auxiliary verb from the box.

| am/is/are | do/does | did have/has |

Example

I ___**am**___ listening to music.

1 Look at those children – they _____ smoking
  cigarettes!
2 _____ your daughter speak French well?
3 _____ you learn German when you were at school?
4 _____ Ben ever been to India?
5 We _____ never played volleyball.
6 I _____ going to have driving lessons soon.
7 _____ Mark and Jane live near you?
8 _____ John going to phone you tomorrow?
9 When _____ you start work? A long time ago?
10 _____ you written to thank Sue and Bill yet?

| | 10 |

Vocabulary – word groups

Put the words in the correct column. Each column has a different number of words.

| quiet day return annoying jumbo jet departure lounge worried niece station husband arrival hall platform tiring aunt flight grandson badly-behaved boarding pass gate widow lovely |

Travel by train	Travel by plane	Adjectives	Family

| | 20 |

Prepositions

Complete the sentences with the prepositions in the box.

| about in out of by on for to from |

Example

Pamela lives ___**on**___ the second floor.

1 I'm reading a book _____ the history of France.
2 *Oliver Twist* is a book _____ Charles Dickens.
3 Is it far _____ your house to the station?
4 Is Mexico City the biggest city _____ the world?
5 Jane's worried _____ her exam.
6 What's _____ television tonight?
7 Are you interested _____ politics?
8 She works _____ a big company.
9 Can I speak _____ you for a moment?
10 He drove _____ the garage and down the street.

| | 10 |

| TOTAL | 100 |

TRANSLATE

Translate the sentences into your language. Translate the *ideas*, not word by word.

1 Tim drives carefully. Tim's a careful driver.

_____

2 Have you ever been to China? I went to China last year.

_____

3 He hasn't finished his homework yet.

_____

4 I've just finished my homework.

_____

5 I want to go home.

_____

6 I'm interested in animals.

Progress test 1

Exercise 1 Asking about people

Surname	Smith
First name	John
Country	Britain
Age	30
Address	94 East St, Oxford OX1 9HJ
Job	Teacher
Place of work	School in Oxford
Married	No
Free time	Football

Read the information about John Smith. Write the questions.

Example
What's his first name?
His first name's John.

1 _____
His surname is Smith.

2 _____
He's from Britain.

3 _____
He's 30.

4 _____
94 East St, Oxford OX1 9HJ.

5 _____
He's a teacher.

6 _____
In a school in Oxford.

7 _____
No, he isn't. He's single.

8 _____
He plays football.

8

Exercise 2 Word order

Put the words in the correct order.

Example
you from are Where?
Where are you from?

1 do at What weekends you do?
_____

2 work she does Where?
_____

3 a television There photo is the on
_____

4 near there chemist a Is here?
_____

5 Coke please I a Can have?
_____

6 children How they do have many?
_____

7 skiing in Hans Switzerland teaches
_____

8 any Is milk the there fridge in?
_____

9 not work Rosy go by does to car
_____

10 Sue going Dave and the opera like to
_____

10

Exercise 3 Questions

Match a line in A with a line in B to make a question. Then find an answer in C.

A	B	C
Who	do you do on Sundays?	At seven o'clock.
How much	do you meet on Saturday evenings?	To the theatre.
What	do you go on Friday evenings?	My friends, Dave and Paul.
Where	do you get up?	I play tennis.
How	is a ham sandwich?	By bus.
What time	do you travel to work?	£1.80.

5

Exercise 4 *some*, *any*, *a*, and *an*

Complete the sentences with *some*, *any*, *a*, or *an*.

Example

There are ___**some**___ flowers in the garden.

1 There are _____ pictures on the wall.
2 Can I have _____ apple, please?
3 Are there _____ books in the living room?
4 There aren't _____ good restaurants in our town.
5 There's_____ newsagent's opposite the post office.
6 John has _____ trees in his garden.
7 Are there _____ Japanese students in your class?
8 There's _____ orange on the table.
9 There aren't _____ photographs on the wall.
10 There are _____ plates next to the sink.

[10]

Exercise 5 Present Simple

Complete the text with the correct form of the verb in brackets.

I (1)_____ (have) two brothers, Simon and Chris. They (2)_____ (live) in London. Simon (3)_____ (be) a pilot and Chris (3)_____ (work) in a garage. Simon (5)_____ (like) flying, but Chris (6)_____ _____ (not like) mending cars. At weekends I (7)_____ (go) to London and I (8)_____ (stay) with them. We (9)_____ (go) to the theatre or to the cinema on Saturday evening, and on Sunday we (10)_____ (walk) in Hyde Park.

[10]

Exercise 6 *be* and *do*

Complete the sentences with a verb from the box.

Example

Peter ____**is**____ a teacher.

am / am not	does / does not	is / is not
do / do not	are / are not	

1 I _____ hungry. Can I have an apple?
2 How _____ you travel to work?
3 Rome _____ in Spain. It _____ in Italy.
4 Mary and Sarah _____ like milk.
5 _____ James have two jobs?
6 Ben _____ like travelling by bus.
7 We aren't from Spain – we _____ from Portugal.
8 '_____ you like ice-cream?' 'No, I _____ .'

[9]

Exercise 7 Plural forms

Write these sentences in the plural.

Example

She's a doctor.   They *'re doctors* .

1 I go swimming on Saturdays.

_____

2 He watches TV every day.

_____

3 The dictionary is over there.

_____

4 This watch is expensive.

_____

5 Look at that lovely flower.

_____

6 Do you have a stamp?

_____

7 She's our child.

_____

8 He's an interesting person.

_____

9 That man is American.

_____

10 The school doesn't have a computer.

_____

[10]

Exercise 8 Prepositions

Complete the sentences with the correct preposition.
Write one word on each line.

1 There are two chairs _____ the living room.
2 The sofa is _____ _____ the table.
3 There's a lamp _____ the sofa.
4 There's a picture _____ the wall.
5 The chairs are _____ the television.
6 There's a cat _____ _____ _____ the fire.
7 The telephone is _____ the table.

☐ 7

Exercise 9 Choose the correct sentence

Tick (✓) the correct sentence.

Example
Let's go to home.
Let's go home. ✓

1 a Kate and Ann are students in Cambridge University.
  b Kate and Ann are students at Cambridge University.
2 a Let's go out to the pub!
  b Let's go out at the pub!
3 a On Thursdays I get home at six o'clock.
  b In Thursdays I get home at six o'clock.
4 a Richard lives at London.
  b Richard lives in London.
5 a To weekends I go swimming.
  b At weekends I go swimming.

☐ 5

Exercise 10 Which one is different?

Underline the different word.
Example
Cambridge London Oxford Rome

1	magazine	pen	newspaper	book
2	milk	apple	ice-cream	ham
3	house	palace	street	flat
4	actor	dentist	policeman	teach
5	boring	interesting	like	funny
6	father	sister	mother	man
7	house	bathroom	kitchen	living room
8	often	near	next to	opposite
9	France	England	American	Hungary
10	my	we	his	your

☐ 10

Exercise 11 Adjectives

Match the opposites.

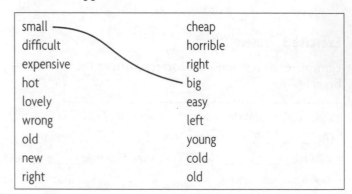

small	cheap
difficult	horrible
expensive	right
hot	big
lovely	easy
wrong	left
old	young
new	cold
right	old

☐ 8

Exercise 12 Words that go together

Match a verb in A with a line in B.

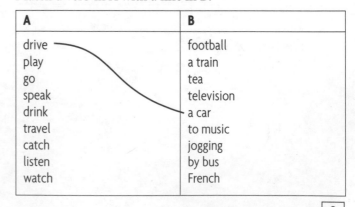

A	B
drive	football
play	a train
go	tea
speak	television
drink	a car
travel	to music
catch	jogging
listen	by bus
watch	French

☐ 8

☐ TOTAL 100

Progress test 2

Exercise 1 The past tense of the verb *to be*

What are the past tense forms of the verb *to be*?

		Positive	Negative
Example	I	was	wasn't
1	You	_____	_____
2	He/She/It	_____	_____
3	We	_____	_____
4	They	_____	_____

8

Exercise 2 *can* and *can't*

Read the information, then complete the sentences with *can* or *can't* and a verb.

	swim	play tennis	speak German	speak Italian
Sylvia	✓	✗	✓	✓
Linda	✓	✓	✗	✓
Marianne	✗	✗	✓	✓

Example
Linda **can swim** and she **can play** *tennis*.

1 Sylvia can swim, but she _____ .
2 Marianne _____ and she
   _____ .
3 Linda _____ , but Sylvia and
   Marianne can.
4 Everybody _____ .
5 Only Linda _____ .
6 Sylvia and Linda _____ , but
   Marianne can't.

7

Exercise 3 Past Simple

Write the Past Simple of these verbs.

Regular			Irregular		
1	work	_____	6	have	_____
2	live	_____	7	come	_____
3	earn	_____	8	give	_____
4	move	_____	9	go	_____
5	stay	_____	10	buy	_____

10

Exercise 4 Past Simple and Present Simple

Complete the text with the correct form of the verb in brackets: the Past Simple or the Present Simple.

My friend Jack is 40. He (1)_____ (leave) Britain when he was 20 and (2)_____ (go) to Italy. He (3)_____ (work) in Naples for ten years, then he (4)_____ (move) to Rome. There he (5)_____ (meet) Antonella. They (6)_____ (get) married in 1982 and now they (7)_____ (live) in Florence. Jack (8)_____ (teach) English in a language school. And what (9)_____ (do) Antonella do? She (10)_____ (sell) computer software.

10

Exercise 5 Past Simple: negative

Make these positive sentences negative.

Example
He bought a new shirt. **He didn't buy a new shirt.**

1 We enjoyed the film.
_____

2 I took a photograph of my sister.
_____

3 Angela wrote a letter to her friend.
_____

4 Charles Dickens became a journalist when he was 18.
_____

5 Germany won the World Cup in 1986.
_____

6 Her father died when she was 14.
_____

7 I lost £10 last night.
_____

8 People flew by plane 100 years ago.
_____

9 That book was very interesting.
_____

10 We arrived at school at eight o'clock.
_____

10

Exercise 6 would like

Tick (✓) the correct sentence.

Example
A Would you like | a drink? ✓
  Do you like | ✗
B No thanks, I'm not thirsty.

1 A Would you like | some fruit?
    Do you like |
  B Yes. An apple, please.

2 A Would you like | windsurfing?
    Do you like |
  B Yes, but I prefer swimming.

3 A What | do you like | for dinner this evening?
        | would you like |
  B Steak and chips.

4 A Would you like | Mr Brown?
    Do you like |
  B No. He's not very nice.

5 A Can I help you?
  B Yes. | I like | a bottle of mineral water, please.
       | I'd like |

5

Exercise 7 Countable and uncountable

Write C next to the count nouns and U next to the uncount nouns.

Example
book **C**   rice **U**

1 pencil ___   5 apple ___
2 music ___   6 money ___
3 rain ___   7 bread ___
4 flower ___

7

Exercise 8 some, any, or a

Write some, any, or a in the gaps.

Example
Do you have ___**any**___ rice?

1 I've got _____ pens in the office.
2 Can I have _____ can of Coke, please?
3 There isn't _____ sugar in the dining room.
4 Have you got _____ photographs of Jim?
5 I'd like _____ fruit, please.
6 Peter put _____ water and _____ glasses on the table.
7 There wasn't _____ petrol or oil in the car.

8

Exercise 9 How much and How many

Complete the questions with How much or How many.

1 _____ milk is there in the fridge?
2 _____ stamps do you need?
3 _____ oranges and apples are there on the table?
4 _____ Coke is there in the kitchen?
5 _____ money did you take to France?

5

© Oxford University Press **Photocopiable**

Exercise 10 Comparatives and superlatives 1

Read about the castles.

Abergoran Castle
Price: £200,000
Built: 1072
Rooms: 0

Footleby Castle
Price: £10 million
Built: 1835
Rooms: 160

Haywood Castle
Price: £2 million
Built: 1450
Rooms: 20

These sentences are false. Correct them.

Example
Abergoran Castle is more modern than Haywood Castle.
No, it isn't. It's older.

1 Footleby Castle is cheaper than Haywood Castle.
_____

2 Abergoran Castle is bigger than Footleby Castle.
_____

3 Abergoran Castle is the biggest.
_____

4 Abergoran Castle is more expensive than Footleby Castle.
_____

5 Footleby Castle is the cheapest.
_____

6 Footleby Castle is older than Haywood Castle.
_____

7 Abergoran Castle is the most modern.
_____

7

Exercise 11 Comparatives and superlatives 2

Complete the chart.

Adjective	Comparative	Superlative
_____	more dangerous	_____
_____	_____	best
bad	_____	_____
interesting	_____	_____

8

Exercise 12 Ordinal numbers

Write the ordinal numbers in words.

Example
6th   **sixth**

1 1st   _____
2 2nd   _____
3 3rd   _____
4 12th _____
5 20th _____

5

Exercise 13 Opposites

Choose a word from the box and write it next to its opposite.

Example
big   **small**

interesting	old	buy	before	start
quiet	east	day	new	same

1 boring   _____
2 stop   _____
3 night   _____
4 sell   _____
5 different _____
6 noisy   _____
7 old   _____
8 modern   _____
9 west   _____
10 after   _____

10

TOTAL 100

Progress test 3

Exercise 1 Present Continuous: -*ing* form

Write the correct -*ing* form.

Example
walk   **walking**
smoke   **smoking**

1 drive   _____
2 stop   _____
3 work   _____
4 use   _____
5 look   _____
6 get   _____
7 buy   _____
8 think   _____
9 swim   _____
10 cry   _____

☐ 10

Exercise 2 Present Continuous

Complete the sentences with the Present Continuous form of the verb in brackets.

Example
Julie **is wearing** earrings. (wear)

1 I _____ on holiday tomorrow. (not go)
2 A Why _____ you _____? (smile)
   B Because Mr Black didn't give us any homework.
3 A Where's Richard?
   B He _____ next to Jane. (stand)
4 Tom _____ at his desk. (not sit)
5 A What _____ Sue _____? (eat)
   B A tuna sandwich.
6 A What _____ you _____ ? (do)
   B I _____ my shoes. (clean)
7 I can't phone my wife. The telephone_____.
   (not work)

☐ 8

Exercise 3 Present Simple and Continuous

Complete the sentences with the Present Simple or the Present Continuous form of the verbs in brackets.

Example
'Be quiet! I **'m watching** (watch) this film!'

1 We usually _____ (take) the bus to town, but today we _____ (go) by car.
2 A Where _____ you usually _____ (go) on Friday evenings?
   B To a disco.
3 A It's 11.30. Why _____ you _____ (work) so late?
   B Because I _____ (have) a lot of homework.
4 A Where _____ your parents _____ ? (live)
   B In a small village near Oxford.
   A _____ they _____ (like) living in the country?
   B Yes, they do.
5 A What _____ you usually _____ (have) for breakfast?
   B Toast. But today I _____ (have) some fruit because there isn't any bread.
6 A The telephone _____(ring). Can you answer it?
   B OK.

☐ 10

Exercise 4 Possessive pronouns

Write the sentences using a possessive pronoun.
Example
It's my pen. **It's mine.**
They're her socks. **They're hers.**

1 It's your newspaper.
   _____

2 They're his books.
   _____

3 It's her T-shirt.
   _____

4 They're our videos.
   _____

5 This is their house.
   _____

   | 5 |

Exercise 5 *going to*

Make positive sentences, negative sentences, and
questions using *going to*.
Examples
she / pilot **She's going to be a pilot.**
he / not / bus driver **He isn't going to be a bus driver.**
you / hairdresser? **Are you going to be a hairdresser?**

1 they / architects
   _____

2 he / not / ballet dancer
   _____

3 you / pilot?
   _____

4 I / not / policeman
   _____

5 we / athletes
   _____

6 she / not / chef
   _____

7 he / vet?
   _____

8 I / actress
   _____

9 he / not / travel agent
   _____

10 you / English teacher?
   _____

   | 10 |

Exercise 6 Infinitive of purpose

Rewrite these sentences using the infinitive of purpose.
Example
I went to Holland because I wanted to see the tulips.
I went to Holland to see the tulips.

1 I'm going to Moscow because I want to see the
   Kremlin.
   _____

2 Paul is going to London because he wants to buy
   some clothes.
   _____

3 Roger went to India because he wanted to visit
   the Taj Mahal.
   _____

4 Tracey often goes to the disco because she wants
   to dance.
   _____

5 Tim is going to America because he wants to see
   the Niagara Falls.
   _____

6 Frank is learning French because he wants to get
   a better job.
   _____

7 Peter is saving money because he wants to buy a
   car.
   _____

8 Henry went to Japan because he wanted to visit
   Kyoto.
   _____

9 Chris went to the newsagent's because he wanted
   to buy a newspaper.
   _____

10 Brian and Jane are going to Paris because they
   want to climb the Eiffel Tower.
   _____

   | 10 |

Exercise 7 Adverbs

Write the adverbs next to the adjectives.
Example
quick *quickly*

1	slow	_____	5	hard	_____
2	early	_____	6	sudden	_____
3	careful	_____	7	fast	_____
4	good	_____	8	bad	_____

   | 8 |

Exercise 8 Question words

Complete the questions with a word from the box.

Example
A ___How___ tall is your sister?
B 1m 52.

Where	Which	Why	How	Who	What	When

1 A _____ often do you go to the cinema?
  B About once a month.
2 A _____ time does the programme start?
  B At nine o'clock.
3 A _____ did you close the window?
  B Because I'm cold.
4 A _____ colour is Angela's new car?
  B Red.
5 A _____ did you go to town with?
  B Jim and Lucy.
6 A _____ newspaper do you want – the Italian one or the English one?
  B The English one.
7 A _____ is Edinburgh?
  B It's in Scotland.
8 A _____ are you going to clean your room?
  B When this film has finished.
9 A _____ is your favourite season?
  B I like summer best.

9

Exercise 9 Past Simple and Present Perfect

Write the Past Simple and the Past Participle of these verbs.

Example
stay *stayed* *stayed*
sing *sang* *sung*

1 eat   _____   _____
2 win   _____   _____
3 live _____   _____
4 have _____   _____
5 do   _____   _____
6 cook _____   _____
7 go   _____   _____
8 drive _____   _____

8

Exercise 10 Present Perfect and Past Simple

Tick (✓) the correct sentence.

1 a I went to London last week.
  b I have been to London last week.
2 a Have you ever been to France?
  b Did you ever go to France?
3 a Kate has finished her homework two hours ago.
  b Kate finished her homework two hours ago.
4 a Did he go to the dentist last week or the week before?
  b Has he been to the dentist last week or the week before?
5 a I haven't seen that film yet.
  b I didn't see that film yet.
6 a I've just bought my plane ticket to Paris – here it is!
  b I just bought my plane ticket to Paris – here it is!
7 a Jim and Cathy won £1,000 last month.
  b Jim and Cathy have won £1,000 last month.

7

Exercise 11 Word groups

Put the words in the correct column.

blue	T-shirt	foggy	green	jumper
tie	sunny	brown	cloudy	snowing
pink	suit	skirt	yellow	windy

Colours	Clothes	Weather

15

TOTAL 100

Answer keys

Answers to the reading

2 **A** How do you spell it?
3 **B** Glasgow, in Scotland.
4 **A** How old are you?
5 **B** Yes, I am.
6 **A** What's your husband's name?
7 **B** He's a teacher. (He teaches blind children.)
8 **B** Yes, I do. I have two sons and a daughter.
9 **A** Do you have any brothers or sisters?
10 **B** Yes, I do.
11 **A** Why do you enjoy your job?
12 **B** In London and Glasgow.
13 **B** Yes, I/we do.
14 **A** What do you like doing in your free time?

Song – Colours

1 Yellow
2, 3 In the morning
4 I love the best
5 Green
6, 7 In the morning
8 I love the best
9 word
10 time

Answers to the reading

1 4 Seoul
3 1 the day of any date in any year; the teams and the scores of every football match in every World Cup.
   2 He remembered the order of 35 packs of playing cards.
   3 No, he wasn't. He couldn't remember his lessons.
   4 They said he was stupid.
   5 Four years ago. He saw a programme on TV which showed people how to improve their memory.
   6 Because he can remember every card.
   7 Seven.
   8 Three. The other four clubs knew him and didn't want him to play.
4 1 What day was April 21, 1876?
   2 When did he become world champion?

3 How much can he earn a day on European TV programmes?
4 What does his wife do?
5 How much did he win?
6 What does he like doing in his free time?
5 1 He remembered the order of 35 packs of cards.
   2 Dominic is 34 years old.
   3 He won £1,000 a night.
   4 He went to 7 clubs (with the interviewers).
   5 He had £1,250 in his pocket.
   6 Children can learn to improve their memory from the age of five.

Song – I Just Called To Say I Love You

1 Day   9 care
2 hearts   10 mean
3 sing   11 warm
4 day   12 moon
5 flowers   13 leaves
6 wedding   14 fly
7 true   15 thanks
8 words   16 heart

Answers to the reading
Vocabulary

Flowers	Colours	
tulip	pink	red
rose	yellow	gold
daffodil	orange	white
snowdrop	brown	
primrose	grey	

(Note that *pink* is also a flower, a type of carnation, but it is not necessary to mention this.)

Comprehension check

1 She's an artist. Her hobby is gardening.
2 To make her garden beautiful. / Because she wanted to make her garden beautiful.
3 Summer, because there were hundreds of red, white, and pink roses.
4 Because she wanted a bigger house.
5 Yes, they did. (They fell in love with it immediately.)
6 Because there was no garden, just a brown field with some stones and rocks. Also there weren't any flowers or trees.

7 £1,000.
8 She's going to plant all the flowers and trees again and she's going to have a pond with some goldfish.
9 They're going to see their solicitor.

Language work

1 2 Which was the prettiest season?
   3 Why did a lot of people come to the village?
   4 Was the cottage easy to sell?
   5 Why did Mr and Mrs Grey want to move from London?
   6 When did they move?
   7 What was the garden like?
   8 Has Verena got a bigger house (now)?
   9 What is she going to do (with it)?
   10 Who are Mr and Mrs Grey going to see?

2 1 **Present**
      I've got a much bigger garden
      Past
      She had flowers and plants for every season
      … *we didn't have* a garden there.

   2 It was *more beautiful than* the park.
      … she would like to move to a ·*bigger* house.
      …I'm going to make it even *more beautiful than* my first garden.

   3 Summer was *the prettiest season of all.*

   4 *spent, had, grew, bought, came, fell, left, (was/were).*

   5 *I'm going to make* it even more beautiful than my first garden
      I'm going to plant all the flowers and trees again.
      I'm going to have a pond.
      We're going to see a solicitor.

   6 She spent ten years and thousands of pounds *to make* her garden there beautiful.
      A lot of people came to the village especially *to see* Verena's garden.
      Mr and Mrs Grey came *to see* it.

   7 There was a brown field with *some stones and rocks.*
      I'm going to have a pond with *some goldfish.*

   8 There weren't *any flowers or trees* and there wasn't *any grass!*

Song – Wonderful tonight

1d 2b 3c 4a 5f 6h 7e 8g 9j
10k 11i 12n 13l 14o 15m

Extra ideas Units 13–14

Answers to the reading

1 1 divorced   5 hard   9 worried
   2 interested   6 exciting 10 had
   3 appeared   7 easy   11 yet
   4 immediately 8 never   12 about

2 1 March 12, 1946.
   2 Judy Garland.
   3 Her parents divorced.
   4 MGM.
   5 Two and a half.
   6 Six.
   7 1963.
   8 No, she hasn't. She has been married three times and she has had problems with alcohol and drugs.

Language work

1 1 How many children did her mother have?
   2 What was her father's job?
   3 How many times did her mother marry?
   4 What did she win in 1973?
   5 How many films has she made?
   6 When did she make *Stepping Out*?

2 **Past Simple**
   was, divorced, spent, liked, enjoyed, learned, said, went, practised, appeared, danced, knew, wanted, saw, looked, told, decided, won, were, made
   Present Perfect
   has won, has made, has had, has (not) been, have lasted, hasn't ended

Song – Summertime

1 The letter *g* is missing.
2 1 easy   3 rich   5 mornings
   2 high   4 cry   6 sky

Stop and check 1

Correct the mistakes

1 London is a very big city.
2 My mother works in a hotel. She's a receptionist. *or* My mother is a receptionist in a hotel.
3 My father watches TV in the evening.
4 He likes watching football.
5 On Sundays we go to a restaurant.

6 Hans is a businessman.
7 Your family is very nice.
8 I like listening to music.
9 Our school has a lot of students.
10 The children go to school near here.
11 We have dinner at 7.00.
12 Buses in London are red.
13 My brother doesn't have a job.
14 Do you want an ice-cream?
15 My flat is near here.

Word order

1 John is a policeman from New York.
2 Is your sister married?
3 My sister goes skiing in the mountains.
4 English coffee isn't very nice.
5 What is your teacher's name?
6 How do you spell your surname?
7 I often go swimming at weekends./I go swimming often at weekends.

Choose the correct sentence

1b 2c 3a 4b 5c 6a 7b 8c

Questions

1 Where do you go on holiday?
   What time do you go to bed?
   Who do you usually sit next to?
   How much is a cup of coffee and a sandwich?
   How many languages do you speak?
2 a What time does Peter start work?
   b Where do Sylvie and Jacques come from?
   c What's your wife's name?
   d How many children do you have?
   e Do you like gardening?

Prepositions

1 in   8 at   15 to
2 with   9 to   16 at
3 at   10 On   17 in
4 at   11 in/at 18 In
5 for   12 after 19 After
6 to   13 by   20 about
7 for   14 at

Vocabulary

Things to read	Professions	Things to eat
menu	scientist	egg
letter	accountant	tuna
dictionary	journalist	cake
magazine	interpreter	chicken
newspaper	nurse	orange

Places	Verbs	Adjectives
hotel	collect	favourite
island	want	easy
pub	deliver	expensive
beach	sell	friendly
office	listen	busy

am/ is/ do/ does (not)

1 is   6 doesn't doesn't
2 are   7 'm is
3 'm not   8 do
4 is/isn't 9 don't aren't
5 does/is   10 isn't

Translate

The idea behind this is that students begin to be aware of similarities and differences between English and L1. Emphasize that they must not translate word by word. Obviously it will only be possible to check their answers in a monolingual class but even in a multi-lingual class students can discuss their answers together in nationality groups.

Stop and check 2

Correct the mistakes

1 There isn't a supermarket. *is no supermkt.*
2 Look at this picture/these pictures.
3 Is there a bank near here?
4 I arrived at Heathrow airport at ten o'clock last night.
5 She could speak three languages when she was ten.
6 Where did you go last night?
7 The plant is in front of the window.
8 I can't go out because I have a lot of homework.
9 There is a table in the kitchen.
10 I went to the cinema last weekend.
11 Who are those people over there?
12 I bought a new video.
13 Did you watch the football on TV last night/yesterday evening?
14 Italian people are very artistic.
15 I like cities because I can go to the theatre.

Past Simple

1 studied   6 thought
2 began   7 didn't go
3 didn't finish 8 wrote
4 was   9 didn't understand
5 wanted   10 could

Irregular verbs

1 gave   5 lost   9 won
2 left   6 made   10 took
3 sold   7 broke
4 spoke 8 met

can/ could/ was/ were (not)

1 wasn't was
2 was could
3 can
4 were weren't was
5 couldn't was

Questions and negatives

1 Is there a good restaurant in this town?
   There isn't a good restaurant in this town.
2 Are there any eggs in the fridge?
   There aren't any eggs in the fridge.
3 Can you speak French?
   You can't speak French.
4 Was he born in 1985?
   He wasn't born in 1985.
5 Could she play the piano when she was three?
   She couldn't play the piano when she was three.
6 Were they in class last week?
   They weren't in class last week.
7 Did your parents study German at school?
   Your parents didn't study German at school.
8 Did the students go to the theatre last night?
   The students didn't go to the theatre last night.

some/ any/ a/ an

1 any
2 a some
3 an
4 some any
5 any
6 some

Vocabulary – connections

(Suggested answers but do award points for any sensible alternatives!)

Easter Day – egg
computer – Internet
2nd – second
telephone – operator
fridge – kitchen
son – sun
season – month
Congratulations! – wedding
ticket – plane
chemist – aspirin
soldier – war

Vocabulary – opposites

clean – dirty   happy – sad
win – lose   poor – rich
old – modern   on – under
near – far   begin – finish
before – after   right – left

Translate

See note about translation on p156.

Correct the mistakes

1 It's very hot today – would you like something to drink?
2 Peter's got a lot of books because he likes reading.
3 How many children have you got/do you have?
4 How much money has he got?
5 Whose is that new car?
6 I'm going home now because it's late.
7 Last night I went to a café to meet my friends.
8 We're going to have a test next week.
9 I'm wearing old clothes because I'm going to clean the car.
10 Pierre is French, he comes from Paris.
11 What are you doing tonight?
12 My sister is older than me.
13 I think it is going to rain.
14 Your house is bigger than mine.
15 Who is the richest person in the world?

Questions and answers

Whose is this coat? – It's Jane's.
How many cats have you got? – Three.
How much did your bike cost? – £195.
Could you help me, please? –
   Yes, of course. What can I do for you?
Would you like some more to eat? –
   No, thanks. I'm full.
Do you like Henry? –
   Yes. I think he's very nice.
Where are you going on holiday? –
   To Turkey.
Why are you going to the chemist's? –
   To buy some toothpaste.
What did you do last night? –
   I stayed at home.
Who's the new teacher? –
   Her name's Mrs Taylor.

Comparatives and superlatives

Adjective	Comparative	Superlative
big	bigger	biggest
beautiful	more beautiful	most beautiful
bad	worse	worst
exciting	more exciting	most exciting
noisy	noisier	noisiest

Comparing hotels

1 a The Strand is bigger than the Ritz.
   b The Ritz is more expensive than the Strand.
   c The Strand is nearer the sea than the Ritz.
   d The Strand is farther from the town centre than the Ritz.
   e The Strand is more modern than the Ritz.
2 a The Strand is the biggest.
   b The Star is the most expensive.
   c The Star is the nearest to the sea.
   d The Strand is the farthest from the town centre.
   e The Strand is the most modern.

some/ any/ a

1 a   5 a some
2 some   6 a
3 any   7 any
4 some   8 some any

Present Simple and Present Continuous

1 smokes isn't smoking
2 are looking don't like
3 wear 'm wearing
4 are you going go
5 works 's writing

going to

1 Peter **is going to buy** some bread at **the baker's**.
2 I **am going to borrow** some books from **the library**.
3 We **are going to see** a play at **the theatre**.
4 They **are going to have** a holiday in **Florida**.
5 I **am going to write** a letter to **my friend**.

Vocabulary

Clothes shop	Food	Drinks
a dress	fruit	wine
a suit	mushrooms	milk
a shirt	cheese	beer
a jumper	rice	water
shorts	meat	juice

Translate

See note about translation on p156.

Correct the mistakes

1 Why do you want to learn Portuguese?
2 She hasn't ever been to Madrid./She has never been to Madrid.
3 I've written to her three times and she hasn't answered yet.
4 I didn't enjoy the film. It was very boring.
5 How many times have you been to Greece?

6 I'm very excited about my holiday.
7 The students worked very hard.
8 Tell me when you want to stop for lunch.
9 What sort of books do you like reading?
10 Have you ever been to Ireland?

Questions and tenses

1 Why **is she tired**?
2 How **do you go to work**?
3 Whose **is this pen**?
4 Who **did** you **meet**?
5 What sort **of car did she buy**?
6 Where **did** you see **him**?
7 What **is she watching**?
8 Where **are they going**?
9 Why **did he leave**?
10 How much **wine did she drink**?

Past Simple and Present Perfect

1 1 met   4 ate
   2 has never been 5 climbed
   3 haven't finished

2 1 went   4 did … live
   2 Have … eaten   5 haven't read
   3 have … been

Adverb or adjective?

1 quiet   4 well
2 slowly   5 healthy
3 good

Word order

1 How many cousins have you got?
2 They have just arrived in Rome.
3 You speak English very well.
4 The man walked quickly along the road.
5 Have you ever seen a play by Shakespeare?
6 The students had a difficult exam yesterday.
7 Did you check your work carefully?
8 Please do this exercise quickly.
9 How many people are you going to invite to your party?
10 She is tired because she got up early.

Auxiliaries

1 are   6 am
2 Does   7 Do
3 Did   8 Is
4 Has   9 did
5 have   10 Have

Vocabulary – word groups

Travel by train	Travel by plane
day return	jumbo jet
station	departure lounge
platform	arrival hall
	flight
	boarding pass
	gate

Adjectives	Family
quiet	niece
annoying	husband
worried	aunt
tiring	grandson
badly-behaved	widow
lovely	

Prepositions

1 about   5 about   9 to
2 by   6 on   10 out of
3 from   7 in
4 in   8 for

Translate

See note about translation on p156.

Progress test 1

Exercise 1

1 What's his surname?
2 Where's he from?
3 How old is he?
4 Where does he live? / What's his address?
5 What does he do? / What's his job?
6 Where does he work / teach?
7 Is he married?
8 What does he do in his free time?

Exercise 2

1 What do you do at weekends?
2 Where does she work?
3 There is a photo on the television.
4 Is there a chemist near here?
5 Can I have a coke, please?
6 How many children do they have?
7 Hans teaches skiing in Switzerland.
8 Is there any milk in the fridge?
9 Rosy does not go to work by car.
10 Sue and Dave like going to the opera.

Exercise 3

How much is a ham sandwich?   £1.80.
What do you do on Sundays?
    I play tennis.
Where do you go on Friday evenings?
    To the theatre.
How do you travel to work?   By bus.
What time do you get up?   At seven o'clock.

Exercise 4

1 some   6 some
2 an   7 any
3 any   8 an
4 any   9 any
5 a   10 some

Exercise 5

1 have   6 doesn't like
2 live   7 go
3 is   8 stay
4 works   9 go
5 likes   10 walk

Exercise 6

1 am   5 Does
2 do   6 does not
3 is not, is 7 are
4 do not   8 Do, don't

Exercise 7

1 We go swimming on Saturdays.
2 They watch TV every day.
3 The dictionaries are over there.
4 These watches are expensive.
5 Look at those lovely flowers.
6 Do you have any stamps?
7 They're our children.
8 They're interesting people.
9 Those men are American.
10 The schools don't have any computers.

Exercise 8

1 in   5 near
2 next to   6 in front of
3 behind   7 on
4 on

Exercise 9

1b 2a 3a 4b 5b

Exercise 10

1 pen (You can read the others.)
2 milk (You can drink milk.)
3 street (The others are buildings.)
4 teach (The others are professions.)
5 like (The others are adjectives.)
6 man (The others are names of family members.)
7 house (The others are rooms.)
8 often (The others describe position.)
9 American (American is an adjective.)
10 we (The others are possessive adjectives.)

Exercise 11

difficult – easy
expensive – cheap
hot – cold
lovely – horrible
wrong – right
old – young
new – old
right – left

Exercise 12

play football
go jogging
speak French
drink tea
travel by bus
catch a train
listen to music
watch television

Progress test 2

Exercise 1

1 were   weren't
2 was   wasn't
3 were   weren't
4 were   weren't

Exercise 2

1 can't play tennis
2 can speak German / can speak Italian
3 can't speak German
4 can speak Italian
5 can play tennis
6 can swim

Exercise 3

1 worked   5 stayed   9 went
2 lived   6 had   10 bought
3 earned   7 came
4 moved   8 gave

Exercise 4

1 left   5 met   9 does
2 went   6 got   10 sells
3 worked   7 live
4 moved   8 teaches

Exercise 5

1 We didn't enjoy the film.
2 I didn't take a photograph of my sister.
3 Angela didn't write a letter to her friend.
4 Charles Dickens didn't become a journalist when he was 18.
5 Germany didn't win the World Cup in 1986.

6 Her father didn't die when she was 14.
7 I didn't lose £10 last night.
8 People didn't fly by plane 100 years ago.
9 That book wasn't very interesting.
10 We didn't arrive at school at eight o'clock.

Exercise 6

1 Would you like …
2 Do you like …
3 What would you like …
4 Do you like …
5 Yes. I'd like a bottle …

Exercise 7

1C   2U   3U   4C   5C   6U   7U

Exercise 8

1 some   5 some
2 a   6 some   some
3 any   7 any
4 any

Exercise 9

1 How much
2 How many
3 How many
4 How much
5 How much

Exercise 10

1 No, it isn't. It's more expensive.
2 No, it isn't. It's smaller.
3 No, it isn't. It's the smallest.
4 No, it isn't. It's cheaper.
5 No, it isn't. It's the most expensive.
6 No, it isn't. It's more modern.
7 No, it isn't. It's the oldest.

Exercise 11

Adjective	Comparative	Superlative
dangerous	more dangerous	most dangerous
good	better	best
bad	worse	worst
interesting	more interesting	most interesting

Exercise 12

1 first   4 twelfth
2 second   5 twentieth
3 third

Exercise 13

1 interesting   6 quiet
2 start   7 new
3 day   8 old
4 buy   9 east
5 same   10 before

Progress test 3

Exercise 1

1 driving   6 getting
2 stopping   7 buying
3 working   8 thinking
4 using   9 swimming
5 looking   10 crying

Exercise 2

1 am not going   5 is … eating
2 are … smiling   6 are … doing
3 is standing   am cleaning
4 isn't sitting   7 isn't working

Exercise 3

1 take are going
2 do … go
3 are … working have
4 do … live Do … like
5 do … have am having
6 is ringing

Exercise 4

1 It's yours.   4 They're ours.
2 They're his.   5 It's theirs.
3 It's hers.

Exercise 5

1 They're going to be architects.
2 He isn't going to be a ballet dancer.
3 Are you going to be a pilot?
4 I'm not going to be a policeman.
5 We're going to be athletes.
6 She isn't going to be a chef.
7 Is he going to be a vet?
8 I'm going to be an actress.
9 He isn't going to be a travel agent.
10 Are you going to be an English teacher?

Exercise 6

1 I'm going to Moscow to see the Kremlin.
2 Paul is going to London to buy some clothes.
3 Roger went to India to visit the Taj Mahal.
4 Tracey often goes to the disco to dance.
5 Tim is going to America to see the Niagara Falls.
6 Frank is learning French to get a better job.
7 Peter is saving money to buy a car.
8 Henry went to Japan to visit Kyoto.
9 Chris went to the newsagent's to buy a newspaper.
10 Brian and Jane are going to Paris to climb the Eiffel Tower.

Exercise 7

1	slowly	5	hard
2	early	6	suddenly
3	carefully	7	fast
4	well	8	badly

Exercise 8

1	How	6	Which
2	What	7	Where
3	Why	8	When
4	What	9	Which
5	Who		

Exercise 9

1	ate	eaten	5	did	done
2	won	won	6	cooked	cooked
3	lived	lived	7	went	gone
4	had	had	8	drove	driven

Exercise 10

1a   2a   3b   4a   5a   6a   7a

Exercise 11

Colours	Clothes	Weather
blue	jumper	cloudy
yellow	skirt	snowing
pink	T-shirt	foggy
green	tie	sunny
brown	suit	windy